Fascis

Fascist Europe

The Rise of Racism and Xenophobia

Edited and with an Introduction
by Glyn Ford

LONDON • BOULDER, COLORADO

This edition first published 1992 by Pluto Press
345 Archway Road, London N6 5AA
and 5500 Central Avenue, Boulder, Colorado 80301, USA

First published 1991 by the European Parliament
as the Report drawn up on behalf of the Committee of Inquiry
into Racism and Xenophobia on the findings of the
Committee of Inquiry

British Library Cataloguing in Publication Data
A catalogue record for this book is available from the British Library

ISBN 0 7453 0667 5 hb
ISBN 0 7453 0668 3 pb

Library of Congress Cataloging-in-Publication Data

Fascist Europe: the Rise of Racism and Xenophobia/edited and with an Introduction by Glyn Ford.
p. cm.
Includes bibliographical references and index.
ISBN 0-7453-0667-5 (HB).–ISBN 0-7453-0668-3 (PB)
1. European Federation. 2. Fascism–Europe. 3. Racism–Europe.
I. Ford, Glyn.
JN15.F34 1992
321′.04′094–dc20 92–6123
CIP

Typeset from author's disks by Archetype.
Printed in Finland by WSOY.

Contents

Abbreviations

ACP	African, Caribbean and Pacific
ANS	Actiefront Nationaal Socialisten
ARC	Rainbow Group in the European Parliament (Groupe Arc-en-Ciel au Parlement Européean)
B	Belgium
BNP	British National Party
BSS	Bevara Sveriga Svenkst
CAHAR	Ad Hoc Committee of Experts on the Legal Aspects of Territorial Asylum and Refugees and Stateless Persons
CARM	Campaign Against Racism in the Media
CCME	Churches' Committee for Migrants in Europe
CD	Centrumdemokraten
CDS	Centre des Démocrates Sociaux
CDU	Christian Democrat Union
CEDADE (Portugal)	Círculo Europeu de Amigos de Europa
CEDADE (Spain)	Círculo Español de Amigos de Europa
CERD	(UN) Committee on the Elimination of Racial Discrimination
CG	Left Coalition (Coalition des Gauches)
CMDG	Committee of Experts on Community Relations of the European Committee on Migration
CNIP	Centre National des Indépendants et Paysans
CPBF	Campaign for Press and Broadcasting Freedom
CRE	Commission for Racial Equality
D	Germany (Deutschland)

DNSB	Dansk Nasjonal Socjalistik Bund
DR	Technical Group of the European Right (DROITES)
DVU	Deutsche Volksunion
E	Spain (España)
EC	European Community
ED	European Democrat
EEC	European Economic Community
ENEK	Ceniaio Ethnikistiko Kinema
EPEN	Greek National Political Society
EPP	European People's Party (British Conservatives)
ESC	Economic and Social Committee
EUL	European Unitarian Left
F	France
FAN	Fédération d'Action Nationale et Européene
FAP	Freiheitliche Deutsche Arbeiten Partei
FMI	People's Movement Against Immigration
FN	Front National
FNE	Faisceaux Nationalistes Européenes
FPIP	Fédération Professionnelle Indépendante de la Police
FPÖ	Freiheitliche Partei Osterreichs
FRG	Federal Republic of Germany
GDR	German Democratic Republic
GRAEL	Green–Alternative European Link
GRECE	Groupement de Recherche et d'Etudes pour la Civilisation Européene
HR	Hessischer Rundfunk
ILO	International Labour Organization
JCWI	Joint Council for the Welfare of Immigrants
LBR	Landelijk Buro Racismebestrijding
LDR	Liberal, Democratic and Reformist Group
LICRA	La Ligue Internationale Contre le Racisme et Antisémitisme
MEP	Member of the European Parliament
MRAP	Mouvement Contre le Racisme et pour l'Amitié entre les Peuples
MSI	Movimento Sociale Italiano
NAR	Nuclei Armati Rivoluzionari
NF (Norway)	Nasjonalt Folkepartei

NF (UK)	National Front
NF (FRG)	Nationalistische Front
NFV	National Front Vlaanderen
NL	Netherlands
NOLS	Nouvelle Organisation de Liberation de Schaarbeek
NPD	Nationaldemokratische Partei Deutschlands
NSIWP	National Socialist Irish Workers' Party
NSP	National Socialist Party
PCF	Parti Communiste Français
PFN	Parti des Forces Nouvelles
PLO	Palestine Liberation Organization
PNFE	Parti Nationaliste Français et Européen
PRL	Parti Réformateur Liberal
PS	Parti Socialiste
PSC	Parti Social-Chrétien
PSR	Partido Socialista Revolucionacio
PvdA	Partij van de Arbeid
RDE	European Democratic Alliance (Rassemblement des Démocrates Européens)
REP	Republikaner Partei
RPR	Rassemblement pour la République
S	Socialist
SAI	Social Action Initiative
SIS	Schengen Information System
SMP	Suomen Maaseudun Puolue
SPD	Social Democratic Party
SSA	Supplementary Schengen Agreement
UDF	Union pour la Démocratie Française
UNHCR	United Nations High Commissioner for Refugees
UVF	Ulster Volunteer Force
VB	Vlaams Blok
VMO	Vlaamse Militanten Orde
VVN/BdA	Vereinigung der verfolgten des Naziregimes/ Bund der Antifaschisten
WUNS	World Union of National Socialists
YES	Youth for Europe

Introduction

Recent events have fully vindicated the compilation and, now, this publication of the Report of the European Parliament's Committee of Inquiry into Racism and Xenophobia.[1]

From the moment of the Committee's inception in October 1989 through to the parliamentary presentation of its Report in October 1990, Europe witnessed a series of incidents of the kind to which the report sought seriously to give attention and which, as the Committee's rapporteur, I believe we ignore at our peril.

The wave of fascist-inspired anti-Jewish violence and racist vandalism which swept across France in May 1990, precisely at the time when the Committee's fact-finding investigation was under way, understandably caused acute shock and grief throughout Europe.

In the most notorious of these attacks, at the Jewish cemetery in Carpentras, near Avignon in the south of France, 34 graves were desecrated and the corpse of a recently-buried 81-year-old Jewish man was dug up, violated and impaled on a parasol stick. Following that outrage, further graveyard attacks took place in Clichy near Paris, in Wissembourg in Alsace and in the city of Quimper in Brittany, where Jewish-owned shops were daubed with the Star of David.

Sadly, the violence did not stop there but spread across the continent with further antisemitic outbreaks as far apart as East Berlin, Lund in Sweden, Naples in Italy, Wejherowo in Poland, Leningrad in the USSR, St Gallen in Switzerland and Tirgu Mures in Romania.

This widespread violence, regrettably, came as no surprise to those of us from all parties across the political spectrum who have both closely observed and tried to warn of the parallel upsurge of racism and the extreme right as a *pan-European phenomenon* in recent years.

As early as 1984–5, via the work of the European Parliament's pioneering Committee of Inquiry into the Rise of Racism and Fascism in Europe, we had begun to sound the alarm and to show that, in Western Europe, nationalism of the most reactionary kind had begun to re-assert itself and that violence against immigrants and asylum-seekers by fascist and racist gangs was prevalent.

The final report of that Committee, the Evrigenis Report, named after its author the late Dimitrios Evrigenis, a Greek Christian Democrat, did far more, however, than alert attention to a deepening problem within European society. It documented the process and argued persuasively that positive action 'at the institutional level', 'at the level of information', 'at the level of education' and 'at the level of social forces' was a necessity if the associated problems of racism, xenophobia and fascism were to be dealt with.

In this sense, the Report not only followed and described events but to a certain extent anticipated the difficulties which would increase if action was not taken.

Forty concrete recommendations were made and overwhelmingly adopted by the Parliament itself. Also, a Joint Declaration against Racism and Xenophobia was adopted and signed by all the key component parts of the European Community: Parliament, the Council and the Commission. The tenor of the Declaration was that racism and xenophobia had to be eliminated.

In reality, however, by 1989 so little had been done to implement the recommendations and Declaration and so much was happening in the wider political context that a new survey was urgently required to measure developments since the Evrigenis Report.

Three new factors had emerged. Firstly, the appearance of an antisemitism more overt than at any time since the Second World War; secondly, the clearly definable spread of racist violence and fascist organization to the countries of the former Communist bloc; and thirdly an electoral breakthrough by the extreme right in Germany.

All three factors, of course, have deep-seated causes, but what is motivating them? In his submission to the Committee of

Inquiry into Racism and Xenophobia, West German Social Democrat Willi Rothley attempted a partial answer. The cause of the rise of racism and right-wing extremism is, he wrote, 'the trend towards individualization inherent in the process of modernizing society. The loosening of ties to the family, vocation, work and company, the church, parties and trade unions has produced increasing uncertainty and lack of direction. There is a growing susceptibility to political platforms offering security by emphasizing the national aspect or providing scapegoats (foreigners).'

This contains a considerable degree of truth. There is no doubt that the 're-structuring' of European industrial societies with its attendant social strains – de-industrialization, unemployment, the labour movement's loss of its traditional working-class constituency – coupled with the collapse and de-stabilization of the former Communist bloc have created new anxieties whose profundity democracy has not yet fully grasped. One product has been a gravitational shift rightwards on a continental scale.

In the five short years since Evrigenis, France and West Germany, in particular, have witnessed the spectacular re-habilitation of the extreme right and its appearance on the mainstream political stage, through exploitation of the deep-rooted social worries and via the legitimization of racism so succinctly analysed by Willi Rothley. Inevitably, a sustained spate of violence has followed this process.

This is most evident in France, the scene of some of the worst incidents, where the Front National (FN), led by Jean-Marie Le Pen, runs a formidable political operation enabling it to control over 30 city and town councils and to hold 10 seats in the Strasbourg European Parliament.

Nakedly and unashamedly racist, the FN's politics centre on demands for the removal of France's entire non-European population. Only thus, argues the charismatic and controversial Le Pen, can France's acute jobs and housing problems be solved. Indeed, one of the Front's posters sums up its argument: 'Two million immigrants equals two million unemployed', with the message that expelling the foreigners will provide jobs for the French.

Such slogans have found a ready reception in the job-starved social wastelands of north and north-eastern France and around

Paris where heavy industries like coal and steel have ceased to exist and where the traditional parties of the Left, the Socialist Party and the Communist Party, have lost the confidence of working people who, understandably, fear for their future and that of their children.

This relative success has not appeared from thin air but is the result of a massive input since the early 1970s by French 'New Right' intellectuals such as Alain de Benoist into the FN's view of the world. Moreover, since the early 1980s, there has been a wave of publications by other intellectuals, such as Lyons professor Robert Faurisson, denying the material facts of the Nazi genocide against the Jews.

This has not been without consequences; the potency of the extreme right's propaganda was illustrated by an opinion poll in March 1990 conducted by the Information and Documentation Service of the French Socialist Prime Minister Michel Rocard which found that 76 per cent of French people think there are too many Arabs in France, 46 per cent too many black people and 24 per cent too many Jews.

The fact is that the FN now has the backing of wide sections of the French working class, especially among the youth who provided up to 18 per cent of Le Pen's 4.3 million vote in the April 1988 French Presidential election first round.

This was a vote for a candidate who consciously manipulated concern that soon France will become an 'Islamic nation', who says that there is 'a Jewish International which operates against the French national interest' and for whom the Nazi Holocaust against the Jews was 'only a detail in the history of the Second World War' – a statement for which he was convicted and fined heavily in March 1991.

In addition, it should be pointed out that 4.3 million French people voted for a man who, as well as holding these fascist views, is also a criminal, having been convicted for racism, antisemitism and for selling discs and cassettes of speeches by Nazi leaders and of war-time Nazi marching songs. That they cast their votes in this way is a measure of the depth of the social and political crisis in France.

The revulsion at the wave of antisemitic outrages which, in part, stemmed form the hot-house racist and antisemitic atmosphere he has created, of course, did not help Le Pen but neither have they done him lasting damage. He kept a low profile and the incidents were forgotten within a few weeks. As in the past, Le Pen has revealed a remarkable immunity to a 'bad press'. We can be sure that the Front National is now a force to be reckoned with and that we have not seen the last of it.

Nor is the kind of racist programme propagated by Le Pen confined to France. Quite the contrary, because in the European Parliament he leads the 17-strong Group of the European Right which is composed of Euro-MPs from other EC countries, represents around 5 million voters and which, as a recognized parliamentary group, has access to massive funds.

Six of these Euro-MPs belonged, until recent internal ructions, to another fascist party, the Republikaner Partei (REP) in Germany. The REP's rise to prominence was truly meteoric. Until the start of 1989 the party was almost unknown within Germany as well as outside the country. However, breakthroughs in Berlin and other cities, anticipating the nationalist groundswell that led to the astonishingly speedy re-unification of Germany in October 1990, thrust the REP into a surprisingly strong position.

The REP's leader is the former top TV broadcaster Franz Schönhuber, who, in addition, served during the war as a volunteer in the Charlemagne Brigade, Nordland Division of the criminal and murderous Waffen-SS. Schönhuber openly and proudly admits his Nazi past; indeed, his party's politics are a continuation of it.

Since the Report was written, however, Schönhuber's star has been in the descendant. In the summer of 1990, he resigned as leader of the REP in a clever tactical manoeuvre aimed at re-establishing his position against more openly neo-nazi factional opponents and then later was re-elected. This, however, was at the price of estrangement from his fellow REP members in the European Parliament who, in early 1991, consummated the split with the formation of the Deutsche Allianz. The new group is led by Schönhuber's erstwhile protégé and Euro-MP Harald Neubauer, a man with a long record of involvement in extreme groups.

The split has been damaging but the underlying trend is more significant. In 1989, the REP, a self-styled 'law and order' party, gathered the votes of more than two million Germans in the European elections on a programme that openly advocated the abolition of trade unions, the destruction of social welfare, censorship and the wholesale 'de-criminalization' of German history. These remain, without exception, traditional themes.

The German extreme right as a whole exercises its influence in a number of important ways. For example, in the academic world its ideas heavily colour discussions on such issues as psychology, genetic theory, AIDS and sexuality and, above all, euthanasia, on which an active debate is taking place on whether 'valueless life' – this means handicapped children – should be allowed to survive because of the long-term expense to the state.

The main thrust of the REP's, and now the Deutsche Allianz's campaigns, however, are those which focus on demands for the repatriation of Germany's four million immigrants, guest workers and asylum-seekers to their countries of origin and for a united Germany within its Nazi-established 1937 frontiers.

Ironically, it was the rapid move towards a re-unified Germany which did most to short-circuit the REP's progress towards becoming a major electoral force and to induce a political crisis in their ranks. In Germany's first truly national elections since 1933, held in December 1990, the REP suffered heavy losses and saw its vote slashed by more than half to just under a million.

For the moment at least, German Chancellor Helmut Kohl and his ruling Christian Democrats (CDU) have been able to ride on the rising tide of revived German nationalism and to parade themselves as the architects of German re-unification. Nevertheless, as the most strident advocate of re-unification within pre-war borders, the REP was universally recognized as the 'hidden hand' behind Kohl's long refusal to give a concrete guarantee of Poland's existing western frontiers. It was when, and only when, the electoral threat from his Right had definitely receded that Kohl finally made the kind of guarantees that international diplomatic opinion, including the Polish, British and Danish governments, had been demanding, and signed a treaty with Poland recognizing the Oder–Niesse line frontier.

In the long-term, however, the German extreme right has grown quite independently of electoral fluctuations and the decline of the REP's fortunes. According to the official report of the Office for the Protection of the Constitution (Verfassungsschutz), in 1989 there were over 38,500 extreme-rightists in the then West Germany.

This figure did not include the REP's membership because, despite its fascist programme, the Verfassungsschutz does not regard the REP as 'extreme right'; but it does include the 27,000 who belong to the Nationaldemokratische Partei Deutschlands/ Deutsche Volksunion (NPD/DVU) alliance, which gained 455,000 votes in the June 1989 Euro-elections.

At the end of 1990, a mere six weeks after the presentation of this Report to the Parliament in Strasbourg, the Verfassungsschutz's deputy-president Peter Frisch issued a new estimate. The number of right-extremists, he declared, had doubled in 1990, the year of re-unification, and there were now as many in the five new east German states as in the western ones.

Rightly, Frisch dubbed this 'an alarming situation' and his remarks were echoed in April 1991 by Bernd Wagner, the senior criminal police officer for the east German states, who has special responsibility for monitoring the activity of right-wing extremists. The east of Germany is now the major growth area for racist and fascist organizations, yet, at the end of 1991, Wagner's office is to be closed down and its functions terminated.

Between the REP, the Deutsche Allianz, the Deutsche Volksunion and violent groups like the Freiheitliche Deutsche Arbeiten Partei (FAP) and the Nationalistische Front (NF) there are proven connections. Frequently, these 'militant' organizations provide security for meetings of the other parties.

It is a measure of the violence of these groups that in May 1990 in Amberg a key FAP and NF activist, Josef Saller, was imprisoned for 12 years for murdering four people, three of them Turks, in a fire-bomb attack. Such groups are heavily oriented towards the skinhead scene which is overwhelmingly neo-nazi, extremely violent and has mushroomed in eastern Germany.

A skinhead FAP member is, at the time of writing, awaiting trial for the brutal murder of a 21-year-old Bundeswehr soldier in Göttingen at the beginning of January 1991 and others have been at the forefront of a veritable blitz against guest workers' hostels and refugee centres in eastern Germany. In March 1991, skinhead fascists murdered 28-year-old Mozambican Jorge Gomondai by savagely beating him and then hurling him out of a moving tram in Leipzig. And, when the Polish–German frontier was opened in April 1991 to visa-free traffic, an assortment of fascist groups responded to the appeal of the late neo-nazi leader Michael

Kühnen and created border incidents serious enough to warrant a summons of Germany's chargé d'affaires in Warsaw to hear forceful protests from the Polish authorities.

The collapse of the East Bloc has thus not been a totally negative experience for the German far-right, even if the REP vote has plummeted as a result and the party is in what appears to be terminal disarray.

All the fascist parties and groups have made interventions in east Germany despite their dubious legal status, and church, refugee, trade union and even police organizations there warn constantly that the ground is fertile for the growth of the most extreme nationalism. In particular, the highly respected Evangelical Church Youth Commission has published a survey showing that 'tens of thousands of youth are potentially on the extreme-right'.

The leaders of Germany's 30,000 Jews have issued similar sombre warnings that unless the economic and social misery there – unemployment could rise soon to over 50 per cent – is alleviated the situation could 'develop out of control' and into what the respected German Foreign Minister Hans-Dietrich Genscher has termed 'the danger of civil war'.

The growth of right-extremist tendencies in Europe has not, of course, been by any means uniform. Quite the contrary, it has been piecemeal and contradictory.

In Great Britain, for instance, the scene of a dramatic emergence of the National Front in the late 1970s, the fascists have been more or less eclipsed and reduced to the albeit no less hateful tactic of desecrating Jewish and Islamic religious premises and cowardly hit-and-run assaults on Jews, black people and anti-fascists.

At most, the active right-wing extremists number fewer than 10,000, gathered in organizations like the British National Party, the National Front 'Flag' group and in what is, perhaps, the biggest movement, the skinhead 'Blood and Honour' network.

Electorally, their approach has become low key. The National Front pledged to field 60 candidates in the 1992 British General Election but, for the most part, they pinned any ballot-box hopes on the future introduction of proportional representation.

Italy, too, has seen momentous changes in the structure of the extreme-right with the Movimento Sociale Italiano (MSI) going into irreversible decline. Results from May 1991's elections in 29

Italian municipalities showed a dramatic slump in support for the MSI, but, more disturbingly, a transfer of their vote to ultra-rightist regionalist groups like the Lega Lombardia. In Valenza Po in Lombardy, the Lega Lombardia separatists grabbed a shock 23 per cent of the vote – up from its last score of only 2 per cent – while the MSI plunged into virtual collapse.

Both parties continue to be represented in the European Parliament. The Lega Lombardia has two seats and the MSI four, with the latter rather isolated, having left Le Pen's Technical Group of the European Right because of differences with its German contingent over the disputed South Tyrol region.

In Italy, too, where fascists were responsible for so much bloody terrorism in the 1970s and 1980s, including the infamous Bologna bombing when 86 people were killed, large-scale violence has receded. However, another disturbing phenomenon has arisen there for the first time: racist attacks directed at foreigners from Africa and the Maghreb.

Elsewhere in Europe, racist and populist far-right parties have made headway but nothing like on the French and German scale. Even within a country, it can be difficult to gauge their progress. Belgium is a good example of this. There, the Vlaams Blok, a party of clearly discernible fascist origin, pulls in roughly 20 per cent of the vote in the Dutch-speaking region around the northern city of Antwerp. The Vlaams Blok is avowedly racist and Karel Dillen its one member of the Strasbourg parliament belongs to Le Pen's fraction. However, it is far from clear how much support this party would gain if it was to field candidates on the other side of the Dutch–French linguistic divide in Belgium.

What is most disturbing about the overall picture in Europe, apart from the direct evidence in the shape of fascist parties and groups, is the tacit acceptance of the authorities that there is an 'acceptable' level of racism and the suggestion, implicit in the refusal to tackle issues like racist violence, that it can even function as a social safety-valve.

It can be argued that the growth of the fascists in western Europe has produced a measure of impotence amongst the politicians of the traditional conservative Right who are afraid of losing voters and that this weakness lies behind the authoritarian agenda for 1992 on issues like immigration and the right of asylum.

It is generally accepted amongst race/community relations experts across Europe that repressive measures to curb immigration – which anyway effectively no longer exists in the EC countries – and the right of asylum give ground to and buttress so-called 'popular racism'. A whole wider European discussion, indeed, now centres on future policy after 1 January 1993 when the internal borders of the European Community will officially come down to facilitate free movement of capital, services and, nominally, people.

It is this last point – people – that has proven most contentious and there exist already inside the EC various mechanisms like the TREVI Group of Ministers and the Schengen Accords which appear to regulate immigration policy at state level but are not remotely accountable. Both these mechanisms portray immigration and asylum policy as 'law and order' issues, alongside less savoury matters like drug-trafficking, organized crime and international terrorism, confirming widely-held suspicions that the current agenda on immigration and asylum is an authoritarian one.

Under the 1990 Schengen Agreement, signed by France, Germany and Benelux countries, relaxation of internal border controls between the signatory states will be complemented by much more stringent checks at the external frontiers. It will be far more difficult for non-Europeans to enter the Schengen countries in the first place and the five signatory states are currently devising a common visa policy that will apply to citizens of no fewer than 115 other states, mainly in the Third World.

Enforcing this will be the Schengen Information System, which will share and distribute data on 'undesirable aliens', asylum applications, patterns of asylum-seeking and people under surveillance by national security services.

And, this is by no means all. The sensitive issues of immigration and asylum have been the subject of wider all-EC discussions. In June 1990, in Dublin, EC Interior and Home Affairs Ministers began the signing of a new European convention on asylum which again tightens already existing rules under the guise of simplifying them and which marks the first step towards an all-embracing EC policy.

Two matters in particular arouse concern over the convention. Firstly, that the standard policy will be fitted to the most restrictive national policies rather than the most liberal ones, and secondly that, by 'zooming in' on immigration and asylum policies in this way, such measures at state level identify immigrants and refugees as 'the problem', fuelling the popular racism they are designed to appease and leading to more strident racist demands for ever tougher curbs on the right of entry to the EC countries.

Europe's agenda will have to change decisively and the problems of the EC's 'thirteenth state' – the Community's 12 to 14 million foreigners – will have to be faced if serious structural dislocation is to be avoided beyond 1992.

The portents are not good and the crisis in the former communist bloc states can only exacerbate the problems. Already very large-scale westward population movements from these states have been predicted.

Nowhere is this illustrated better than in the former Soviet Union where a majority of the country's 2 million Jews now want to leave. This wish stems from a real physical anxiety about what will result for them from the chaos into which the CIS seems to be falling.

So far, the CIS governments have done little to control or combat the CIS's home-grown, black-shirted fascist 'Pamyat' movement, despite the fact that this mass organization has publicly announced its intention to launch a campaign of terror against Communists and Jews and despite the fact that racist murders have been carried out by Pamyat followers (see Chapter 2, p. 41 below).

Neither is Pamyat an isolated case. Almost incredibly, the official Soviet Novosti Press Agency hosted a conference in Moscow of the Moon organization, which is closely linked with the up-market fascists of the World Anti-Communist League.

Similar tendencies are at work in Hungary, Romania and Poland. For example, in Hungary, Democratic Forum, the party which won the 1990 elections, has within its top leadership men like Istvan Czurka who have publicly expressed antisemitic views (see Chapter 2, p. 40).

In Romania, the situation is, if anything, even worse. There, in Bucharest, the notorious antisemitic forgery *The Protocols of the Elders of Zion* is on public sale and a strong fascist movement, Vatra Romanesca, with tens of thousands of members, has been formed to conduct what it says will be 'a bloody struggle against Hungarians, Germans, gypsies, Jews and other minorities'.

Finally, in Poland, there have been serious outbreaks of fascist violence against left-wing and Jewish members of 'Solidarity', and in May 1990 a large force of skinheads attacked demonstrators who had gathered to protest at a Warsaw meeting of seven different extreme-right groups. Poland's President Walesa and his allies in the Roman Catholic hierarchy have not helped to allay fears by playing with the antisemitic sentiments which, according to a May 1991 survey, are held by more than a third of Polish people.

In the East, the main forms of racism exhibited are antisemitism and anti-Romany and -Sinti prejudice with the Jews and 'gypsies' taken as scapegoats for the massive crisis left behind by the collapse of the communist regimes, whereas in the West the racism is directed more at black, non-European immigrants and asylum-seekers.

There is growing evidence of collaboration between racists and fascists in the East and West of Europe. The skinheads in East Germany and Hungary are known to have close contact with skinheads in West Germany, Austria and, it is reported, with the British international skinhead network 'Blood and Honour', which is led by ex-National Front member and 'Skrewdriver' lead singer Ian Stuart.

At other levels, too, there is active cooperation. The French Front National has numerous contacts in Poland and journalists from its daily paper *Présent* are frequent visitors, while at the Polish University of Radom, literature from the US 'Third Way' nazi Gary Gallo is used as course material by sympathetic academics.

The picture presented here is not a comforting one and reflects a radically different Europe – one of racism and violence – from the vision of ever-expanding harmony that is supposed to appear magically from the first minute of 1993.

The difficulty is that the colossal and dramatic upheavals since 1989 have brought with them the re-appearance of aggressive nationalism and xenophobia.

De-stabilization also produces mass insecurity which, combined with the structural crisis of European society and economy (one in every four young people aged between 18 and 25 is jobless within the EC), is leading millions to seek an explanation and a solution. The racists and fascists begin to give those answers – however bizarrely irrational and grotesque.

Today, we are at the beginning of this process. Millions are alienated from the dreams of 1992 as presented by many leading politicians and, through the extreme right and prejudices like racism and xenophobia, are beginning to express themselves autonomously and to make up their own minds. They are starting to make the leap to acceptance of what are enormously complex, inhuman and logic-defying racist answers to concrete social, economic and political problems.

Thus, it would be wrong to see right-wing extremism and fascism as some kind of puppets of a faceless 'Big Business'. That time may come but has not arrived yet, and there is no evidence to prove such a link at present.

What *has* arrived, however, is a mushrooming of fascism based on and utilizing already existing and powerful undercurrents of racism and xenophobia within our societies. It is there and growing like a cancer; unless we diagnose it properly, we shall be powerless to challenge and defeat it.

A pre-condition for these actions is to be informed and the publication of this Report can help perform this function. It is packed with information and provides an essential and timely overview. The purpose is to reproduce for public consumption a popular version of the Committee of Inquiry as ratified by the European Parliament. Thus the report remains in its original version. It is to be hoped that it will be widely read and will lead to positive social action and engagement along the lines of the 77 very practical recommendations contained in its final chapter.

If only a fraction of these are implemented, we can begin to climb out of the rising quagmire of racism and xenophobia, promoted by right-wing extremism, into which our societies run the risk of sinking and we can turn the existing difficulties and problems into opportunities for cultural diversity and enrichment.

The choice may be a hard one but it cannot much longer be evaded. This Report can help us in making the choice. Positively.

Glyn Ford

Note

1. The chapters which follow have been adapted from the Committee of Inquiry's Report. The text was completed in June 1990 and thus predates political developments since that time, including the re-unification of Germany on 3 October 1990.

1
General Considerations

Between 1984 and 1989 the European Parliament had to contend with an increased presence of elected representatives of extreme right-wing groups in its own chamber. This, amongst other factors, encouraged it to devote considerable attention, in its second legislative period in particular, to the increase of racism in Europe and to the rise of such extreme groups, which are the political expression, the result and to some extent the cause of this increase.

The upshot was the establishment of a committee of inquiry to study the rise of fascism and racism in Europe and to submit a report to Parliament. Mr Le Pen brought an action before the Court of Justice of the European Communities in Luxembourg, on behalf of the Group of the European Right, requesting it to annul the European Parliament's decision to appoint a committee of inquiry, but the Court declared the action inadmissible.

The report (the Evrigenis Report) was submitted in December 1985 and discussed in plenary in January 1986. On re-reading it one is struck by the fact that it is still an extremely valuable analysis of the phenomena of fascism and racism, their ideological and social roots and the objectives of the groups which they have produced.

The creation of the Committee of Inquiry and its report were contributory factors to the Joint Declaration against Racism and Xenophobia which was signed on 11 June 1986 in the chamber of the European Parliament in Strasbourg by the Presidents of the European Parliament and the Council, the representatives of the Member States meeting within the Council and the Commission. The declaration makes it incumbent on the institutions, and also the individual Member States, to take appropriate measures to combat all forms of intolerance, hostility and use of force against persons or groups of persons on the grounds of racial, religious, cultural, social or national differences. On the day the declaration was signed Parliament adopted a resolution approving the declaration.

Since then, almost every available opportunity has been seized in the European Parliament to denounce expressions of racism and fascism and to remind the European institutions and the governments of the Member States of their responsibilities in this respect, as solemnly stated in the Joint Declaration. Parliament has also been concerned with Community and national legislation on the right of asylum, identity checks and the social rights of immigrants; fields in which the principles of the Joint Declaration can be given concrete expression.

In addition to all the oral and written questions and resolutions on these subjects, the reports by the Committee on Legal Affairs and Citizens' Rights on the right of asylum (the Vetter Report), the Commission proposal on the fight against racism and xenophobia (the Medina Ortega Report) and the report of the Political Affairs Committee on the Joint Declaration (Van der Lek Report) should be cited as particularly significant contributions to the ongoing debate.

However, some three years after the signing of the Joint Declaration, Parliament felt there was a need for a more comprehensive report, which would both take stock of how the declaration had been implemented and present a kind of synthesis of a number of aspects directly concerned with this subject and stressed in previous reports adopted by the European Parliament. It was also felt necessary to update and supplement the factual information contained in the Evrigenis Report; since December 1985, when the original report was submitted, the situation had undergone a radical change in some Member States, e.g. the Federal Republic of Germany and Italy, whilst Spain and Portugal had now joined the Community.

Nor was it possible for the 1985 report to take account of the signing of the Single European Act and the plans in 'operation 1992/93' to hasten the removal of intra-Community borders. By the late 1980s it had become quite clear what impact the compensatory measures which would have to be taken in this connection might have on immigration policy in respect of persons from third, non-European countries and on their legal position and freedom of movement within the Community. Although this is, to a large extent, a matter for some of the permanent committees of the European Parliament, there were sound reasons for establishing a separate framework for looking at the measures and comparing them with the principles enshrined in the Joint Declaration of 1986.

Now, in 1990, the governments of all or some of the EC Member States are jointly planning measures which could have far-reaching consequences for the lives of millions of persons living in their countries, but the preparation of these measures is beyond all parliamentary control. National parliaments can only say yes or no to the international agreements embodying the results of the international negotiations; the European Parliament may possibly be able to take some action pursuant to its powers by virtue of the Single European Act, but on the whole in matters such as this it can exercise only a verbal control. This weakness can, however, be a strength in some instances. Monitoring and presenting well-documented evidence of cross-border incidents, the complex nature of which is beyond the control mechanisms of the national parliaments, can in itself exercise a significant corrective function.

The result of the foregoing was that in August 1989 a motion for a resolution by Mr Glinne, Mr Cot, Mr Ford and Mr Romeos, and bearing the signatures of 147 Members, was tabled, and submitted to Parliament's enlarged Bureau. It proposed setting up a committee of inquiry 'to assess the situation in the Member States in the light of the declaration of 11 June 1986 and to take stock of any violations'. It found that 'measures which could be described as racist and xenophobic are being taken in some Member States, especially by local authorities'.

The composition of the Committee, as proposed by the Bureau and approved in plenary, was as follows: six members were nominated by the Socialist Group, three by the Group of the European People's Party, one by the Liberal Democratic and Reformist Group, one by the European Democrat Group, one by the Green Group, one by the Group of the European Unitarian Left, one by the European Democratic Alliance and one by the Left Coalition.[1] The constituent meeting was held on 23 November

1989, at which Glyn Ford, Chairman of the previous Committee of Inquiry into the Rise of Fascism and Racism in Europe, was appointed rapporteur.[2]

The Committee of Inquiry held thirteen meetings between 23 November 1989 and 17 July 1990, including two hearings. The Committee bureau, together with the rapporteur and several members, held two working meetings, once in London and once in Luxembourg. The Committee as a whole met once outside the normal places of work of Parliament in Marseilles. The rapporteur paid an exploratory visit on behalf of the Committee of Inquiry to West and East Berlin. From the outset the Committee decided to meet in public. Exceptions were made to this on only two occasions: the hearing in late January 1990, which at the request of the guest participants was closed to the press and public, and in Marseilles, where only part of the meeting was closed to the public.

The Committee adopted virtually the same approach for gathering information as its predecessor which had produced the Evrigenis Report:

- by holding ordinary meetings in Brussels, including exchanges of views with the representatives of other institutions;
- by holding public or private hearings;
- by asking for written submissions;
- by visits of the whole committee or of the enlarged bureau to a number of towns and conurbations.

The rapporteur was also helped in his fact-finding by two organizations: *Migrants Newssheet* (published by the Brussels-based Churches' Committee for Migrants in Europe) and Searchlight, a London-based institute which collects systematic information on fascists and other extreme right-wing groups and organizations in Europe. The rapporteur is particularly grateful for their help. He would also like to express his appreciation to the Institut für Migrations- und Rassismusforchung (Institute for Research into Migration and Racism) in Hamburg, which provided similar assistance, and to the Anne Frank Foundation in Amsterdam.

Central to the Committee's terms of reference was the task of investigating the extent to which the signatories to the Joint

Declaration in June 1986 had implemented what had been agreed. Setting aside the question whether the Joint Declaration can be deemed to be Community legislation and whether non-implementation of the intentions and principles of the declaration can be regarded as an infringement in the legal sense, the Committee believes there was every reason to carry out an in-depth survey of whether the European institutions and the governments of the Member States had fulfilled the obligations they had solemnly entered into.

The first stage in the inquiry was to invite the responsible ministers to cooperate in a hearing held in Brussels with national civil servants responsible for combating racism and forming legislation in that field. This hearing took place on 29–31 January 1990.[3] The Committee then organized a second hearing, this time in public, in Brussels, from 9 April 1990, to look into the broad field of the fight against racism and xenophobia and the way in which it is actually implemented in terms of facilities for refugees, immigrants and ethnic minorities.[4]

At its ordinary meetings in Brussels the Committee received information from the responsible Members of the European Commission, Mrs Vasso Papandreou and Mr Martin Bangemann. Prior to this there was a more detailed exchange of views with officials representing the Commission on issues such as the European Migrants Forum and the Rhodes Group, etc. It also received evidence in Brussels from Mr Piet Stoffelen, Vice-President of the Parliamentary Assembly and Chairman of the Legal Affairs Committee of the Council of Europe, Mr Houshmand, head of the International Instruments section of the United Nations Centre for Human Rights in Geneva, and Professor Michael Banton of the University of Bristol.

During its meeting in Marseilles from 17–19 April 1990 the Committee received detailed information on the situation of local immigrants from the Mayor of Marseilles, Mr Robert Vigouroux and his staff, and from mayors and town councillors from the Marseilles area, the prefect of the Rhone-Alpes-Côte d'Azur region, Mr Claude Bussiere and other police and judicial authorities, etc. There was an invitation to the members of the Committee to attend a reception and working meeting at the Regional Council by its Chairman, Mr Jean-Claude Gaudin. Three members participated, but the majority decided to boycott it because of claims that Mr Gaudin's Administration was formed with support from the Front National.

There was also a lengthy (and at times emotional) exchange of views in Marseilles at a public hearing with the representatives of mainly local organizations for immigrants and foreigners. The Committee also received information from Mr Jean Kahn, Chairman of the Conseil Représentatif des Institutions Juives en France (CRIF: Representative Council of Jewish Councils in France), who had initially been invited to the public hearing on 9–11 April but had been unable to attend.

During its meetings in London (24 and 25 May 1990) and Luxembourg (28 June 1990) the Committee's 'enlarged' Bureau had detailed discussions with ministers, local councillors, Members of Parliament, representatives of interest groups for immigrants and experts, etc. There was a meeting in the House of Commons in London with three black MPs: Mr Paul Boateng, Mr Bernie Grant and Mr Keith Vaz. There was an in-depth exchange of views between the Bureau and Mr John Patten, Minister of State at the Home Office with responsibility for race relations. In Luxembourg the Bureau and the accompanying members received information from Mr Jacques Poos, Deputy Prime Minister and Minister for Foreign Affairs, Mr Marc Fischbach, the Minister of Justice, Mrs Würth-Polfer, Mayor of Luxembourg city, representatives of employers and employees' organizations and of immigrant workers. In London, as in Marseilles, the Committee established contact with the immigrants in their own communities.

It was not until 17 July 1990, i.e. at its last meeting, that the Committee was able to hold talks with the President-in-Office of the Council of Ministers of the European Communities. The Committee considered talks with one of the signatories to the Declaration of 11 June 1986 to be of major importance for its inquiry and had therefore sent an invitation, as early as the beginning of December 1989, to the then French Presidency of the Council, but, despite oral assurances from officials of the French Permanent Representation that the President-in-Office would attend the committee's meeting of 20–21 December 1989, the latter cried off just before it was due to take place.

The Committee then immediately approached the Irish Presidency but during its six-month term of office the latter completely boycotted the inquiry, despite repeated requests and invitations from its chairman, Mr Nordmann, and Parliament's President, Mr Barón Crespo, to the Irish Foreign Minister, Mr Gerard Collins. The rapporteur and the Committee therefore express their particular appreciation to the Italian Presidency which, almost immediately upon taking up office, declared itself willing to appear before the Committee. The talks held on 17 July with Mr Claudio Vitalone, Italian Under-Secretary of State for Foreign Affairs, were most useful and informative but, owing to the circumstances described above, came too late to have a significant impact on the content of the report.[5]

At its meeting of 16 and 17 July 1990 the Committee adopted the recommendations by 10 votes in favour, one against and one abstention. A roll-call vote was requested and agreed.[6]

The Committee and its rapporteur believe that even without the cooperation of the Presidency of the Council (which managed to adopt a resolution on the fight against racism and xenophobia without informing or consulting in any way the European Parliament's Committee of Inquiry) it has been able to build up a fairly complete picture of the implementation (or non-implementation) of the Joint Declaration of 1986. Readers of this volume will decide for themselves whether we are justified in this belief.

2

Organized Racism and Right-wing Extremism

Belgium

The current situation of right-wing extremism in Belgium represents a picture of limited progress whose focal point is very much the Vlaams Blok (VB), which doubled its support in parts of Flanders between 1988 and 1990. Antwerp is the VB's strongest centre, a fact reflected in a 21 per cent vote for the party in the June 1989 Euro-elections and its gain of one seat, occupied by VB deputy leader Karel Dillen, in the European Parliament. This success was founded and consolidated on earlier election wins in the Antwerp region since 1986, when, with 10 per cent there, the VB got two seats in the Belgian national parliament, and in 1988, when, with a 17.7 per cent vote, it captured 10 seats in the Antwerp city parliament.

However, its forward march is by no means limited to Antwerp because in other Flemish-speaking centres it registered increased support in June 1989. For example, in Ghent it got 5.2 per cent of the vote and in Mechelen 8.6 per cent after running racist campaigns targeting Moroccan immigrants for its anti-immigration policies.

Its central policies are those of racism and its main slogan is 'eigen volk eerst' ('our own people first'). The Flemish people, the VB believes, are part of the wider German family and one of its leaders, Member of the Belgian Parliament Filip de Winter, has proclaimed on behalf of the VB: 'Our dream is of a greater Netherlands with around 20 million people.' Other areas of activity with which the VB concerns itself are law and order, abortion and drugs. It also calls for a European unity free of Russian and American influence.

The VB's roots can be traced back to the pre-war fascist movement in Belgium, which collaborated politically with the country's nazi occupiers during the Second World War. While it is a legally-constituted political party with three MPs and one Euro-MP, it does have links with the violent Voorpost (Vanguard) organization and its members have been involved in attacks on political opponents. Some within both the VB and Voorpost are former members of one of Belgium's most notorious post-war fascist organizations, the Vlaamse Militanten Orde (VMO), which was founded by ex-collaborators in 1949 and existed right up to the early 1980s, when it was outlawed for its violent actions.

Before being made illegal, the VMO was connected with terror organizations across the entire continent, including the Turkish Grey Wolves, the French organization Féderation d'Action Nationale et Europèene (FANE), the Italian Ordine Nuovo and loyalist paramilitary groups in Northern Ireland. The VMO's terror links came to light accidentally in a trial in Britain of 14 members of the Protestant Ulster Volunteer Force (UVF) some years ago. In court evidence it was revealed that the VMO had tried to do a secret deal with the UVF in which, in exchange for £50,000-worth of firearms, the VMO asked the UVF to launch a bombing campaign against Jewish targets in Britain. The UVF refused.

After the state ban on the VMO many of its members joined the Vlaams Blok while others chose to remain independent and to try to reconstitute the VMO or establish new groups. This has led to the formation of a myriad of extreme-right groups, parties and movements in the Flemish-speaking regions of Belgium. The two most notable of these are the VMO-Odal Group (Odal being an ancient runic symbol that is one of the origins of the swastika) and the Nationaal Front Vlaanderen (NFV).

The VMO-Odal Group is led by the veteran neo-nazi Bert Eriksson. It was founded in 1986 but later split over the issues of whether it should support the Vlaams Blok. The group that split off became the NFV and is led by Werner van Steen, who has a conviction for racial violence. Both groups have wide international contacts and have organized international gatherings in Belgium together. The most important of these were at Antwerp in 1987, Courtrai in 1988 and Alveringhem in 1989. Present at these meetings were extremists and neo-nazis from Britain,

France, the Federal Republic of Germany and the Netherlands. These gatherings took place despite efforts by the authorities to prevent them.

Both groups also have a serious record of violence directed against both migrants and political opponents but are mainly organizations of militants with fewer than 600 members between them and with no electoral presence.

In the French-speaking parts of Belgium the extreme right finds itself divided and lacking in any serious electoral expression, having a total of only three elected representatives. Two of the three sit on the council in Brussels and the other in Molenbeek. All are members of the Front National, which was established in 1984 from a unification of several smaller groups and models itself on the Front National of France with which it has links.

The FN numbers at most 1000 members, of whom only about 250 are active. It has, however, eclipsed the other main right-extremist group, the Parti des Forces Nouvelles (PFN), which was formed in 1982 and largely concentrates its efforts on trying to recruit skinheads and soccer hooligans. Some of its members have been involved in street assaults on immigrants.

Ideologically, the PFN is influenced very heavily by Robert Stuekers of the Belgian 'New Right' who directs publication of the reviews *Vouloir* and *Orientations* and who in February 1990 was a prominent guest at the London conference of the racist *Scorpion* magazine published by the Cologne-based British neo-nazi Michael Walker.

A worrying development in Belgium since 1988 has been the activity of the l'Assaut (Assault) group, which is composed of former VMO and PFN members in the Brussels area. L'Assaut already has a record of violence against immigrants and tries to foster good relations with racist-influenced skinheads. It also has close connections with the Parti Nationalist Français et Européen (PNFE) in France, with skinheads grouped around the fanzine *Le Rebelle Blanc* and with the French chapter of the Ku-Klux-Klan.

According to Marijke Van Hemeldonck, MEP, 'only a few studies of racism have been carried out' but 'they all show that racism in Belgium is very pronounced'. It has been argued that the failure of the extreme right to capitalize on this situation is partly attributable to the linguistic divide between the Flemish and French-speaking communities. Nevertheless the potential dangers have been highlighted by the surge of support for the Vlaams Blok.

Denmark

In Denmark the main neo-nazi group is the Dansk Nasjonal Socjalistisk Bund (DNSB), led by the 30-year-old schoolteacher Poul Riis-Knudsen, who doubles as head of the World Union of National Socialists (WUNS) with a broad range of international contacts.

In 1988 Riis-Knudsen, who claims that more than 1000 members in eight Danish cities belong to his organization, promised that his party would field candidates in local elections in Copenhagen and Aalborg. These would have been the first openly fascist candidates to contest elections in Denmark since before the Second World War. This did not materialize and may have been a tactic designed to win publicity.

Certainly the DNSB was successful in this quest in April 1989 when it won wide media attention for its repeated declarations that it would commemorate the 100th anniversary of Hitler's birth and for its statements that among those invited to the event would be the German neo-nazi leader, Michael Kühnen.

The DNSB not only has contact with Kühnen but is also connected with ex-Auschwitz SS man Theis Christophersen, the author of the infamous book, *The Auschwitz Lie,* who fled to Denmark to escape possible arrest by the German Federal authorities. Christophersen, though elderly, has exercised an important influence on the DNSB and has been instrumental in ensuring that it does not deviate from the nazi ideology. Thus the DNSB's programme is openly nazi and promotes a Denmark purged of immigrants, the death penalty for anyone transmitting AIDS, labour camps for political opponents and compulsory sterilization for non-white adopted children. When Riis-Knudsen proclaimed these points in a televised documentary film, he caused widespread shock in Norway and Sweden where the programme was screened (it was banned in Denmark). Some Danish politicians, like former Communications Minister Arne Melchior, have since urged that Danish law be fully applied to the DNSB.

The DNSB has now been restructured into a cadre organization with three tiers of membership, according to the degree of commitment shown by individual members and supporters.

Despite its publicity-seeking activities, the DNSB exercises little real influence on the political scene. The same can be said of the groups of Greenjackets (a youth group which takes its name from the American airforce style jackets its members wear) who have carried out serious street assaults, including attempted murder, against immigrants.

Of far more concern to those who work closely with immigrants and refugees is the Fremskridtspartiet (Progress party) led by Mogens Glistrup. Ejner Christiansen, MEP, has described the Fremskridtspartiet in the following terms: 'Generally speaking, this party has made hatred of aliens as important a part of its party manifesto as the hatred of the tax system which originally swept the party into the Danish Parliament in 1973 with nearly twice as many votes as the party now obtains.' The current level of popular support for the party stands at around 10 per cent, a figure that corresponds closely with the percentage of Danish people who have decidedly negative attitudes towards foreigners resident in the country.

Since the last two major intakes of refugees in 1985 and 1986, racist attitudes appear to have hardened (46 per cent believing that Denmark accepts too many refugees) and this has been accompanied by a rising incidence of racist assaults and abuse and a mushrooming of racist groups, including the Citizens' List, Stop Immigration, which obtained 5868 votes in Copenhagen, Odense, Aalborg and Frederiksberg in the 1989 local elections. The Citizens' List claims to take the German Republikaner Partei as its model and styles itself as a Danish nationalist party.

Some of the organization's leaders have connections with the Fremskridtspartiet, the cultural Danish Association and the DNSB. More recently, in March 1990 an attempt was made to bring together the various anti-immigration groups under an umbrella organization called the People's Movement against Immigration. However, this foundered when the town council in Fredericia made it clear that it did not want such a gathering in the town and the hotel which was to host the founding meeting cancelled the booking.

The general view of observers in Denmark is that in the last few years racism has become a more serious and pressing problem and conditions are becoming more favourable for a growth of the extreme right.

Federal Republic of Germany

Between 1985, when the Evrigenis Report was published, and the end of 1988 extreme-right organizations in West Germany made little visible progress. However, at the start of 1989 the situation changed rapidly with election breakthroughs in West Berlin, Frankfurt, Cologne, Stuttgart and Düsseldorf and other major cities at municipal level, and also in the 18 June 1989 elections to the European Parliament.

The process began at the end of January 1989 when the Republikaner (REP), led by Franz Schönhuber, from a base of fewer than 300 members in the city, polled 90,000 votes in West Berlin and won 11 seats in the city parliament. Only two months later this process was furthered in Frankfurt with the REP's neo-fascist rival, the Nationaldemokratische Partei Deutschlands (NPD), gained 7 seats in the city parliament and re-established a presence there for the first time since the late 1960s.

By June 1989 the mounting electoral support for extreme-right parties was demonstrated to be a new social and political tendency in the European Parliament elections in which the REP gained over two million votes and 6 seats in Strasbourg. The combined vote for the whole West German extreme-right in that election added up to more than 2,655,000 and indicated the extent of the rightwards shift in West German politics.

Finally, in later elections in the West German provinces of North Rhine Westphalia and Baden-Württemberg the REP piled up impressive votes and saw its candidates elected in a whole series of major cities: Cologne, Düsseldorf, Gelsenkirchen, Stuttgart, Mannheim and Karlsruhe.

These successes of the REP have provided it with immense resources with which to pursue its racist and anti-foreigner campaigns. From Federal German funds alone it received almost DM 16 million and its membership of the Group of the European Right in the European Parliament gives it access to additional revenue. This money will be put to effective use by the REP, whose grasp of propaganda techniques has so far been revealed as very skilful. During its election campaign in Berlin and for the

European Parliament the REP's ability to popularize its ideas was put to striking effect with highly professional television spots. The ideas transmitted – for a strong Germany, for reunification within Germany's pre-Second World War frontiers, for national self-determination and spiritual and moral renewal and above all for tighter controls over foreigners – touched deep chords within the West German population.

Willi Rothley, MEP, has argued that a population insecure and directionless after modernization has dissolved traditional ties is particularly susceptible to the apparent 'security' offered by the nationalist and xenophobic message of the extreme right (see Introduction, p. xiii above).

German political analysts have rejected the view that the re-emergence of the extreme right is only a protest at the failure of the mainstream political parties, by pointing to a firm base of support among young working-class men attracted by the macho images of strength and power projected by the REP.

Detailed studies of extreme-right voting patterns indicate that while the REP draws the bulk of its support from disenchanted Christian Democrat (CDU) supporters, it also finds backing from people who previously voted for the Social Democrats (SPD). Other surveys, for example one by the SPD-aligned police trade union, suggest that support for the REP among policemen is especially strong. In Bavaria, for example, more than 50 per cent of policemen declared support for the REP while in Hesse more than 60 per cent of officers expressed similar loyalties. In addition the REP now has serious backing in the Federal Republic's armed forces with more than 1000 serving soldiers in party membership. The demands for a strong Germany are obviously paying dividends.

The tactics employed by the REP's leader, Franz Schönhuber, are robust and win publicity. For example, when he was accused of antisemitism, Mr Schönhuber declared that although he 'liked certain Jewish writers and composers, that did not mean he had to like Mr Galinski' (the leader of West Germany's tiny Jewish community). Later, in autumn 1989, he stated that there were 'five occupying powers in Germany: the USA, the USSR, France, Great Britain and . . . the Central Council of German Jews'.

Mr Schönhuber does not conceal his wartime record of service as a volunteer in the Waffen-SS, an organization branded as criminal in the Nuremberg trials of top nazi war criminals after the war. In 1982 he published his memoirs of that period in his life under the title '*Ich war debei*' ('I was with them'), an action which reportedly resulted in him losing his position as a television journalist.

The REP's ideas bear an uncomfortably close resemblance to the policies of Hitler's nazis and propose among other things:

- subordination of trade unions to the state;
- compulsory training of girls for the roles of wife and mother;
- censorship;
- withholding social security and political rights for foreigners.

These ideas are advocated publicly from party publications and platforms, but REP members have also argued that HIV virus carriers should have their genitals tattooed and that the now-abandoned nuclear power plant at Wackersdorf should be transformed into a labour camp for political opponents.

Claudia Roth, MEP, has stated that 'on no other political theme is there such consensus among West Germans as on the issue of xenophobia and racism'. She cited a survey published in *Der Spiegel* in September 1989 which revealed that no fewer than 79 per cent of Germans took the view that too many foreigners live in the Federal Republic. The impact on these attitudes of the momentous events in East Germany and the rapid moves towards German re-unification remains to be seen, but there is evidence that there is also prejudice against ethnic German immigrants from Poland, Romania and the USSR. However, paradoxically, the REP, along with other extreme-right groups, has seized on the collapse of the German Democratic Republic to spread propaganda and establish (illegal) organizations there.

The REP's main impact generally, however, seems to have been to push the axis of political discussion in West Germany to the right, a fact exemplified by the presence of three Federal Republic government ministers on the platform at the Hanover rally of German nationalist Silesian exiles in August 1989. This caused some public concern as did the claim by official government spokesman Hans Klein that the Waffen-SS was 'a group of fighting soldiers who defended the fatherland'. Such positions taken by German politicians have not diminished support for the

REP but rather have served to legitimize many of its ideas in the public mind.

One notable consequence of the REP's emergence has been a weakening of other sections of the neo-nazi right, not least the Deutsche Volksunion (DVU) led by Gerhard Frey. The DVU commands large resources including a medium-sized press empire which enabled it to mail over 24 million homes with printed propaganda in the June 1989 European elections. The European elections provided a testing ground for the DVU and the REP and the latter emerged as the clear winner, leaving it in a strong position to contest the 1990 Federal elections.

To illustrate the dramatic character of the rise of the REP it is worth noting the observation of the European parliament's report of its Committee of Inquiry into the Rise of Racism and Fascism in Europe. The report, issued in December 1985, said: 'In the middle term organized German right-wing extremism has no chances in electoral politics.'

Although, because of its crashing electoral breakthroughs, much media and public attention focuses on the REP, this organization is in fact only the tip of a very large extreme-right iceberg in West Germany.

The DVU, in alliance with the NPD, fielded candidates in the June 1989 European elections under the title 'Liste D' – the 'D' standing for Deutschland (Germany). Although eclipsed by the heavy REP poll, Liste D still managed to get 455,000 votes. This exercise cost the DVU more then DM 18 and it will be able to reclaim more than DM 2.4 million from state funds.

Liste D's programme differed little from that of the REP in proposing the expulsion of foreigners as the answer to West Germany's jobs and housing crises. Its appeal is directed at those who want to give voice to growing anxiety about the future by looking outside the established democratic political framework. Thus its slogans, 'Germany for the Germans', 'Germany first, then Europe' and 'Proud to be German', find a ready hearing among younger people as well as the older generation who grew up under the influence of nazi indoctrination in the Third Reich.

The main handicap of the DVU/NPD alliance is its more overt neo-nazi image. Its leader, Dr Gerhard Frey, is not, unlike the REP leader Franz Schönhuber, a former Waffen-SS man, but he controls a press empire which publishes an endless stream of material seeking to revise Germany's wartime history and expunge nazi war guilt. The flagship of this empire is the *Nationale Zeitung*, a weekly paper with sales of 120,000 copies.

Frey's papers also concentrate on antisemitic themes and maintain a relentless hostility towards the country's small Jewish population. In fact the DVU and NPD sympathize with denials that the Holocaust ever took place and the DVU on more than one occasion has prominently featured the revisionist British historian David Irving to give weight to such denials. Irving's books, which almost all centre on providing an 'objective' history of the nazi regime, are bestsellers in West Germany and even more extreme historical revisionist texts also sell in large numbers. For example, the book *The Auschwitz Lie* by Thies Christophersen (see p. 11) sold over 80,000 copies despite being illegal.

The DVU/NPD alliance has a combined membership of about 27,000 and is particularly strong in southern Germany and in the poorer north where in 1987 it captured two seats in the city parliament in Bremerhaven, a city badly hit by shipyard closures. The DVU and its NPD partners, who won seats in the Frankfurt city parliament and gained 9.3 per cent of the vote in the Baden-Württemberg town of Tuttlingen in October 1989, have, however, both lost many members who have defected to the now larger REP (approximately 30,000 members) and form its basic activist cadre.

Though the DVU/NPD alliance and the REP disclaim links with the more terroristically-inclined groups like the 1500-strong Freiheitliche Deutsche Arbeiter Partei (FAP) and the 500-strong Nationalistische Front (NF), members of these organizations are frequently found stewarding meetings of both movements.

Inside the NPD there are sharp divisions over how to respond to its REP rivals and there is also a Third Position 'neither capitalism nor communism but national revolution' – a faction which liaises with the Political Soldiers of the National Front in Britain and acts as an outlet for the writings of Colonel Gadaffi of Libya.

The whole of Liste D is virulently antisemitic, but the NPD is more forthright in this regard. Already one of its elected representatives in Frankfurt, Erich Gutjahr, has been disqualified from taking his city parliament seat after a public outburst in which he said: 'The Jews are robbing us again' and went on to claim: 'The Jews have bought up half of Frankfurt.'

An additional side-effect of the general electoral progress of the REP is that to date there is not the slightest chance of unity between Liste D and the REP because of mutual dislike between their leaders. The REP's rise appears to be Liste D's fall.

The militant, street-active, neo-nazi groups like the FAP, the NF and the Deutsche Alternative, which is largely inspired by several-times-convicted ex-Bundeswehr officer Michael Kühnen, have, like their French counterparts, been overshadowed by the electoral successes of more respectable racists. These groups, noted for their ability to gather huge caches of arms, organize skinheads and football hooligans for assaults on foreigners and Jewish property and to plant bombs and murder, as in the 1980 Munich Beer Festival attack when they killed 12 people, have been pushed firmly on to the sidelines by the REP and have even urged their members to support Schönhuber.

Equally marginalized are the heavily-armed and well-organized so-called military sports groups like the now-defunct Wehrsportgruppe Hoffman, which in the early 1980s received military training in the Lebanon from both the PLO and its enemies in the Christian Phalange. The Hoffman Group's leader, Karl-Heinz Hoffman, who also admires Schönhuber, was recently released from prison after serving a sentence for serious crimes including possession of weapons.

Other terror groups, which earlier in the decade bombed over 100 US military installations in a bid to cause destabilization, still exist but have largely gone underground. Some members in these groups who are wanted by the police, like Walter Kexel and Ulrich Tillman, fled to England to be safe-housed by the British fascists of the League of St George.

Another of Germany's most wanted neo-nazi terrorists, Odfried Hepp, was arrested by French police in the Paris apartment of the French representative of the Palestine Liberation Front, the organization that later hi-jacked the cruise ship *Achille Lauro*.

Though neo-nazi terror is no longer either fashionable or politically useful in the Federal Republic, this does not mean that the most violent wing of German right-wing extremism has renounced its activities. As recently as April 1989, police raids discovered large quantities of illegally-held arms in the hands of neo-nazis in Frankfurt and Munden.

Violence also continues and Claudia Roth has remarked: 'The rise in the REP's political significance has been paralleled by a rise in the number of violent attacks on foreigners in the FRG.' In particular, violence has been carried out and provoked in Hanover and Göttingen by neo-nazi affiliated skinhead groups who have singled out Turks for assaults.

Action by the authorities can contain this problem. Electoral success embracing millions cannot, however, be so easily handled by police action and West Germany now faces a very serious problem of right-wing extremist advances, even if election results in Saarland, Bavaria and Schleswig-Holstein in early 1990 point to a downturn in electoral support for the REP.

Already the state's constitutional watchdog, the Bundesverfassungsschutz security service, which monitors both the left and right, has charted an increase in the number of hard-core fascist activists from 22,000 in 1988 to more than 30,000 in 1989. This figure, however, does not include members of the REP, which is regarded by the Bundesverfassungsschutz as right radical rather than right-extremist. The Bundesverfassungsschutz in Bavaria has characterized the REP as 'unfriendly to the constitution' and in Hamburg has declared its intention to place the REP under observation, but it remains a measure of the state's priorities that its most recent report (for 1988) devoted 142 pages to left extremism and only 42 pages to the extreme right.

Greece

In recent years there has been a number of far-right groups which, apart from their activities against Jews, gypsies and Muslims, have also participated in acts of economic sabotage in an attempt to destabilize the former socialist government. In particular the Fourth of August Movement has burned down forests. The Ceniaio Ethnikistiko Kinema (ENEK) had links with the League of St George in Britain.

Since the mid-1980s, the extreme-right political party, the Greek National Political Society (EPEN), has seen its fortunes recede to the point where it has lost its one seat in the European

Parliament and in the 1990 elections polled less than 1 per cent of the vote.

France

The resurgence of the extreme-right in France can be effectively charted from 1984 when, against expectations, the Front National (FN) gained 10 seats in elections to the European Parliament. Although the 10.9 per cent vote for the anti-immigration FN was viewed as a protest phenomenon, its progress was later confirmed in March 1986 when it won more than 2.7 million votes in the elections to the French National Assembly and secured 35 seats.

The first round of the French Presidential elections in April 1988 saw the FN's support further consolidated when, running against Socialist President Mitterrand, the FN's candidate and leader, Jean-Marie Le Pen, gained 14.4 per cent of the vote and caused profound shock throughout France. The percentage may have masked the real scale of support for the FN. Analysing the votes cast, the measure of the FN's success can be estimated. Le Pen's total vote of 4,367,926 indicated that his party's concentration on anti-immigration themes had gained ground among French people.

The Le Pen vote extended right across the entire French social and geographical spectrum and suggested that large sections of the French public were willing to identify with the FN policy of demanding the removal of France's large immigrant population.

Brief examination of the extreme-right vote in the April 1988 election highlights this clearly. An article in *Le Monde* of 27 April 1988 shows that Le Pen secured the votes of:

- 31 per cent of small business owners;
- 21 per cent of professional people (doctors, lawyers, etc.);
- 21 per cent of shop workers;
- 19 per cent of unemployed people;
- 18 per cent of farmers/agricultural workers;
- 16 per cent of factory workers.

With this broad social cross-section of support the FN established itself as a permanent fixture in French politics. Despite some setbacks stemming from adverse publicity, the loss of some electoral support and the death of its deputy leader, Jean-Pierre Stirbois, the signs are that the FN has recovered and consolidated a hard-core electoral base. This was reflected in the June 1989 elections to the European Parliament, when, despite a record level of abstentions, the FN won 10 seats, polled more than two million votes and pushed up its percentage share to 11.3 per cent.

Later, in November 1989, the FN's candidates won votes of 61 per cent and 47 per cent in Dreux and Marseilles respectively in parliamentary by-elections, securing the election of Mr Stirbois's widow, Marie-France Stirbois, to the French National Assembly, only the second FN member to be elected since the voting system was changed in 1988.

In part much of this recovery can be attributed to the FN's powerful organizational machine and massive resources which enable it to run heavy-weight and relentless propaganda campaigns against immigration, foreigners and what Le Pen calls Marxism and the Islamicization of France. The resources of the FN include:

- 100,000 members;
- 200,000 sympathizers;
- a sympathetic daily paper, *Présent*, with a circulation of 100,000;
- its own weekly, *National Hebdo*, with 200,000 readers;
- influence in the police, the judiciary and the armed forces;
- 842 elected representatives at local level;
- a growing following in the universities and academic circles fostered by intellectuals like Alain de Benoist and the far-right think-tank, GRECE (Groupement de Recherche et d'Etudes pour la Civilisation Européenne).

The size and scale of the FN's organization and activities give the party considerable strength, especially in the south of France, where in Perpignan, for example, it takes almost 30 per cent of the vote and in Marseilles it always polls heavily. But it is not just in the south that the FN is strong. In the depressed steel and coal regions of northern and eastern France, regions suffering all the pain brought about by slow de-industrialization, it challenges the declining Parti Communiste Français (PCF) for the working-class vote. This challenge even extends into the historic heartland of French communism, Seine-St Denis in the red belt around Paris.

There the FN has twice won more votes than the PCF from working people who are disillusioned with the left.

By presenting itself as the voice of the working man against big capital on the one hand and red manipulation on the other, the FN has had a potent effect. The desperate crisis of the badly-divided French trade union movement, to which only 20 per cent of workers now belong, has helped the fascists to penetrate deeply into the most disadvantaged social layers.

At the same time a legacy of racist and nationalist policies, such as the bulldozing of an immigrant workers' hostel in Vitry, pursued by the PCF in the late 1970s and early 1980s, has found an outlet now in the FN. Racism has seduced many people in France and exists there in abundance, notwithstanding the efforts of numerous anti-racist movements such as SOS Racisme and France Plus. In reality it seems that such movements have not significantly dented support for the FN, whose politics centre on existing racism against North Africans, black people and, sporadically, Jews.

Apart from outbursts of antisemitism, Le Pen and the FN constantly claim that France is in acute danger of becoming an Islamic nation and that the real immigration figures are concealed. They advocate that foreigners, particularly Muslim ones, should be encouraged to leave.

The orthodox conservative reaction to the consolidation of the FN has been mixed. Many politicians like Simone Veil, herself a nazi concentration camp victim, have condemned the FN, but at local level, especially in the south of France, the traditional conservative parties, the Rassemblement pour la République (RPR) and the Union pour la Démocratie Française (UDF), have often made informal electoral pacts with the FN to guarantee the election of conservative candidates. Such deals, plus its ability to get its members elected and even win control of local administrations – the party currently controls 30 town councils – have enabled the FN to become the vehicle for the French extreme-right's biggest post-war successes and have led to its legitimization.

This process of acceptance of the FN as part of the political framework in France has marginalized the more hard-line neo-nazi groups like the Parti Nationaliste Français et Européen (PNFE), which vegetate on the edge of legality. These groups command little influence. However, police action against the PNFE at the end of 1989 indicated its propensity for violence when 18 of its members were arrested in connection with an attack on an immigrants' hostel in Nice in which one person was killed and twelve people severely injured. Among those held was Serge Lecanu, the general secretary of the extreme-right police trade union Fédération Professionnelle Indépendante de la Police (FPIP), to which about 6.9 per cent of French police officers belong.

The PNFE is closely connected with groups elsewhere in Europe, especially in Belgium, West Germany and Great Britain. It participated at gatherings in 1988 in Belgium attended by members of the British National Party, supporters of the banned Belgian Vlaamse Militanten Orde (VMO) and West German neo-nazis. Its journal, *Tribune Nationaliste,* openly promotes the organization's ideas: 'a strong and hierarchical New Order, based on the nationalist ideal, social justice and racial awareness'.

Several organizations carry out propaganda for similar ideas and compete, for example, for the support of the growing skinhead sub-culture. One such group is the Faisceaux Nationalistes Européennes (FNE), the successor organization to the Fédération d'Action Nationale et Européenne (FANE), whose leader, Marc Frederiksen, was involved in terrorist activities. The FNE continues its monthly publication, *Notre Europe Combattante,* and in April 1989 organized a meeting in Metz to commemorate the centenary of the birth of Adolf Hitler.

Other groups that still have a public profile include Troisième Voie, with its journal *Jeune Solidariste,* which is racist and antisemitic in content, and a youth movement, the Jeunesse Nationaliste Revolutionnaire, which is active among skinheads who have been responsible for violent onslaughts in Lille, Brest and Rouen against homosexuals and black people. It has links with other Third Way groups in West Germany, particularly the Nationalistische Front.

These groups and others, like the now semi-defunct Groupe Union Défense, have small numbers of followers in comparison with the FN and feud bitterly among themselves. Interestingly, while some, like the Parti Nationaliste Français, advise their followers to vote for the FN, others oppose such a stance.

All have a proven capacity for violence. This extends as far as the FN itself and can be catalogued from the numerous racist crimes committed against North Africans, black people and Jews that have come before French courts. There is also random racist violence which in March 1990 led to a whole series of incidents in which immigrants were attacked and in three cases killed.

Ideologically, the whole of the extreme-right spectrum in France continues to draw sustenance from the 'New Right', especially from GRECE, which publishes the journal *Eléments* and emphasizes a racist view of history. This outlook finds an echo in the activities of the historical revisionists whose driving forces are Paul Rassinier, Professor Robert Faurisson and Henry Roques, who have all written extensively in furtherance of the claim that the nazi Holocaust never took place. In November 1989 Faurisson took part in an international assembly of revisionists in Haguenau together with the West German neo-nazi Ulo Welendy and the British historian David Irving. It should be noted, however, that in 1986 the Universities Minister, Mr Devaquet, blocked the award of a degree for Mr Roques's thesis. More recently a prominent French revisionist, Alain Guionnet, was arrested after being caught by police while pasting up wall-stickers denying the existence of the nazi gas chambers.

The extreme right in France presents a diffuse picture but certain clear characteristics are visible: antisemitism (Le Pen currently faces prosecution for his remarks containing a slur on the name of the Jewish former government minister Mr Durafour); racism and a belief that France's problems can be solved by expelling the country's 4 million immigrants; hostility to homosexuals; and opposition to abortion rights. It is also highly flexible, as is shown by its increasing preoccupation with economic and green issues and, in the case of the FN, in its ability to use the media, for example over the issue of the rights of Islamic girl students to wear traditional head-scarves in French schools.

For its ideas and programme it retains the support of 31 per cent of people who, according to a survey by the respected SOFRES polling organization, say they agree with statements by Le Pen on immigration. This same trend has been confirmed by the Information and Documentation Service of the French Prime Minister, Michel Rocard (see Introduction, p. xiv).

Although there are obvious paradoxes in that other surveys indicate that 51 per cent of people believe that immigrants are victims of scandalous racism on the part of many French people, the situation and the way in which the extreme right uses it to profit politically continues to give rise to serious concern, exemplified in the establishment of a National Consultative Committee on Human Rights.

Republic of Ireland

Although the persistence of certain forms of racial prejudice, intolerance and xenophobia in a significant minority of the Irish population has been documented in a recent study by the anti-racist group Harmony, the country has a very small number of immigrants and refugees, and racist sentiments tend to be directed against the native gypsy or traveller community. In any event, such attitudes are very rarely expressed in public discourse and almost never within the political mainstream. The principal exception concerns the very few neo-nazi groupings in the country, none of which has more than a couple of dozen adherents. These groups have undergone a bewildering series of changes in name and leadership in recent years and there would appear to be no immediate prospect of them coalescing or otherwise developing into a significant political movement.

The National Socialist Irish Workers' Party (NSIWP), a strongly antisemitic white supremacist organization, was active mainly in Dublin from the early 1970s until the late 1980s. The NSIWP split in the mid-1970s, with one faction, allied with a British racist group, calling itself the NSIWP NSPUK. Both sections made contact with foreign racist groups and dealt extensively in racist literature, taking advantage of the absence in Ireland at that time of legislation (since enacted) against incitement to racial hatred. Both factions produced magazines and stickers abusing Jews, black people and travellers. The NSIWP appears to have ceased to exist in its original form, although its propaganda is still occasionally seen around the capital and several of its members remain active in racist or extreme right-wing politics. A number of its leading activists have served in the Irish armed forces.

John Kane, the last known leader of the NSIWP, which in line with its strongly nationalist philosophy sought to organize on an all-Ireland basis, lives in Northern Ireland. Following the failure in 1987–8 of his attempt to establish a racist National Workers' Party, he was associated in 1989 with a faction of the British National Front.

Late in 1986 a more sophisticated white supremacist organization, the Social Action Initiative (SAI), arose under the leadership of a seaman in the Irish Navy from Cork. The SAI produced a journal espousing pan-Celtic ideas and made contact with a number of UK and other racist groupings, but it probably had fewer than 10 members when it was disbanded in 1988 after an investigation by the Naval Service.

The National Socialist Party (NSP) arose around 1987 as a semi-autonomous section of the NSIWP and was based in the city of Kilkenny. When the NSIWP became leaderless around 1988 the NSP was for a time the only organized racist party in the Republic, but its propaganda activity was minimal and rather crude.

A group of perhaps 20 racist youths from the Cork area and nearby Kinsale, some of whom had been associated with the SAI or with a short-lived National Socialist Party of Ireland, later came together under the leadership of an English immigrant to form a uniformed racist group, usually called the World SS. This body became in effect the paramilitary wing of the NSP, whose leader it recognized as 'Führer' of the Irish national socialist movement. The 'Führer' of the NSP and World SS had a crisis of conscience in late 1989 and rejected the movement. It has sought to regroup under the Cork SS leader as the International SS Movement but has had little or no success.

Among other very small political formations are a few that have right-wing or ultra-nationalist orientations including elements of racism or xenophobia. There are occasional reports of racist violence and slogan daubing by street gangs in Dublin and a number of known instances of intimidation, harassment, violence and discrimination against travellers by elements in the settled communities.

Italy

Italy is one of the few European countries in which right-wing extremism was able to maintain a continuous parliamentary presence in the post-war period. This was achieved by the Movimento Sociale Italiano (MSI). Despite its claims to parliamentary respectability, however, the MSI has always had a certain connection with violence. For example, the recently released Massimo Abbatangelo, who was accused of involvement in the 1985 bombing of an express train near Florence in which 17 people were killed and more than 200 injured, has just become an MSI member of the Italian Parliament. Like Abbatangelo, most of Italy's notorious right-wing terrorists started in the MSI before moving on to such groups as Ordine Nuovo and the Nuclei Armati Rivoluzionari (NAR), which bombed Bologna railway station in August 1980 killing 86 people.

The MSI today is in crisis. Many of the party's problems stem from the death in 1988 of its long-time leader and former Mussolini minister, Giorgio Almirante, which provoked a leadership struggle. In the 1989 Euro-elections the MSI saw its vote drop from 6.5 per cent to 5.5 per cent, as a result of which it lost one of its five seats in the European Parliament. Moreover, its paper, *Il Secolo d'Italia*, sells only 30,000 copies and does not appear regularly, whereas formerly it was a daily. Also the party's membership has fallen from more than one million in the 1960s to around 350,000.

Because its new leader, Giancarlo Fini, lacked Almirante's charisma and was unable to unite the party behind him, he has been replaced by Pino Rauti. Rauti thinks the party must find a 'third way' by re-orientating itself to green politics and focusing on social issues and conditions. He has been especially critical of the MSI's connection with the French Front National, because of its racism. Italian fascism's main preoccupation has always been anti-communism and Rauti wants to find a road to those who feel that the Communists and Christian Democrats have disappointed them. Nevertheless the last five years have seen the adoption by the MSI of a more racist, xenophobic style with demands for Italian jobs for Italian workers.

How far this process will advance is not yet clear but Italy, a country hitherto regarded as not having a racist problem, has since the beginning of 1990 seen racism erupt with a spate of racist attacks and graffiti in Florence in particular. The violence precipitated a major crisis in the city, resulting in the resignation of the mayor after protests at his toughening of measures against immigrant street traders. It also sparked off a wave of racist attacks, including arson, in other Italian cities with incidents reported in Caserta, Catania, Livorno, Matera, Milan, Rome, Varese and Turin. The main objects of these assaults were Africans from Senegal and the Ivory Coast and Moroccans.

The dissemination of racist literature has also become widespread for the first time. For example, in Trento the Partito Autonomista (Autonomous Party) published a pamphlet against migrants from the Third World, accusing them of carrying AIDS and drugs and being a source of insecurity and criminality. In Milan leaflets with swastikas and signed 'Aryan Order' appeared in March 1990 threatening Africans and Jews, while the Archbishop of Ravenna issued a statement warning that Europe is being Islamicized and suggesting that it is impossible for people of different culture, religion and race to live together.

Opinion polls have also tended to highlight the growing racist trend, with 51 per cent in one poll saying that the influx of foreigners should not be encouraged.

Luxembourg

Luxembourg, the smallest country in the European Community, is not one noted for racial tensions or extreme-right organizations. However, this does not mean that these are absent. Quite the contrary, because in a country with a population of only 377,000 there are at least six discernibly extreme-right organizations.

Two of these, Nouvel Acropole and the Cercle Luxembourgeois des Amis de la Revue Eléments, are pseudo-academic associations and maintain a very low public profile. Nouvel Acropole was described by Michel Neyens (Policy Adviser to the Ministry of the Family and Social Solidarity of the Grand Duchy of Luxembourg) as an extremely hierarchical and paramilitary organization whose members are in favour of an aristocratic totalitarian regime. The Cercle Luxembourgeois des Amis de la Revue Eléments is closely allied to the French neo-fascist group GRECE.

The other organizations – Greng National Bewegung, Eislecker Freiheetsbewegung, Lëtzeburg de Lëtzeburger and the Lëtzeburger Partei – are more active. However, their success in electoral terms has been negligible. In the elections to the European Parliament on 18 June 1989, Lëtzeburg de Lëtzeburger, whose members number only a few hundred, obtained only 2.19

per cent for its list of candidates. The other parties stood in elections to the Luxembourg Chamber of Deputies on the same date but failed to secure the election of any of their candidates.

Of all the parties and groups the most recently formed is the Lëtzeburger Partei, which has links with the National Front in Britain. Founded in November 1989, its self-declared aims include working together with nationalist forces throughout Europe, reducing the number of foreigners living in Luxembourg, establishing the death penalty and building a 'Europe of Nations'. As to activities, all these groups have campaigned against the presence of foreigners and have opposed any steps towards granting foreigners the right to vote. They have also widely circulated stickers bearing the slogan 'I am proud to be a Luxemburger'.

Although there have been sporadic incidents of racist action, like the daubing of roadsigns with racist slogans and the scrawling of antisemitic insults in the Jewish cemetery (both in 1988), there is no evidence at the moment to link these acts directly with the assortment of nationalist groups.

One positive feature of the situation is that when nationalist and extreme-right tendencies began to appear in the late 1980s, the traditional political parties signed a joint declaration to establish an anti-racist and anti-xenophobia consensus.

The Netherlands

The far right in the Netherlands has enjoyed a partial revival since the autumn of 1989, when, after an interval of three years, it won a seat in the Dutch Parliament with the election of Hans Janmaat, leader of the Centrumdemokraten (CD), a party whose leaders have been convicted on several occasions for racism.

In comparison with similar organizations in France and West Germany, the CD is small with a total membership of just over 1000 of whom only 100 are active. However, despite its small size, the CD has seats in 11 town councils, following municipal elections in March 1990 in which extreme-right parties made their biggest breakthrough since the Second World War.

The CD has rivals on the far right including Centrum Partij '86, which is all that remains of the Centrum Partij formerly led by Janmaat. Centrum '86 proclaims itself national democratic and is racist and antisemitic. It, too, is represented at municipal council level with four members in various localities. The party works closely with the German NPD, but is small and estimated to have only about 75 members.

There are three more open neo-nazi groups in Holland: the Jongeren Front, the Actiefront Nationaal Socialisten and the Consortium de Levensboom.

The Jongeren Front is a small but highly active neo-nazi group about 50-strong. Its leader, Stewart Mordaunt, is also a member of Centrum Partij '86 and is a city councillor in The Hague. Members of this group have been regularly convicted for racism and illegal possession of arms and they promote their racist policies among skinheads and soccer hooligans. In addition the organization is closely linked to the international neo-nazi group, Euro-Ring (see below).

The Actiefront Nationaal Socialisten (ANS), the Dutch wing of the banned German organization ANS, is small but violent. One of its leaders, Eite Homann, functions as an occasional bodyguard for German neo-nazi Michael Kühnen, while another, Et Wolsink, is closely linked to the violent neo-nazi British Movement. Both men were arrested in November 1989 in a raid on the home of an ANS member in Purmerend in which drugs, firearms and nazi literature were seized. One of the six people arrested has since been elected to the town council in Purmerend.

The other neo-nazi group, the Consortium de Levensboom, is more a sect than a political party. Consisting largely of elderly people, its leader is Florie Rost van Tonningen, the widow of one of the leading Dutch collaborators with the nazis during the war, who is internationally respected in neo-nazi circles. Mrs van Tonningen has been prosecuted and convicted several times for publishing antisemitic books and leaflets. In 1985 the organization had 450 members but since then it has diminished.

In the Netherlands ethnic minorities form only 5 per cent of the population and there is evidence of discrimination in jobs and housing. Popular racism is reported to be increasing and the success of racist parties in local elections tends to confirm this.

Portugal

Despite, or possibly because of, its long history of quasi-fascist government and colonialism, racist and xenophobic movements have had little influence or electoral significance in Portugal since the democratic coup of 1974. There are, however, many Portuguese residents of African or Chinese origin or descent and they have been the target of racist propaganda and abuse from a number of fringe political groupings and from unorganized hooligan elements, notably skinheads professing nazism.

A youth-oriented white supremacist group, the Círculo Europeu de Amigos de Europa (CEDADE-Portugal, European Circle of Friends of Europe), was formed around 1980 as an affiliate of the Spanish nazi group CEDADE. It has publication exchanges and other contracts with that group and other racist formations in Spain, France and elsewhere. Strongest around Oporto, it espouses traditional Hitlerite beliefs and has a paramilitary structure but a small membership, probably in the low hundreds.

The Movimento Acção Nacional (National Action Movement), an authoritarian grouping with ultra-nationalist and xenophobic tendencies, draws much of its inspiration from nostalgia for the Salazar era. It has aligned itself with racist and ultra-right groupings in other EC countries, including the UK National Front, Parti des Forces Nouvelles in Belgium, the Spanish Falange and Bases Autónomas, and the French grouping Troisième Voie.

Other antisemitic, white supremacist and fascist organizations active in recent years, often in close cooperation with CEDADE-Portugal, have included the Mocidade Patriótica (Patriotic Youth, based in Amadora), the Círculos Nacionalistas (Nationalist Circles), Ordem Nova (New Order, Lisbon) and the União National (National Union, Lisbon and Oporto). The composition of the racist fringe in Portuguese politics is somewhat fluid and other small groups (such as the Movimento Nacionalista, Nationalist Movement, and Acção Nacional Popular, an attempted revival of the pre-1974 ruling Popular National Action movement) appear to have become defunct.

None of these movements has achieved a significant membership or electoral following; indeed, of all the Portuguese parties of the radical right, it is only the least overtly racist of them, the monarchist movement, which has managed to retain an electoral support above 2 per cent. Several racist groups have, however, developed international links through publication exchanges and attendance at international rallies.

The various political organizations are supported by a number of magazines and publishing houses advancing racist or xenophobic views, often within the context of extreme right-wing ideology.

Spain

In Spain, as in Ireland, the largest ethnic group to suffer racial discrimination and harassment is the native gypsy population, numbering about 300,000. Occasional violent attacks on gypsy camps have, however, tended to arise locally and without the involvement of political movements. Other communities suffering racism and xenophobia include Portuguese and Moroccan workers in seasonal or permanent low-paid, low-status employment, and the Jewish community.

Racism is not a major feature of Spanish political life. The extreme right – that end of the political spectrum where racism and xenophobia are most often found – is no longer a mass movement, with barely 1 per cent of the electorate. Parties within it (such as the Frente Nacional and Solidaridad Española) tend to focus on nostalgia for the Franco dictatorship and opposition to liberalization, democracy and abortion rather than on racial concerns. That is not to say, of course, that individuals within such parties do not have, or do not express, racist and antisemitic attitudes; and some parties (such as the Falange Española, a signatory of the 'Manifesto of the European Nation', and the Frente Nacional, linked with Le Pen) have active contacts with foreign groupings of an overtly racist nature. Similarly, although supporters of the various movements in favour of, or against, regional autonomy or independence may hold or express views in respect of their co-nationals which can be equated with racial prejudice, they fall outside the scope of the present study.

National socialist organizations in Spain espousing white supremacist and anti-Jewish ideas include the Círculo Español de Amigos de Europa (CEDADE, Spanish Circle of Friends of Europe). Based in Barcelona, CEDADE is one of the oldest (formed in 1965), largest (possibly 1500 members) and most active neo-nazi groupings in the EC. It is of particular interest because of its policy of forging extensive links with racist organizations in other countries – there are in fact several groupings in Portugal,

France and elsewhere which are explicitly modelled on CEDADE and bear similar names – and also because it was one of the first racist organizations to adopt the rhetoric and concerns of the ecologist movement in order to find a new vehicle for racist and xenophobic theory. In the European context this is expressed in terms of a 'Europe of the peoples', that is a confederation of ethnic or linguistic statelets rather than the present nationalities. CEDADE, which produces explicitly Hitlerite propaganda, has uniformed paramilitary sections in many Spanish cities and numerous associated or front groups, including a youth wing called the Juventudes Nacional-Revolucionarias (National-Revolutionary Youth).

Other racist and xenophobic groups on the nazi fringe include the Centro Unitario Nacional Socialista (National Socialist Unity Centre), formed in Barcelona in 1984 as an offshoot of CEDADE with a particular brief to promote international liaison among white supremacists. The Centre appears to be a service unit rather than a membership organization. There are also a number of independent journals and publishing houses advocating or providing a platform for racist ideas, such as antisemitic conspiracy theories, in the context of Francoist, neo-nazi or Catholic fundamentalist beliefs.

The Spanish enclaves of Ceula and Melilla in North Africa have witnessed some racist agitation by local groupings opposed to the granting of Spanish citizenship to the Arab residents.

United Kingdom

Britain still has an intolerably high level of racial harassment and violence. For the most part it is directed at Asian members of the community and to a lesser extent at Afro-Caribbeans. In the last twelve months, however, there is strong evidence, not only in Britain but also internationally, of a rising tide of antisemitism. Monitoring bodies such as the Anti-Defamation League in the USA have reported in early 1990 on very significant increases in such activity.

In the summer of 1989 the Commissioner of the Metropolitan Police in London, Sir Peter Imbert, stated that racial crime in the capital had risen by 60 per cent in the first quarter of the year (see also pp. 77–78). Certainly some police forces in Britain are now gathering much more accurate figures for such crimes and positive steps have been taken, such as the production of multi-lingual pamphlets sent out to all households encouraging people to report these crimes. Within the police, training in this area of crime is being addressed in a more considered way, although racism in the lower echelons of the police is still a real problem.

A very welcome development was the announcement by Home Secretary David Waddington in late April 1990 that all 43 district police forces in England and Wales must make racial attacks a top priority and methods of reporting and monitoring such incidents must be stepped up. He went on to express his very strong abhorrence of such crimes.

Complaints from members of the black communities and a number of Members of Parliament have also highlighted a very serious problem in the country's armed services with regard to racial discrimination. Some élite regiments remain totally white.

Since December 1985 major changes have taken place in organized racism in Britain. The series of splits in the National Front (NF) continued and after 1986 two major groups bearing the NF name appeared. One became known as the Flag Group and the other as the Political Soldiers.

The first took on the appearance of the traditional National Front, contesting elections, organizing marches and, under the leadership of two young men, Martin Wingfield and then Ian Anderson, building an image not dissimilar to the Front National of France but without the mass following. With re-recruitment of former NF members they have raised the membership to around 3500. The Flag Group publish three journals: *The Flag*, a monthly newspaper, *Vanguard*, a monthly magazine, and *Lionheart*, a quarterly magazine. The circulation of these journals does not extend much beyond their own members. However, their various racist leaflets have a far wider range and hundreds of thousands are distributed each year. The group's election results have been insignificant. In March 1990 they stood in a Parliamentary by-election in the Midlands, an area where they have one of their largest branches, and gained only 311 votes.

Their former partners, the Political Soldiers, a number of whose key members have gained convictions for violence, sometimes against the police, became more and more extreme in both their thinking and their connections. Praise for Iran and Libya and their failure to condemn the terrorists on both sides of the Northern Ireland conflict led to the loss of the bulk of the already diminishing membership of the organization. Moreover, their connection with Italian far-right terrorist exile Roberto Fiore only did them harm when it was revealed that he had been an agent of British Intelligence Section M16 since the early 1980s. They claimed that they wanted to develop friendly contacts with black and Jewish nationalist extremists, but when seriously challenged over these relationships, said they still believed in racial separate development.

The Political Soldiers have tried unsuccessfully to set up front organizations in areas of growing interest in Britain such as green politics and animal rights. The group has declared that it has no interest in parliamentary democracy.

In October 1988 a programme called 'Disciples of Chaos' was transmitted by Channel 4 television in its 'Despatches' series. This gave a detailed history of developments in the two National Fronts. It was followed by the Searchlight booklet *From Ballots to Bombs*, published in January 1989, which revealed the Political Soldiers operation from the inside with the use of internal documents.

In January 1990 the Political Soldiers split again. One group led by Derek Holland and Nick Griffin left for France where they have set up a far right commune and Patrick Harrington took the fifty or so remaining members into a group calling itself the Third Way.

The British National Party (BNP) has around 1500 members, of which more than 10 per cent are activists. It has developed rapidly since the mid-1980s led by John Tyndall, an active nazi since the age of 19 and leader of the National Front in its heyday in the early to mid-1970s. Tyndall broke away from the NF in 1979 and re-formed the BNP in 1981. It is an openly nazi party. There is no elected leadership or committees; Tyndall is in sole command.

Like Tyndall himself the key men in the leadership (there are no women) have serious criminal convictions. Their crimes range from bomb-making, organizing illegal paramilitary groups, possession of firearms and a series of convictions under the Race Relations and Public Order Acts.

The BNP has targeted schools for its racist material. Apart from probably a quarter of a million racist and antisemitic stickers, it produces videos and sound tapes and runs a book club that helps it circumvent the laws against the distribution of racist material. It also produces *Spearhead,* a monthly magazine, and *British Nationalist,* a monthly newspaper. Both publications are uninhibited in their racist style and report unashamedly on their members stabbing black people.

The Salman Rushdie affair has been a catalyst for all the racist groups in Britain but none more so than the BNP. It has used the upheaval in Britain's large Muslim community to provoke serious confrontation and in 1989/90 organized marches in areas with a large Muslim population. On several occasions this has led to serious disorder.

In addition the BNP is responsible for the distribution of antisemitic tracts and papers such as *Holocaust News,* which denies that the nazi death camps ever existed. These are sent unsolicited to schools, Members of Parliament, various institutions and members of the Jewish community.

At one time Tyndall was not interested in any overseas connections except with nazis in the USA and South Africa. Today the BNP is part of the Odal Ring, which is based in Belgium and run by Werner Van Steen, a Belgian who has a conviction for his racist activities.

Apart from the formal racist parties a whole range of smaller but sometimes no less vocal groups exist, such as Lady Jane Birdwood's Self Help and British Solidarity organizations and her paper, *Choice,* which, along with about ten different antisemitic and racist leaflets, is circulated free of charge all over the country in huge numbers.

Don Martin's British League of Rights is tied to similar racist and anti-Jewish groups in Australia, Canada and South Africa. In each of these countries they have publishing houses and hold international gatherings.

The British far right's links with the 'New Right' in Europe are by means of a glossy magazine called *Scorpion* run by Michael Walker, a close associate of Alain de Benoist in France and Robert Stuekers in Belgium. Walker is a former National Front officer who now lives in West Germany. *Scorpion* holds at least two international gatherings each year and is at present very keen to develop links with ultra-nationalist and antisemitic groups in Russia and Eastern Europe.

In 1986 Colin Jordan, the former leader of Britain's nazis, wrote in *National Review*, the influential journal of the League of St George, about his ideas for the movement in the last years of this century. He called for the building of a party of men and women prepared to take up an underground struggle as soldiers of the cause. The result of this call has been the re-emergence of Jordan's old organization, the British Movement, and within it a cell-structured secret group called the British National Socialist Movement, which has very strong links abroad. Contacts are strongest with Michael Kühnen's group in West Germany and Et Wolsink's organization in Holland. A connection also exists with the American Ku-Klux-Klan.

The choice of *National Review* for this rallying call was important, because although the League is an élitist group with only about 50 members, they are in the main very wealthy and it is the most respected of the pure national socialist groups in Western Europe.

Austria

The most dramatic development in Austria since the publication of the Evrigenis Report in 1985 has been the meteoric rise of the Freiheitliche Partei Österreichs (FPÖ) led by the man who has been dubbed the yuppie fascist, Jorg Haider. Despite the FPÖ's affiliation to the Liberal International, the party stands on the extreme right of the Austrian political spectrum and pursues racist policies against foreigners generally and, in its stronghold of Carinthia, the Slovene minority in particular.

In this province the FPÖ has established itself firmly in the political framework and in elections in 1989 it won 29 per cent of the vote there as against 10 per cent nationally. Haider is now chief minister in Carinthia, which before the Second World War was a centre of nazism, and has used the region as a power base from which to project himself as a nationally known and even popular political figure.

Only 40 years old, Haider was earlier involved in several far-right groups before joining the Liberals. As a journalist he edited an antisemitic paper, *Carinthian News*, which defended war-time collaboration with Hitler's nazis. He is reported to be proud of the fact that both his parents were nazis and some of his considerable personal wealth stems directly from ownership of forest land expropriated from its Jewish owners in 1940.

Haider has never concealed his nazi associations. He has been a regular visitor to annual reunions of ex-SS veterans and has lent his support to campaigns for amnesty for nazi war criminals. With this background it is not surprising that since taking over the leadership of the FPÖ he has set it on an extreme-right course and has made antisemitic statements.

The character of the FPÖ is above all revealed by the company it keeps. In 1989 its leader held at least one meeting with Jean-Marie Le Pen of the French Front National and Franz Schönhuber, the Republikaners' leader.

There has been a tradition of antisemitism and fascist organization in Austria since the 1930s, when the Austrian Nazi Party was over 500,000 strong. While through its elected representatives at national and local parliamentary level and the fact that it holds state office in Carinthia the FPÖ is the most prominent organization on the far right, it is by no means the only one. Indeed, the far-right groups proliferate and, according to evidence given by police in the 1985 trial of nine neo-nazis for a series of bomb attacks on Jewish-owned property, the number of extreme-right activists is estimated at about 20,000. These belong to a variety of organizations, some of them cultural, of which the biggest is probably the National Democratic Party (NPD), which averages about 3 per cent of the vote when it contests elections.

The former leader of the NPD, Dr Norbert Burger, was once convicted for terrorism in the disputed South Tyrol region. More recently he has figured as the director of the Commission for Truth in History, which is a historical revisionist association that denies the nazi genocide of the Jews and entertains links with like-minded people elsewhere in Europe, including the British historian, David Irving.

In 1986 former United Nations Secretary-General Kurt Waldheim was elected national President with 53 per cent of the vote, despite massive publicity about his nazi and allegedly war-criminal past. Waldheim's election and the continuing evidence of racism and antisemitism shown in numerous opinion surveys indicate that in Austria there remains fertile soil for the growth of nazism once more.

Eastern Europe

The political changes that have swept Eastern Europe since the midsummer of 1989 could not have been anticipated even by the most informed experts. Nevertheless it is now becoming clear that the removal of dictatorship in East Germany, Hungary, Poland and Romania has brought extreme-right, nationalist and antisemitic tendencies to the surface.

In East Germany extreme-right organizations have publicly proclaimed their existence despite being in violation of the law. For example the Republikaner claim groups in East Berlin, Leipzig, Dresden, Karl-Marx-Stadt, Gorlitz and other cities. Other groups, like the Deutsche Alternative led by hardline neo-nazi Michael Kühnen, have also established local organizations and function openly. Material evidence of this presence has been gathered at the regular weekly demonstrations in Leipzig and Dresden which preceded the elections of 16 March 1990.

The fascist skinhead scene has grown quickly with groups reported in East Berlin, Rostock, Weimar, Leipzig and Dresden. These groups draw their political inspiration from the extreme right and operate as activists for the Republikaner. In April 1990 there were clashes between police and groups of over 300 skinheads who had gathered in East Berlin to commemorate Hitler's birth. In these incidents homosexuals were attacked and passers-by greeted with nazi salutes.

Social scientists and Church organizations have expressed anxiety about the growth of right-extremist tendencies and have noted a rise in the number of assaults on black students and Vietnamese guest workers, as well as a wave of politically-inspired vandalism against Jewish cemeteries and Soviet war memorials.

Similar tendencies have surfaced in Romania with pogroms in which several members of the Hungarian minority were killed in March 1990 and the re-emergence of antisemitism on such a scale that the Romanian Chief Rabbi, Moses Rosen, has warned of the serious dangers facing Romania's 20,000 strong Jewish population. Attacks on Jewish property have been reported from the town of Oradea in northern Romania.

Visible signs of extreme-right organization have included the appearance of the notorious antisemitic forgery, *The Protocols of the Elders of Zion*, on public sale in Bucharest and the formation of the organization Vatra Romanesca, which is a successor organization to the pre-war and wartime Iron Guard movement.

Vatra Romanesca is openly racist and proclaims its intention of waging a violent struggle against the Hungarian, German and gypsy minorities, which it regards as racially impure. The organization claims to have received support from as yet unidentified Canadian and French organizations.

In Hungary, too, the collapse of the communist regime has opened the political arena to right-extremist trends. Skinhead groups have appeared and leaflets bearing the imprint of the traditional Hungarian Arrow Cross movement have been circulated. More worrying is the fact that the leading political party in Hungary, Democratic Forum, contains within its leadership individuals who have made public their antisemitism. For instance, Istvan Czurka has blamed Jews for the problems that Hungary has suffered since the Second World War and such statements have created a climate in which Jewish property has been vandalized in Budapest, Debrecen and Tab; groups of skinheads, who are in contact with their East German, Austrian and British counterparts, have also become active.

In Poland the hatred of the former communist rulers has expressed itself with both anti-Russian nationalism and antisemitism, despite the now minuscule size of the country's Jewish population. Nevertheless, prominent Jewish members of Solidarnosc have been singled out as targets for anonymous propaganda leaflets and graffiti. There is also evidence that fascist material from the US Third Way neo-nazi group led by Gary Gallo has been circulated at the University of Radom by Sociology Professor Mieczyslaw Trzeciak and that initiatives have been taken to establish groups of the US fascist LaRouche organization in Poland.

The fragility of the overall atmosphere was brought home in the summer of 1989 in the controversy over the Carmelite nunnery at the site of the former nazi death camp at Auschwitz. The head of the Roman Catholic Church in Poland, Cardinal

Glemp, issued statements accusing Jews of 'orchestrating an international campaign' against the nunnery, which sparked off a wave of antisemitic vandalism.

In the USSR the Russian nationalist and antisemitic Pamyat organization has continued to develop. It has particular centres of strength in Moscow and Leningrad where it has around 30,000 and 40,000 members respectively and has whipped up an atmosphere of terror among Jews and other national minorities. In Leningrad Pamyat has recently been registered as a legal organization under the name Republican People's Party of Russia.

Pamyat faces prosecution for inciting national and racial hatred after calling, in an election manifesto, for the 'de-Zionization' of Russia and for a legal ban on Jews holding government posts. The organization has begun to cooperate closely with other groups like the Fatherland organization and the hardline nationalist United Workers' Front movement in a bid to broaden its popular base. In April 1990 it was announced that five such groups including Pamyat had formed an alliance, called the People's Russian Orthodox Movement, to campaign for the restoration of the tsar. It attributed Russia's problems to the Jews. Internationally, it has been confirmed that Pamyat has formed links with extreme-right individuals in London

Violent antisemitic attacks including murder have taken place in Moscow and Leningrad since autumn 1989. Despite promises that the authorities will take action against racist violence, the appointment of two known antisemites, Valentin Rasputin and Veniamin Yarin, to President Gorbachev's 15-strong Presidential Council has reinforced anxiety as has Pamyat's large-scale penetration of the USSR's biggest green group, Volga.

Norway

In Norway since the Evrigenis Report there has been a definite expansion of racist prejudice and activity. In particular this has been exploited by the Fremskrittspartiet (Progress Party) of Carl I. Hagen, which in the 1989 general election took 13.7 per cent of the vote. With its 22 seats in Parliament it holds the balance of power.

The Fremskrittspartiet has made no secret of its desire to see tighter curbs on immigration and acceptance of refugees and its popular support was held to have worried the previous Labour government enough to have pressured it into passing the Aliens Law to enact tougher controls. These measures did little to silence the racist clamour and especially gave new encouragement to the People's Movement Against Immigration (FMI), a far-right pressure group that has managed to gather support from the more extreme fringes of the Fremskrittspartiet at the same time as winning over many members of the overtly fascist Nasjonalt Folkeparti (NF).

Recently the FMI has seen its support dwindle after its leader, Arne Myrdal, was sentenced to one year's imprisonment for his part in a conspiracy to bomb an immigrant centre. The NF, too, was similarly affected after 11 of its members were charged with the bombing of an Oslo mosque and found to be in possession of arms and explosives. Clear association with violence has tended to be a weakening factor for the extreme right in Norway but the extremists themselves are not deterred and constantly attempt to renew their organization and activities.

In the latest guises the extreme right has organized itself into two new groups that perform different functions: the National Democrats and Zorn 88.

The National Democrats are an off-shoot from the Stop Immigration Party, which put up candidates in the 1989 general election but failed to win any seats in Parliament. As so often is the case with such groups, failure led to factional warfare and splits. The breakaway element felt disillusioned at Stop Immigration's attempts to win respectability by attempting to use the democratic process, even if for clearly racist and undemocratic objectives.

These aims were clearly demonstrated when members of the newly-formed party took part in February 1990 in a peak-time television programme about asylum-seekers and declared themselves national and socialist. Moreover, the party bears the stamp of its two main leaders, Hoge Bortland, notorious for his aggressive racism, and Erik Gjems-Onstad, a lawyer who is well known as a defender of South African apartheid.

Zorn 88, a violent nazi group claiming over 200 members, was also scheduled to receive television airtime, but these plans were frustrated by concerted public protest. Its main theses are the promotion of antisemitism and Holocaust revisionism, which resulted in March 1990 in the daubing of Jewish-owned property with nazi insignia. The group is led by Erik-Rune Hansen, who has a long record of anti-Jewish activity.

During the 1970s Erik Blucher was Norway's most notorious neo-nazi but in recent years he has kept a low profile. However, he is believed still to be an influential figure.

Despite the efforts of the hard-line racists and neo-nazis, it seems that the racist tide will continue to run with the Progress Party for some time to come.

Sweden

The extreme right in Sweden has been undergoing a process of regroupment after the dismal failure of its previous endeavour to construct a united party, the Sweden Party, founded in 1986 from a fusion of three different racist and neo-nazi groups. The main reason for the Sweden Party's rapid demise was the unrelenting campaign conducted by anti-racist groups who were able to bring to public attention the organization's connections with violence and its close ties with the British National Front.

The outcome of the latest series of splits and fusions has been the formation of the Sweden Democrats led by the erstwhile leader of the Sweden party, Leif Zeilon. Their membership, which is claimed to number more than 2000, is comprised largely of former members of the racist and violent Bevara Sverige Svenskt and the remnants of the openly fascist Nordiska Rikspartiet.

The new organization has contested elections but has signally failed to make any visible impact or to profit from the outburst of populist racism that broke out in 1988 in the southern agricultural town of Sjöbo, where a clear majority of citizens voted in a town referendum to refuse to accept any refugees under the Swedish government's quota regulations. Equally, in a bid to present themselves as a legal and democratic organization, the Sweden Democrats have alienated many of their former skinhead supporters who remain under the influence of racist and fascist ideas but are no longer willing to act as 'arrest fodder' for any group.

Other fascist groups, like the Sveriges Nationella Forbund, do exist but have an elderly and inactive membership. Of interest, however, is the continued existence of the Sveaborg organization of Swedish former Waffen-SS volunteers. This highly secretive organization is widely believed to have a hand in providing the finance for the activity of young extreme rightists and also to have provided the funds for the printing of Holocaust revisionist literature on the printing presses of Dietlieb Felderer in Taby.

Felderer has an international reputation as a publisher of such material and has long had ties with the Spanish group CEDADE and other neo-nazi groups in Europe. He prints large amounts of neo-nazi and antisemitic tracts and in addition promotes his own irregularly produced journal under the title *Revisionist History*.

The far right, however, does not just rely on the printed word to make propaganda but also uses the community radio, Open Forum, to broadcast its racist and antisemitic message. On several occasions this radio station has run foul of the law but so far its licence has not been revoked.

Generally Sweden has been able to avoid the kind of racist problems that have afflicted other countries largely because of its relative wealth, strong social net and high living standards – but ominous signs like the Sjöbo vote have begun to appear. It was in response to racist undercurrents that the Swedish government took action in December 1989 to tighten drastically its asylum policy, a move that drew fierce protests from the Church and anti-racists alike.

The International Skinhead Movement

By far the most worrying development in the non-parliamentary field since the last Committee of Inquiry report has been the rapid growth of the skinhead movement. Britain has had an appallingly unsuccessful record for exports in recent years but in one field it has done remarkably well, namely in spreading the racist and violent sub-culture of the skinheads. Skinheads first appeared in Britain in the late 1960s and were involved in what was known as 'Paki bashing'. This included not only assaults but also some murders. In the early 1970s they went into decline but found a natural home in the British Movement from the late 1970s until about 1982 when that organization itself went into temporary decline.

Over the next five years the racist skinheads built up their organization by means of a series of bands playing racist music. These developed a following who wore an unofficial uniform of T-shirts and badges sporting racist slogans, black jackets and steel-capped 'Doc Martin' boots. The biggest international distributor of their records is a West German company, Rockarama Records.

The key group formed around the band 'Skrewdriver'. In 1988 the leader of the band broke away from the Political Soldier wing of the National Front. However, he did not set up his own organization; 'skins' tend to be very nihilistic and would not join anything organized. Instead he produced a magazine, *Blood and Honour*. The British Movement, which was then re-forming, and the BNP started covertly to support his activities.

During the 1980s the skinhead cult spread from Britain to West Germany, Belgium and Holland and then to Scandinavia. The cult also gained popularity among young unemployed racists in France, and it eventually reached Hungary, Poland and East Germany, where skinheads were involved in brutal attacks on guest workers and overseas students. They appeared to awaken some of the pre-war antisemitism in these countries.

The very rapid development of the skinhead movement has been followed closely by *The Monitor*, the publication of the Center for Democratic Renewal in the USA, and in an Anti-Defamation League pamphlet, *Shaved for Battle*. In Britain the skinheads' activities have been watched closely by the national press and by *Searchlight* on a regular basis.

One of the most startling developments has been the success of the skinheads in the USA. Around 1987, when they first appeared on the US racist scene, they had around 400 followers. Within a year this had grown to about 4500 and they have increased rapidly in numbers since then. As in the rest of the world they have engaged in racial attacks including murder.

In the USA, Canada and Sweden they have dealt with their own dissident members with real brutality. In one instance a young man was crucified in a car park in California when he wanted to break away from them.

The established racist groups see the skinheads as a potential recruitment ground and as cannon fodder for street actions, which can cross international borders, such as attendance at international football matches. They are also viewed as a huge financial benefit for the racist movement. In Britain they are capable of generating income to the tune of around one million pounds a year from sales of concert tickets, videos, T-shirts, boots, records and tapes. They also sell protection for other people's concerts and public events. Most, if not all, of this income is not declared to the Inland Revenue and is therefore not taxed.

In Britain and the USA the skinheads have formed a recruitment pool for the Ku-Klux-Klan, in particular the Klan group of James W. Farrands, who visited Europe on at least two occasions in 1989/90.

Under the social security systems in Western Europe the skinheads are able to draw benefits in all the EC countries. In Britain groups of Germans, French, Belgians and Dutch visit regularly for periods long enough to carry on political activities. In 1988 it was discovered that there was an organized link with Sweden with full-time political workers from Britain stationed there. Letters spelling out their plans and tactics for future disruption of football internationals exposed some of these links.

Certainly the major figures behind British football violence have far-right and racist links. Martin Wingfield, the former leader of the National Front Flag Group, admitted in an interview with the London magazine *Time Out* that the group had encouraged its members to be active at football stadia and had reaped the benefits from this, both financially and in terms of recruiting new members.

The Searchlight booklet *Terror on the Terraces* published days after the Heysel stadium tragedy produced firm evidence, later incorporated in the Leuven University report, of fascist involvement in the majority of serious disorders at international football matches in recent years. In Britain this kind of activity has spread to cricket and boxing matches and indeed to almost all sporting events.

It was also discovered that young people from Scandinavia were being taken via Britain to Northern Ireland for paramilitary training. Since then it is believed that such training has taken place on a smaller scale in Britain. The Swedish media gave widespread coverage to these illicit international activities.

In the USA groups like White Aryan Resistance, which is run by former West Coast Ku-Klux-Klan leader Tom Metzger and his son John, who is in charge of its skinhead section, have built up international solidarity by leaps and bounds. These are violent operations. At the 1989 gathering of the Klan at Stone Mountain, Georgia, 300 Klansmen took part. Half wore white sheets and the other half were young men and women skinheads in combat clothes. (This area of racial politics is practically the only one in which women are treated as equals and certainly in the US skinhead groups they fight alongside the men.) In almost every speech reference was made to Britain's skinheads, the young people whom Colin Jordan, Britain's most infamous postwar nazi leader, saw as the movement's new recruits for the next century.

Sources

Television Programmes

Disciples of Chaos, Channel 4 television programme in the Despatches series, UK, October 1988.

The Other Face of Terror, Channel 4 television, UK, 1983.

Magazines and Pamphlets

From Ballots to Bombs: The Inside Story of the National Front's Political Soldiers, Searchlight Publication, January 1989.

The Monitor, publication of the Center for Democratic Renewal, USA, issues appearing between 1987 and 1990.

Racial Discrimination in Ireland: Realities & Remedies, A Harmony Report, Dublin, March 1990.

Searchlight magazine, London, issues from 1986 to 1990.

Shaved for Battle, Anti-Defamation League publication, New York.

Time Out magazine, London, various issues 1986 to 1990.

Official Documents

Annual Reports of the Commissioner of the Metropolitan Police, 1987, 1988, 1989.

Home Office Directive to Police Forces in England and Wales, April 1990.

Books

Gerry Gable, *The British Far Right's Third Position Stance,* Longman, London, 1990.

Geoffrey Harris, *The Dark Side of Europe: The Extreme Right Today*, Edinburgh University Press, Edinburgh, 1990.

Ray Hill and Andrew Bell, *The Other Face of Terror: Inside Europe's Neo-Nazi Network*, Grafton Books, London, 1988.

Ciarán O Maoláin, *The Radical Right: A World Directory*, Longman, London, 1987.

In addition, information has been provided by Searchlight's infiltrators operating inside various fascist groups and fascist informants in some of these groups.

Searchlight's network of correspondents have also contributed. They remain unnamed for security reasons.

Other information has come from the following organizations and individuals: MRAP (France); VVN/BdA (Federal Republic of Germany); Celsius (Belgium); Anti-Racist Centre (Norway); Anne Frank Centre (Holland); National Consultative Committee on Human Rights (France).

From the working documents of: Ernest Glinne, MEP (Belgium), PE 139.226 and PE 140.250; Marijke van Hemeldonck, MEP (Belgium), PE 139.154; Ejner Christiansen, MEP (Denmark), PE 139.296; Juan de Dios Ramírez Heredia, MEP (Spain), PE 140.275; Claudia Roth, MEP (Federal Republic of Germany), PE 139.279; Willi Rothley, MEP (Federal Republic of Germany), PE 139.153.

From the contributions of: Mr Jean Kahn, President, Conseil Représentatif des Institutions Juives de France; Ligue des Droits de l'Homme; LICRA; France Plus; SOS Racisme (Marseilles).

3

Country by Country Analysis

Introduction

This chapter will provide a succinct picture of the growing levels of intolerance, xenophobia or racism and discrimination, and their more extreme forms of expression, overt hatred and physical violence against ethnic minorities, leading in numerous cases to senseless murders. Sadly enough, despite the adoption of the Joint Declaration against Racism and Xenophobia back in June 1986, there is still an enormous mass of evidence pointing to the growing strength of racism and xenophobia. The aim of this chapter is to 'highlight' the more serious incidents which have occurred since 1986 and to examine these in view of the recommendations to be formulated.

This chapter will deal only briefly with the numerous forms of legally permitted discrimination, referring to a few of the most blatant cases in which Member State governments may be violating their international obligations. Such brevity should not imply that such forms of discrimination are not important: they contribute to the inferior status of legally residing foreigners and imply government approval of the existence of a category of second-class residents, thus appearing in the minds of ordinary citizens as a licence to practice some degree of discrimination against foreigners.

Moreover, the specific examples of racism and discrimination against Community nationals will not be provided, although these are certainly not exempt from being victims. On the contrary, there is still reluctance – which varies from one to another depending on the composition and importance of foreign population of Community origin – to grant nationals of other

Member States the same rights of residence, employment, education, etc. as those enjoyed by their own nationals. This has led to a number of condemnations by the European Court of Justice against Member States which continued to violate the principle of free movement with discriminatory measures.[1] It must, moreover, be pointed out that with the development of European case law, Community migrant workers are gradually receiving more and more legal protection against discrimination. Besides, with the post-1992 European Single Market, there will no longer be Community migrant workers, but instead 'European Community citizens'.

This does not mean that the obligations of the European Institutions are in any way diminished. For example, the explanation offered by Mr Sutherland, on behalf of the Commission at the June 1987 plenary session of the European Parliament when faced with the question of appointing a European Ombudsman to defend the rights of EC nationals in cases of discrimination, was that 'the differences between the national legal systems and the Community legal system made it impossible to have a European ombudsman'.[2] It can, however, be argued that since most Member States are party to the various international or European human rights conventions (a first step would be to ensure that those Member States which have not yet signed and ratified certain conventions do so as a priority), in particular the UN Convention on the Elimination of All Forms of Racial Discrimination (except Ireland), the Community could set up a structure to monitor how Member States have (or have not) complied with their international obligations in the field of human rights.[3] Such a structure could also serve a surveillance and information agency, closely following events in Member States and reminding the latter of this report's recommendations.

One essential part of this chapter will focus on difficulties in applying the few anti-racism laws in force in some Member States. Sometimes, indeed, these have been perversely applied. This can be largely explained by the fact that racist remarks, abuse, insults, etc. have 'evolved' to a great extent 'like germs adapt to antibiotics'.[4] They have found new means of expression within more legal contexts, frequently abusing, if not making a mockery of, freedom of speech.[5] They also hide behind pseudo-scientific arguments of the so-called school of socio-biology.[6]

The European Community

Belgium

According to the Eurobarometer opinion survey carried out between 17 October and 21 November 1988,[7] the Belgians and Germans have the most difficulties in accepting an existence alongside the differences of the 'other'. However, racial violence and abuse in Belgium are nowhere near the levels in France, the United Kingdom or even in Italy. This paradox can, in part, be explained by the fact that Belgians who dislike foreigners more readily express such a view, even those who may get along quite well with a foreign neighbour. This of course does not mean that racism and/or xenophobia is not widespread in Belgian society, as Ernest Glinne[8] and Marijke Van Hemeldonck[9] have shown.

The 30 July 1981 anti-racism law has in only very rare cases resulted in convictions. In 1985 and 1986, 343 complaints under the 1981 anti-racism law were submitted in Brussels of which 317 were rejected as having insufficient grounds for prosecution.[10] In 1987, the number of cases submitted fell to 93 of which 82 were rejected and three resulted in convictions.[11] The following year, 83 complaints were submitted of which 70 were rejected and only one resulted in a conviction.[12] One of the 'successful cases' in 1987 concerned a North African youth who was convicted for having called a politician a racist.[13]

In another case, seven members of the far-right 'Forces Nouvelles' received light suspended sentences and only one other was sentenced to an immediate four-month prison term for having exerted intensive and continued physical violence against immigrants. The compensation received by one immigrant family was not even enough to pay part of the transport costs for moving to another area.[14]

On the other hand, no political parties in Belgium have ever been convicted for making insulting statements against immigrants, despite complaints lodged. The Parti des Forces Nouvelles (PFN) thus freely distributed leaflets during the 1987 national elections, saying 'Halt the Barbarians' with cartoon drawings of Arabs.

Referring to immigrants, in particular North Africans, Yugoslavs and Turks, as 'barbarians' has become 'acceptable' ever since the Interior Minister in the caretaker government in 1987 did so himself. First he denied this and then said that the word 'barbarian', as he used it, had to be understood in its etymological Greek sense, meaning foreigners.[15]

The Turks and North Africans (they number more or less 300,000) are the most disliked and discriminated against foreigners in Belgium,[16] although with the increasing number of black African asylum-seekers there are more and more serious incidents of violence and/or harassment against this latter group (mainly Zaïrean residents and students and Ghanaian asylum-seekers) in the form of systematic and abusive ID checks[17] and beatings of black asylum-seekers in the detention centre of Brussels Zaventem Airport.[18]

There have also been two deaths of African asylum-seekers: one murder in September 1987 (the racist motive has never been established) and another, on 14 January 1987, concerning a Zaïrean asylum-seeker who was forced to board a plane back to Zaïre under the escort of two police officers. There has never been any plausible evidence to support the authorities' claim that he committed suicide[19] and human rights associations alleged that he was beaten and then subjected to an overdose of tranquillizers.

Ever since the anti-American demonstration on 20 April 1986 against the US bombing of Tripoli in which a minority group of Islamic fundamentalists participated, there has been growing 'Islamophobia' in Belgium with the frequent exaggerated and abusive labelling of the Muslim population and their religious practices as radical fundamentalism. This has been reinforced by the Islamic headscarf affair which was, however, far less controversial than in France. In October 1989, 20 Muslim girls of a technical school started to wear a headscarf within school premises and many others in the same school followed. A Brussels tribunal ruled on 1 December 1989 that female Muslims could wear their headscarves in the presence of a male teacher, but that they had to remove them during physical education, sporting activities, along the school corridors and in the playground.[20]

Although the teaching of Islam in Belgium was officially introduced in 1978, two Brussels boroughs, one run by Mr R. Nols of Schaarbeek, an ex-member of the Parti Réformateur Libéral (PRL)[21] known for his hostility towards immigrants, and another by a Socialist, Mr. C. Picque,[22] refused to allow Muslim courses in local schools until they were ordered to do so by a court ruling in December 1989.[23]

Inter-community relations in the Brussels borough of Schaarbeek are perhaps the worst in the whole country and the former mayor, Mr Nols, contributed a great deal to fuelling the racial hatred and tensions. During Ramadan in 1986 he imposed a one-month ban on gatherings of more than five persons after 10 p.m., just when Muslims gather before their evening meal.[24] At about the same time, some 150,000 copies of his borough's information brochure were distributed to schools, depicting North Africans as terrorists and religious fundamentalists, associated with drug dealing and addiction.[25] At a borough council meeting on 27 April 1988, he openly accused immigrants of being the cause of insecurity and described Moroccans as 'the barbarians of today'.[26] The next month, tensions between the North Africans and the police had reached such a pitch that a violent confrontation was only narrowly avoided.[27] His anti-immigrant measures became the object of ridicule among Belgians living in the borough when he ordered the removal of certain benches near a park; SOS-Racisme in Belgium claimed that it was a form of apartheid to prevent immigrants from using the benches.[28] However, his 'popularity' in Schaarbeek was such that prior to the mid-1988 local elections, both the French and Flemish local Socialist parties tried to reach an agreement with him under the pretext of getting 'inside to change Mr Nols'.[29]

A Royal Decree of 7 May 1985 allowed six Brussels boroughs to refuse to enter certain foreigners in the special aliens register, thereby preventing them from living there. The ban was for a five-year period and expired on 14 May 1990.[30] Politicians from all parties, except the Ecologists (Ecolo/Agalev), have been in favour of the ban, including the present deputy Prime Minister and former Minister of Justice, Mr Philippe Moureaux,[31] who in 1981 got the anti-racist Bill adopted, tabled as long before as 1966 by Mr Ernest Glinne. Although it apparently contravenes the 1950 European Human Rights Convention, several more Brussels boroughs have been in favour of implementing a similar ban, as has also the city of Liège.[32] It should be noted that the immigrants consultative councils have helped integration at local level.

On 9 May, the Government decided to allow five of the six Brussels boroughs to prolong the ban for another two years. The city of Liège has been authorized to implement this ban for one year to enable the local authorities to regularize the situation of some 2234 asylum-seekers there. The sixth borough has to reintroduce its application in the appropriate form. The request by the Brussels borough of Koekelberg to implement the ban was turned down. One positive factor in the Government's decision is that the ban can no longer be applied to non-EEC students. This decision angered the opponents of the ban, as well as its advocates, because of its limited scope and duration.[33]

Relations between the police and the immigrant population are especially bad, in particular with regard to youths of North African origin who are considered to be responsible for the high crime rate. Some police vans actually bear stickers of extreme-right groups. At the end of September 1987, the local police of one borough stood passively by as a band of skinheads got close to attacking a group of youths of North African origin, threatening to disfigure them with swastika signs. The skinheads were stopped by the local people, but attempts to call in the gendarmes were unsuccessful.[34]

In August 1988, all local TV and radio stations broadcast information on a Moroccan youth, hospitalized with a concussion and other injuries following his arrest by the police. Other than resisting arrest, the police brought no other charges against him and dismissed the affair as 'rare'. The new Interior Minister reacted with speed by demanding a report from the police the morning after the incident, but came under criticism from the police, who argued that such a matter should have been dealt with first by the judicial authorities and/or the Ministry of Justice.[35]

Only when the extreme-right party, the Vlaams Blok, tripled its 1982 score at the October 1988 local elections did the Government at last begin to take up the problems of immigrants seriously.[36] It quickly decided to nominate as soon as possible a commissioner to draft a report on the problems of co-existence among ethnic minorities and encourage the peaceful co-existence among peoples of different cultures in large cities.[37] After much delay, the first voluminous report was finally presented on 23 November 1989,[38] outlining the situation and proposing measures on prevention and repression of racism. One of them calls for the setting up of a national centre against discrimination and for the integration of ethnic minorities, comparable to the Commission on Racial Equality in the UK and the Landelijk Buro Racismebestrijding (LBR – National Bureau for Combating Racism) in the Netherlands.[39]

Denmark

Events since 1986 concerning inter-community relations in Denmark have given rise to growing concern as to the extent of racial prejudice. An Australian lawyer requested by the Danish Centre for Human Rights to undertake a three-month study on labour market discrimination has concluded that foreigners are denied equal opportunities, in violation of many international conventions signed and ratified by Denmark.[40] In some state-run job centres employers are actually asked if they want an immigrant to take up a certain job and they are apparently free to refuse a foreigner.

Other than the UN Convention on the Elimination of All Forms of Racial Discrimination, which entered into force in Denmark on 9 January 1972, there is no separate anti-racism legislation. Calls for such legislation during a parliamentary debate on 3 March 1988 were dismissed by the Minister of Justice, who argued that foreigners already enjoyed sufficient protection under existing laws protecting individuals, in particular paragraph 266b of the Danish Penal Code.[41] In the Minister's view, further bans to combat associations professing intolerance towards foreigners might constitute interference in the freedom of expression and of association.

The number of foreigners in Denmark of non-European origin is around 90,000, of whom some 60,000 are immigrants who arrived during the 1960s (mainly from Turkey, Pakistan and Yugoslavia) and about 30,000 are people granted asylum within the last decade. The problems of racism in Danish society began to assume alarming proportions with threats and attacks against immigrants and refugees as of 1985 when an increasing number of asylum-seekers were arriving. During the night of 12/13 July 1986, for example, some 2000 'rockers' launched a concerted attack against a hostel which was accommodating 247 asylum-seekers from Iran, Sri Lanka and Lebanon to protect against the influx of refugees.[42]

A TV journalist who tried to raise awareness of the problem of racist attacks interviewed some 'skinheads' on 21 July 1985. Racist statements were made and the journalist as well as the programme controller responsible were fined for enabling these skinheads to contravene the afore-mentioned paragraph 266b.[43] As for the skinheads themselves, they were convicted on a long series of other charges which had the paradoxical result that no separate penalty was handed down to them for their racist remarks. All means of appeals having been exhausted, the case of the journalist and programme controller has been taken to the European Court of Human Rights.

On 7 March 1988 a group of young people were convicted for violating the said paragraph 266b after they confessed to having burnt a wooden cross near a church accommodating Tamils to frighten them.[44] However, when, on a local radio station, a member of the ultra-right Fremskridtspartiet (Progress Party, see below), referring to refugees prior to the 1987 elections, spoke of 'the vast hordes of terrorists pouring in over us from the Middle East and Sri Lanka' who 'breed like rats', the Public Prosecutor and the Ministry of Justice considered that the remarks did not constitute sufficient grounds for a conviction under the said paragraph 226b in view of the context and the form in which they were made.[45]

Most of the anti-foreigner votes go to the Fremskridt, whose electoral promises include expelling all Muslims and refugees (who, in its view, are all 'false'), and tax cuts. It managed to double its score at the 10 May 1988 elections capturing 9 per cent of the votes (4.8 per cent previously) and now has 16[46] out of a total of 179 parliamentary seats (previously 9).[47] The number of local council seats held by the party fell from 150 during the 1981–5 mandate period to 35 during the 1985–9 period, before making a spectacular rise to 235 at the 1989 elections.

The party's international affiliations are not clear-cut. At a meeting of extreme-right movements in Copenhagen during the weekend of 12/13 May 1990, in which Mr Le Pen of the French Front National and Mr Schönhuber of the German Republikaner participated, members of the Fremskridt surprisingly refused to take part.[48]

According to an opinion survey carried out in March 1988 by the Kaspar Vilstrup Institute, between 30 and 35 per cent of Danish adults had a positive view on immigrants and refugees,

10 per cent were quite negative and the remainder either had intermediate views or no opinion at all.[49] The 10 per cent corresponds more or less to the audience of the Fremskridt and the new Stop Indvandringen (Stop Immigration) party which appeared for the first time at the municipal elections in the autumn of 1989.[50] An attempt to form a nationwide 'People's Movement against Immigration' failed when the organizers were prevented from holding their founding meeting on 3 March 1990.[51]

A new form of xenophobia with 'Christian respect for the cultures of others' (who should remain where they are), advocated by a Lutheran parish priest, Rev. Af. Søren Krarup, is gaining some ground.[52]

One particularly controversial move against immigrants was taken in March 1988 in the borough of Ishøj when the local council voted against having 'even more people of foreign origin take residence in Ishøj'.[53] Another Copenhagen suburb, Farum, decided in March 1988 to hold a referendum on whether the municipality should make 25 homes available to refugees.[54] Fortunately, this matter was not raised again and the referendum was not held.

Federal Republic of Germany

There is still no specific anti-racism legislation in the FRG as the Federal Government considers that the protection against racial discrimination provided for in Articles 1(1) and 3(3) of the Constitution is adequate to combat racism[55] and, as confirmed by the representative of the FRG at the Committee of Inquiry hearing[56], the 'Federal Government considers that the legal instruments in force are sufficient to counter undesirable developments effectively. It did not therefore take any special legislative measures in connection with the adoption of the declaration against racism and xenophobia'. However, it seems that the German Government considers that the constitutional provisions apply only to its nationals.

However, there has been a rise in the number of violent attacks against foreigners since 1986[57] and there continues to be reluctance on the part of the police and the Public Prosecutor's offices to prosecute racially motivated violence or admit that racism was a motive.[58] For example, the two men responsible for the killing of an Iranian asylum-seeker in 1988 were given an 18-month suspended sentence. The court in Tübingen (Baden-Württemberg) accepted the argument from the defence that the two men, employees of a supermarket, had mistaken their victim for a shoplifter and considered that the victim's behaviour contributed to the 'tragic accident'.[59]

Hatred of foreigners has led to actions such as the arson attack on 17 May 1987 in Wuppertal, resulting in the death of a Greek couple and their son and serious burns to 18 other foreigners. A similar incident took place in Schwandorf on 17 December 1988 when a Turkish couple and their son were killed in a fire, as was the father of a German family who happened to be their neighbour. The 19-year-old German youth responsible for the arson attack in Schwandorf was supposedly linked with extreme right-wing groups and the only 'motive' he gave was his hatred of foreigners.[60] In another incident in Hamburg, in October 1988, a group of youths attacked and beat up a Turkish woman before pushing her in front of an oncoming car.[61]

The Turkish population, numbering about 1.5 million, probably bears the brunt of racial harassment, violence and discrimination. This has been well described, documented and exposed by the journalist, Mr Günther Wallraff in his now renowned book and film *Ganz Unten*.[62] Most of them, in fact, form a class of sub-proletariat, with insecure rights of residence, and are quite defenceless against legislation that still treats them as 'guest workers'.[63]

Another group which continues to suffer much discrimination are the Sinti and Roma Community (the gypsies), who number some 60,000 in the FRG (the Nazis exterminated more than half a million).[64] According to Mr J. Ramirez Heredia, MEP,[65] the Bonn Government has systematically refused to agree to any project of the European Social Fund in support of gypsies in the FRG.

There are also the specific problems of the between 40,000 and 50,000 black or Afro-Germans in the FRG, many the offspring of liaisons between black GIs and German women, of whom very little is said. They consider themselves as members of German society, but are not recognized as such.[66]

As in Sweden (see below), the British extreme-right groups have been introducing and propagating racial hatred in the FRG through the distribution and commercialization of racist video games. This was denounced in March 1989 by Mr Ernest Glinne, Belgian MEP,[67] but according to a report in March 1990, pupils in Hesse were still playing with such games.[68]

Antisemitism is far from being eradicated and two studies conclude that as much as 20 per cent of the population still harbours anti-Jewish sentiments, while antisemitism is latent among another 30 per cent.[69] In fact, those who deny the existence of the Nazi gas chambers are speaking out more openly than ever and are now part of an expanding international network with branches mainly in the USA, the UK, the FRG and France.[70]

The massive influxes in 1989 of Germans from the GDR (343,854) and East Europeans of German descent (720,909),[71] together with a record number of 121,318 applicants for asylum (an increase of 18 per cent over 1988),[72] have further aggravated the housing shortages and existing negative sentiments towards foreigners and this in turn has led to the spectacular successes of the Republikaner,[73] with gains in the Berlin municipal assembly and other State Parliaments, as well as six seats in the European Parliament. This party has been brought under surveillance since the beginning of 1990 by the Office for the Protection of the Constitution in Hamburg (Verfassungsschutz).[74] The question of whether to take such a decision at federal level is pending. According to a confidential (provisional) report of the Federal Office for the protection of the Constitution in Cologne (Kölner Bundesamtes für Verfassungsschutz), this party is a threat to the Constitution.[75]

According to an opinion survey issued in September 1989, 75 per cent of West Germans questioned felt that there were too many foreigners in the FRG, 69 per cent agreed that asylum-seekers were unfairly exploiting the social welfare system, and 93 per cent favoured reducing the number of so-called 'economic refugees'. Racial hatred against Africans or Asians was shared by about 20 per cent of respondents, the majority of whom supported the Republikaner. Migrant workers ('guest workers') are rejected to a lesser degree than asylum-seekers. The survey nevertheless confirmed strong negative feelings against the Turks, whose situation is now all the more precarious due to the influx of East Germans and ethnic Germans from eastern Europe. The latter category, especially those from Poland and the USSR, were, according to the poll, accused of unfairly exploiting the social welfare system (54 per cent), aggravating the unemployment situation (61 per cent) and the housing shortages (69 per cent).[76]

Greece

According to Paraskevas Avgerinos[77] and the statement of the Greek government delegate, Mr Ekonomidis,[78] 'Greeks were and are as a rule xenophiles rather than xenophobes'. There are several laws to combat discrimination, including Article 5(2) of the 1975 Constitution.[79]

In fact, other than EC nationals, who number more than 16,000, the foreign (non-EC) population is only double that number, mostly from the Philippines, Poland, Egypt and Iran (in order of importance).[80] However, in January 1990, there were violent riots in Komotini, Western Thrace, with fights between Orthodox Christians and Muslims. The first independent Muslim MP, elected in June 1989, was sentenced to 18 months' imprisonment on 26 January 1990 for disturbing the peace and inciting discord. His imprisonment and that of another Muslim leader sparked off the clashes which resulted in the death of one Orthodox Christian, 19 persons injured, and the breaking of windows of dozens of shops belonging to Muslims.[81] A diplomatic row broke out between Greece and Turkey over the (ethnic) status of the 120,000-strong Muslim minority in Western Thrace.[82] That incident has been considered purely political, between Greece and Turkey.

Under the 1923 Treaty of Lausanne, the rites of worship of Greek Muslims in Thrace were given special protection. However, (Greek) Muslims complain of harassment by the Greek authorities. They speak of bureaucratic obstacles to obtaining permits for building houses and repairing their existing homes where sanitary and heating facilities are often lacking. They also complain of being refused loans from state-controlled banks, denied driving licences and rarely given permission to drive tractors.[83]

These problems and conflicts must also be seen within the context of centuries of bitter, if not hostile, relations between Turkey and Greece, which was colonized for about four centuries by the former. The Greek authorities are, in general, apprehensive of possible Turkish territorial expansion into Western Thrace and this may help to explain the cause of some of the grievances of Greek Muslims.

The Committee received no new specific examples of any problems being encountered by the Jewish and Armenian communities, although the Evrigenis Report did refer to some incidents. As for the gypsies, attempts to assimilate them have not succeeded and the majority still live apart from Greek society.

As the Greek delegate to the hearing quite rightly pointed out, no country could consider itself 'entirely immune' to the dangers of racism and Greece recognized the need 'to be on the alert and exercise vigilance in facing up to such dangerous phenomena as they might also emerge to a greater or lesser extent in Greece in the future'.[84]

Spain

Among the legal forms of protection against discrimination from which foreigners can benefit in Spain are Articles 1 and 14 of the Spanish Constitution and the Organic Law of 25 June 1983. Moreover, there is an Ombudsman (Defensor del Peublo) who is appointed by the Cortes to defend individuals' rights.[85]

Nevertheless, a well-compiled dossier issued by Documentación Social of Cáritas Española in 1987 shows a disturbing degree of racism in Spain.[86] On the other hand, a national opinion survey carried out at the end of 1987[87] concluded that the Spanish people believed themselves to be more racist than they were in reality. It pointed out that apart from gypsies and North Africans, other foreigners (such as Latin Americans and Filipinos) hardly ever complained of racist practices.

The same survey claimed that black people (Africans) complained more of racism in the workplace than elsewhere in society. Hardly four months later, the same review that published the survey ran an article saying that drug trafficking and the high crime rate among foreigners had led to increasing discrimination against black people.[88] Black people with valid residence permits are often persecuted by the police while some have even been deported to their country of origin. The article reported on allegations that police sometimes picked on innocent foreigners and tore up their residence permits. This has been confirmed in the Ombudsman's 1989 Annual Report.[89]

North Africans are probably the worst treated in Spain and gypsies constitute the second most discriminated against group.[90] The latter number about half a million in Spain. Like black people in the US, the gypsies are often only appreciated for their dance and music; problems begin when they leave the theatres and try to be part of Spanish society.

Growing hostility towards foreigners and their families[91] led to the organization on 5 November 1989 of the 'Immigrants Day', during which human rights associations issued a document criticizing the painful situation under which immigrants in Spain live.[92] There have been several scandalous cases of discriminatory treatment in the form of ostracism of black and North African workers.

In the town of Lerida, as nobody wanted to rent accommodation to the black workers there, most of them had to live in wooden huts without gas, electricity or running water. Three of them even sought shelter in a former pigsty. Complaints of racism to the police produced no action. Another article denounced a similar situation confronting the 600-strong Moroccan community in an industrial area in Barcelona. As most of them had no work permits, they did not dare to complain.[93] Local people, meanwhile, often accuse the foreigners of bad behaviour.[94]

Although since October 1985 a far-reaching 'National Plan for Gypsy Development' has been implemented,[95] violent incidents, including arson attacks, have been perpetrated against whole gypsy communities. In one incident in July 1986, more than 30 gypsy families in Andalusia had to flee to a nearby village after their homes were burnt down, only to be refused reception. When they arrived at the next town, riots broke out and they finally ended up sleeping in tents provided by the Spanish Red Cross under the protection of the civil guards. Shortly after the incident, two-thirds of callers during a radio programme admitted that they were racists.[96] Three months later, in the town of Ciudad Real, another group of gypsies had to flee after an arson attack.[97]

In Barcelona and Madrid, there have been cases of gypsy children being prevented from attending schools and on 13 February 1988, the Supreme Court dismissed an appeal by the Madrid municipality against a sentence issued on 15 May 1987 condemning the municipality for continued racist practices against gypsies there.[98]

There are 17 autonomous regions in Spain and the central government has virtually no powers in matters of social and cultural services.[99] The treatment of gypsies varies from one municipality to another and the 'main source of confrontation and discrimination experienced by gypsies in Spain is to be found in the municipalities'.[100]

France

Since 1986 in France about 20 foreigners have been assassinated[101] and all but one (a Romanian)[102] were North Africans or French citizens of North African origin. The racist motive has not been proven in all cases, but in at least half of these killings there was no reason whatsoever other than the desire to kill foreigners. In one case when six youths simply kicked to death a Tunisian father of five children, the arresting police officer said, 'What shocks me the most is that they have the feeling of not having committed anything reprehensible'.[103] In a similar case, three youths shot and killed a Harki[104] youth 'to amuse themselves'.[105] In another, in which a Moroccan youth was simply in the wrong place at the wrong time, his assassin admitted that he had made a 'mistake' because he thought he 'had fired at a Chinese'.[106] Even when there are 'motives', they include reasons such as the victim refused to pay for his bread or his drink, the victim was responsible for breaking a window, of making noise, etc. In an opinion survey after the killing of three youths of North African origin in March 1990 76 per cent of those questioned agreed that 'the behaviour of some of them can justify racist reactions against them'.[107]

Apart from murders, there have been numerous other violent incidents which resulted in amputations, physical and mental handicap and permanent and complete paralysis. A number of these incidents have been attributed to excessive and unjustifiable violence by the police. Almost all go unrecorded, except in cases of death[108] or when the victims are public figures, like a black doctor who suffered substantial injuries inflicted by the police when he tried to respond to an emergency call.[109]

In many cases, the sentences passed or action taken have been very lenient. In one case a policeman responsible for the death of a North African youth received a ten months' prison sentence, four months of which were suspended, although his own defence lawyer requested two years without probation.[110] The resulting outcry and rage among immigrants have been translated into the feeling that there is no justice for them. The Harki father of the youth who died from three shots in the back at close range, who received a series of decorations for his services in the French Army, went on a long hunger strike to protest against the release of the policeman by the examining magistrate, acting against the advice of the Public Prosecutor's Office in Marseilles.[111]

As the French representative at the Committee hearing himself said,[112] 'the enactment of new legislation was not considered a priority', although human rights groups and some prominent politicians from both the Left and Right have pointed to the need for more legislation to plug the significant number of loopholes in the anti-racist law of 1 July 1972.[113]

In France, as in some other Member States, measures against racism have been enacted not with pre-emptive foresight, but only when violence and murders have reached intolerable and embarrassing proportions with protests voiced by the governments of North African countries. Only after the bombing of an immigrant hostel in Nice in December 1988[114] did the Prime Minister decide to set up an interministerial unit to coordinate the campaign against racist violence. Similarly, the decision to enact new anti-racism legislation and measures[115] was made only after the deaths of three French youths of North African origin and when opinion surveys revealed extensive racism in French society and strong aversion against North Africans, gypsies, black people, Asians and Southern Europeans (in order of dislike).[116]

Probably because of a lack of coordination among the various political parties, the anti-racism bill was presented as an initiative of the Parti Communiste Français (PCF) and political considerations unfortunately entered the picture and dominated the debate. Although there was consensus among the leaders of the various political parties, except the Front National (FN), on the proposed measures, including the additional sanction of denying certain civil rights to those convicted of racism, only the Parti Socialiste (PS) and the PCF voted in favour of the bill at its first reading on 3 May 1990 – after complex internal debates, the

Rassemblement pour la République (RPR), the Union pour la Démocratie Française (UDF) as well as the Centre des Démocrates Sociaux (CDS) voted against.

Under the anti-racism bill, persons convicted of racism would be barred from public posts and would not be able to present themselves as election candidates. The bill also introduces the offence of revisionism. However, it hardly provides any solution to the difficulties often encountered by victims of racism and discrimination of proving their case in court.[117]

Human rights associations have pointed out that the 1972 anti-racism law has really only been applied in matters concerning the press[118] and, in going through the case law in this matter, the impression is that this law has served no purpose other than to exacerbate sentiments against immigrants. Judges have given a more and more restrictive interpretation of the 1972 law.[119] For example, the legislation was aimed at protecting 'groups of people' against discrimination.[120] Judges now demand that the term 'groups of people' be clearly determined; thus immigrants do not form a group.

So far, mayors of three municipalities (Beaucaire, Casseneuil, Montfermeil) have openly defied the Ministry of Education in refusing to register non-EC children in local schools to 'shock' the authorities into curbing immigration.[121] One Communist mayor expressed 'understanding' for this kind of action and himself made such a strong attack against black people and Arabs that disciplinary party action was taken against him.[122]

The nationwide controversy that lasted about two months when three Muslim girls in a school in Creil, Northern France, refused to remove their headscarves[123] had serious detrimental consequences for the Muslim population. There has been persistent over-exaggeration of Islamic fundamentalism, giving rise to equally exaggerated fears of an Islamic takeover.

The Front National, which has been losing some ground[124] since capturing 14.38 per cent of the votes in the first round of the presidential elections on 24 April 1988,[125] bounced back with such popularity that many French politicians nowadays, consciously or unconsciously, define their stand on immigration in relation to that of the Front National. President Mitterrand himself caused quite considerable concern when he said that the 'threshold of tolerance' (of immigration) had been reached in the 1970s.[126]

Whatever reasons he could have had for making such a statement, the fact remains that a term which was once considered to have been the exclusive appendage of the extreme right was uttered by the President himself.

With declarations such as: 'Soon, it will be our children who will be integrated by the North Africans', the Front National candidate in Dreux captured 61.3 per cent of the votes and once again the Front National gained representation at the National Assembly.[127]

Its Chairman, Mr Le Pen, who claims to be neither racist nor antisemitic, but who none the less makes remarks against immigrants and Jews that could be considered denigrating and insulting and, at times, an incitement to racial hatred, has been convicted under the 1972 anti-racist law on at least three occasions.[128] In addition, four requests by the Ministry of Justice have been made to the European Parliament to lift his parliamentary immunity in order that legal action be taken against him for racist and other denigratory remarks – two have met with a favourable response and two others are pending.[129]

Although banned from speaking in Geneva in November 1987 for being a threat to public order[130] and prevented the following month by a huge mass of demonstrators from landing in Martinique as well as in Guadeloupe, where the local people threatened to ransack the airport if he dared to leave the plane,[131] Mr Le Pen has been allowed to make anti-immigrant speeches in France, and commands huge audiences. Opinion surveys show that between 73 and 81 per cent of French people consider the Front National to be a racist party, 76 per cent consider that it is incapable of governing and 72 per cent consider it to be a risk for democracy. However, 31 per cent of respondents agree with Mr Le Pen's views on immigration and 18 per cent would favour him as the new 'Immigration Minister'.[132]

The so-called 'Le Pen phenomenon' has brought about some 'respectability' in racist behaviour under the cover of defending Christianity against Islam, and upholding national pride, family values and the 'natural principle' of priority to French people. The FN congress at the end of March 1990 received such support and attention that the opposition right (UDF, RPR, CDS, CNIP), who held their Congress at the same time, proposed certain policy measures on immigration which were the same as those called for by the Front National, such as a referendum on the nationality law, less social security rights for foreign residents, stricter conditions for family reunion, etc.[133]

There has been widespread opposition to the building of mosques in France. In Lille the construction of a mosque has been prevented since 1985,[134] in Charvieu-Chavagneux (S.E. France), the Muslim place of worship was destroyed by a bulldozer 'by mistake' in August 1989,[135] and in Lyons the outspoken Gaullist Mayor, Mr M. Noir (RPR), has come under very strong criticism from a large section of the local population for having signed, on 28 August 1989, the construction permit for the Lyons Mosque.[136]

Other than the racist violence practised by extreme right-wing terrorists, like the 'Commandos de France',[137] 'SOS France' (which 'dissolved itself' when four of its leaders were blown up with their own bomb which they planned to use against immigrants)[138] and some members of the Front National, there are attacks carried out by skinheads[139] and by members of the police involved with the extreme-right Parti Nationaliste Français et Européen (PNFE). Four of these policemen, charged with involvement with the bombing in Nice in December 1988 (see above) and another attack against the magazine *Globe*,[140] were also members of the extreme-right police union, FPIP (Fédération Professionnelle Indépendante de la Police), which has the support of about 6.9 per cent of the police force.[141] The four have been expelled from the force, but FPIP still exists.[142]

Last but not least is the growing frequency of antisemitic statements made in public as well as the anti-Jewish attacks and denigrating graffiti on walls and Jewish cemeteries. The most abject in a series of desecrations of Jewish cemeteries was perpetrated in the night of 9/10 May 1990 in the town of Carpentras (near Avignon), the founding place of Judaism in France. Thirty-four tombstones were damaged and the corpse of an old man who was buried two weeks earlier was removed from the coffin and mutilated.[143] The incident caused great national and international indignation and the leaders of all political parties,[144] excluding the Front National, took part in a massive demonstration in Paris on 14 May 1990. For the first time since the end of the Second World War, a president of the Republic joined the silent procession in Paris composed of some 200,000 participants. In about ten other provincial cities, including Marseilles, Quimper, Rennes, Nantes, Dijon and Rouen, similar demonstrations were each attended by several thousand people. That same evening, another (or the same) group of vandals desecrated another Jewish cemetery, damaging 32 tombstones.[145]

Although the Secretary-General of the Front National, Mr C. Lang, also expressed his indignation over the desecration in Carpentras and the FN Chairman, Mr Le Pen, reiterated that he was not antisemitic, publications related to the FN, especially the party's publication, the *National Hebdo*,[146] and remarks made by its political leaders, including Mr Le Pen, cannot be dissociated from the rise of antisemitism in France. Mr Le Pen has already accused the 'Jewish International' and freemasonry of playing 'a non-negligible role in the creation of the anti-national spirit [in France]'.[147] After saying that Field-Marshal Pétain has been unjustly criticized ('injustement accablé'), he recently affirmed on television that 'Jews have a lot of power in the press'.[148]

A former Front National MEP, Mr C. Autant Lara, even expressed regret that the Nazis failed to exterminate Mrs S. Veil, a former President of the European Parliament.[149] Others close to the Front National, like the Gaullist Mayor of Nice, Mr J. Médecin (RPR), have issued statements considered by many to be antisemitic.[150] The recent report of the Committee on Human Rights[151] points out that anti-North-African racism has 'reanimated' an 'explicit and virulent antisemitism'.

The desecration of the Carpentras cemetery at least had the positive effect of uniting the opposition parties (except the Front National) with the Government to combat racism, antisemitism and xenophobia. The earlier decision of the opposition parties to boycott the Government's second round table meeting on immigration has been reversed.[152] In 'exchange', the Government agreed to postpone the round table meeting, scheduled to be held on 16 May to 29 May 1990, after the parliamentary debate on the same subject on 22 May.[153] The Carpentras incident probably had some influence on the unanimous decision made by the administrative council of the University of Lyon III (Jean-Moulin) to dismiss two extreme-right professors, one of whom is Mr B. Notin, a lecturer on Economics who once wrote a revisionist and antisemitic article.[154]

Republic of Ireland

Ireland has a non-EC population of only about 18,000 and, according to Patrick Cooney,[155] the country 'has been remarkably free' of racism as there is not a large presence of foreigners.

The number of known cases of racial harassment or violence is very small compared to other countries. However, precisely because of the insignificant foreign population, the few cases which this report will mention are indicative of some racism and xenophobia which could reach more dangerous levels if there were more foreigners, in particular non-Europeans.

The cases mentioned in a recent report compiled by an anti-racism group[156] are as follows: Jewish shops in Dublin's south inner city were repeatedly attacked in 1986; a group of travelling people were barred from participating in an anti-racism meeting in a Dublin hotel in September 1987; in November 1987, a Moroccan, his Irish wife and their daughter started suffering from physical and verbal abuse and, in the absence of protection, finally left their council flat; in December the same year, a black man, his Irish wife and three children began experiencing a similar, but more violent, ordeal – they could not even drink in a local pub because the barman could not 'guarantee their safety'.

The single most discriminated against ethnic group is the 'travelling people' who, according to the last official count in November 1988, number 15,888. Like gypsies in other countries, they are considered undesirable neighbours and are usually forced to move out of residential areas. More than 70 per cent now have fixed accommodation.

Although Ireland has not yet signed the UN Convention on the Elimination of all Forms of Racial Discrimination, a positive step forward was made with the enactment of the 'Prohibition of Incitement to Hatred Act' on 29 November 1989 which, *inter alia,* prohibits the preparation or possession of material or recordings of a racist or similarly offensive nature.[157] Police had, on a few occasions, discovered that Ireland was used for printing such material for distribution abroad, but did not have the necessary powers to act.

Italy

The Evrigenis Report noted that 'Italy is certainly one of the countries of Europe with the lowest number of racialist incidents'.[158] At the Committee hearing, Dr A. Cavaterra made similar remarks claiming that Italy 'is not a xenophobic country' and explained that the cases of racial intolerance described by the media were in fact 'instances of petty criminality'.[159] Dacia Valent,[160] however, presents a picture that is very much to the contrary.

The fact remains that at the end of February 1990 at carnival night in Florence some 200 masked people armed with baseball bats and iron bars organized a beating of black people and gypsies in the town centre, severely wounding a number of them.[161] The violence persisted in March and spread to Rome, Varese, Turin, Caserta, Catania, Livorno, Matera, Milan, etc., with incidents of Molotov cocktail attacks against an immigrant reception centre, the burning of four cars belonging to immigrants, skinhead attacks, evictions from rented accommodation and refusal to allow immigrants to rent places. In March 1990, thousands of immigrants who were refused accommodation in Rome had to sleep under bridges and about 1500 were reported to be taking turns to sleep in four-hour shifts in a part of the catacombs.[162]

Racist leaflets issued by new racist groups such as 'Ludwig', 'Falange' and 'Brigata Goebbels' made their appearance. The last urges 'vigilance against the blacks and gypsy pigs and the drug traffickers and the filthy Bolsheviks who protect them'.[163]

While some sectors of the Roman Catholic Church pleaded for tolerance, including the Pope himself, others fuelled the tensions, like the Archbishop of Ravenna, who stated that Europe had been 'Islamicized' during the 1980s and that Italy now risked being 'lebanized' owing to the inability of people of different cultures, religion and races to live together.[164]

The incidents have been mainly interpreted as a sudden revolt against the increasing number of immigrants entering the country, sponsored mainly by shopkeepers and street vendors who felt threatened by the increasing competition of immigrants. The emergency law aimed, *inter alia*, at regularizing the several hundred thousand irregular immigrants, which came into force on 30 December 1989,[165] was criticized by some sectors of being a 'pull factor' in encouraging more irregular migrants to enter. Indeed, the number of irregulars which was once thought to be between 800,000 and one million is now believed to be in the region of one and a half million or even more.

Opinion polls show a growing number of Italians in favour of stopping immigration, and in Florence one survey indicated that 37 per cent of the local people agreed that all immigrants should be repatriated. A poll conducted in 1989 showed that 20 per cent of respondents shared this view.[166]

Apart from the UN Convention on the Elimination of all Forms of Racial Discrimination which came into force in Italy on 2 February 1976, the only other legal protection against discrimination is in the Italian Constitution. No laws or regulations have been implemented since 1986 to combat racism and xenophobia.

The Government's view is that the present problems are due to the ever-increasing number of non-EC foreigners entering the country and 'must be tackled by preventing and eliminating the causes, rather than suppressing the potential effects of uncontrolled migration'.[167] In April 1990, the Deputy Prime Minister and deputy leader of the Partito Socialista Italiano, Mr C. Martelli, caused quite a scandal when he suggested on Italian television that the police were not capable of controlling the thousands of kilometres of Italy's coastal borders alone and that the army should be called in.[168]

There were violent racist incidents prior to those in Florence. In January 1987, the Salvation Army hostel in the San Lorenzo quarter of Rome was raided by about 20 hooded persons who beat up three foreigners and then threw a petrol bomb. The hostel's director described it as an act of hooliganism. The hostel was again attacked in February (and several other times since then), this time with gunfire, but nobody was wounded. 'San Lorenzo 77' claimed responsibility and the racist graffiti against black people this time clearly indicated racist motives.[169]

In May 1988 in Rome, a black Italian woman of Eritrean origin was told by a male passenger to give up her seat to a white. Nearly all the passengers defended this man, except two students and an Indian who sided with her until they realized that they were greatly outnumbered and withdrew. The incident provoked a national scandal as this woman happened to be the cleaning lady of an employee in the news media. The Mayor of Rome made a public apology on television.[170]

In what appeared to be a burglary on the night of 24/25 August 1989, 30 African workers were robbed and one was murdered. As the total amount stolen was so small (180,000–270,000 lire), no one in Italy seriously believed that it was a mere robbery and considered rather that it was aimed at frightening black people away.[171]

These incidents and other attacks against foreigners led to the biggest anti-racist demonstration ever held in Italy in October 1989, which brought more than 100,000 people on to the streets of Rome.[172]

In addition to hostility towards foreigners, there is also intolerance and outright hatred among some Italians in the North against those in the South. In June 1989, a Southern Italian immigrant was beaten to death by a group of Northerners. An opinion poll carried out shortly afterwards indicated that two-thirds of those in the North disliked the Southerners.[173]

Luxembourg

Although Luxembourg has the highest percentage of foreigners (almost 30 per cent), about 90 per cent of them are EC nationals, mainly Portuguese (29 per cent), Italians (20 per cent) and French (12.6 per cent),[174] and there is a large degree of cultural homogeneity in the sense that almost all foreigners are Europeans. The most important groups of non-Europeans are the Capeverdians of Afro-Portuguese origin (just over 1000) and the Iranians (fewer than 500).[175]

It can safely be said that racist or xenophobic incidents like those in other Member States are virtually unknown in Luxembourg. The only two examples of any relevance occurred in 1988 when there were two cases of road signs defaced by racist slogans and one occasion when antisemitic graffiti were scrawled over the Jewish cemetery.[176]

One of the main grievances of the foreign population voiced in the last few years is that they are denied the right to vote. Owing to the high percentage of foreigners in Luxembourg the authorities have been unwilling to grant this. In some boroughs, the percentage is well over 30 per cent. Preparing for the national and European elections which took place at the same time on 18 June 1989, the party list 'Lëtzeburg de Lëtzerburger, National Bewegung' (Luxembourg for the Luxembourgers, National Movement) tried to stir up xenophobia by attacking foreigners over the implications of their right to vote with reference to the 'syndrome of Larochette' (a small borough of 800 inhabitants, 20 per cent of whom are non-Portuguese[177]). This list, however, gained only 2.91 per cent in the European elections and no representation.

Owing to the particular trilingual system of education in the country (German, Luxembourgish and French), foreign pupils, who represent about 40 per cent of the school population, quite often have serious difficulties. But the authorities have paid attention to this matter over the years and classes have been reduced to 15–16 pupils, and teachers have been provided with specialized training courses.

There is no anti-racism law; two articles in the Constitution are considered to provide adequate protection against racism and discrimination. Nevertheless, in May 1989 these articles were declared open to review by the Chamber of Deputies in view of extending the guarantee of fundamental rights to foreigners on equal terms with Luxembourg nationals.[178]

The Netherlands

Ethnic minorities in The Netherlands account for about 5 per cent of the total population and consist of mainly Dutch nationals of Surinamese origin (about 200,000), of West Indian origin (about 60,000), of Moluccan origin (about 60,000), Turks (170,000) and Moroccans (130,000).[179] There are about 300,000 Dutch nationals of Indonesian or 'semi-Indonesian' origin (of mixed descent) who are not, in general, confronted with the same problems as ethnic minorities and are therefore not considered as such.

Compared to countries like the FRG, France and the UK, racism and discrimination take on a less aggressive, though no less harmful, form and ethnic minorities tend instead to be victims of institutionalized and subtle variants of racism.

As pointed out by Maartje van Putten,[180] the unemployment situation for ethnic minorities is 'disastrous' as the average rate among them is three times higher than among Dutch nationals. This has been confirmed by the Dutch Government representative at the hearing of the Committee of Inquiry,[181] who pointed out that 40 per cent of them are unemployed and this percentage reaches approximately 44 per cent where Turks and Moroccans are concerned.[182] Both reports claim that even those who are well educated have the same problem, which refutes assertions by employers that the high unemployment rate among ethnic minorities is caused by poor education and lack of qualifications.

Efforts have been directed to get all national and local authorities to implement a positive action programme, i.e. to ensure that public bodies engage a certain number of people from ethnic minorities whose qualifications satisfy the set criteria. The next step is to get private firms to take similar measures. The institution of 'contract compliance', whereby private firms dealing with the national or local government bodies will be obliged to adopt a non-discriminatory staffing policy or else lose out on government contracts, is also envisaged. Pressure has also been exerted on local authorities and housing associations to ensure that ethnic minorities are not discriminated against in housing allocations – they are required to submit annual or six-monthly reports.[183]

The second half of the 1980s also witnessed a growth of anti-fascist organizations, whether directed at victims (discrimination reporting centres) or at institutional discrimination. One of the more positive actions was the setting up in 1985 of the Landelijk Buro Racismebestrijding (LBR – National Bureau for Combating Racism, similar to the Commission for Racial Equality in the UK).[184] The following year, the Second Chamber of the Dutch Parliament approved by a large majority a bill making organizations whose aims and activities are contrary to public order liable to prosecution and dissolution. Only the Public Prosecutor was given the power to initiate such an order to outlaw and disband racist associations and political parties and he would be able to do so only if one or several of their leading members had previously been convicted of violating the Penal Code.[185] The wording of the bill, however, gave cause for concern that it could lead to abusive interpretation and, as a result, it was considered necessary clearly to define its application, i.e. against what kind of associations or parties. Therefore, the bill became law only in 1989 when it was also approved by the First Chamber.

Steps are now being taken to see how this new law can be used to prosecute and dissolve the extreme-right Centrum Partij '86 (see below), several of whose members had been convicted for offences related to racism. However, it has been very difficult for the police and public prosecutor to provide legally conclusive evidence of racial discrimination and the number of successful convictions is very small.[186] It is interesting to note that the first verdict by the UN Commission on the Elimination of Racial Discrimination in Geneva on a citizen's complaint concerned a Turkish woman in the Netherlands.[187]

A report prepared by the Dutch Research Centre on Social Conflicts which was handed to the Minister of Justice on 10 February 1988 concludes that ethnic minorities tend to come to terms with discrimination instead of using legal means to combat it. The authors point out that ethnic minorities suffering from discrimination at work and in daily life seem to take this as a normal social phenomenon of the 'cold, crude, hard and reserved' behaviour of the Dutch people.[188]

Although not as bad as in some other Member States, there are problems in relations between the police and ethnic minorities. The latter are largely under-represented in the police force, not least because of racial harassment within its ranks.[189]

Extremely violent incidents have been absent for some time. The last one, a bomb which destroyed the façade of a café in Schiedam frequented by immigrants, dates back to 10 August 1986.[190] On the other hand, the far right has gained ground in the election process: the extreme-right Centrumdemokraten gained a seat in the Second Chamber in September 1989. In the municipal elections on 21 March 1990, this party, together with another extreme-right and openly racist party, the Centrum Partij '86, increased their local representation from 2 to 15 council seats, mainly in Rotterdam (7.1 per cent of the vote), Amsterdam (6.8 per cent) and The Hague (6.4 per cent). On the other hand, there was a low turn-out among foreigners, who, for the second time, had the right to go to the polls. The number of elected foreigners fell from 48 (in the 1986 municipal elections) to 33, one reason being the poor results of the Partij van de Arbeid (PvdA – Labour Party), who put up the highest number of ethnic minority candidates.[191]

Portugal

Despite the fact that the Portuguese people are renowned for their mixed cultural and ethnic heritage, having been very open to mixed marriages wherever they established overseas settlements and colonies in the past centuries, and the Portuguese Constitution and laws provide for substantial protection against racism and discrimination,[192] it would be quite wrong to assume that the country enjoys racial harmony.[193]

It would not be exaggerating to say that children of mixed parents are more easily accepted in Portuguese society than in other countries and that racial discrimination or rejection is quite often related to the 'degree of blackness', i.e. someone born of one black parent would be more acceptable than someone both of whose parents were black.

At present, the population of African origin is not very large, numbering about 50,000 including the irregular immigrants. The majority of them (about 30,000) are from Cape Verde and the rest are from Angola, Mozambique, Guinea-Bissau, Sao Tomé and Principe.[194] They mostly belong to the poorer classes in society and live in the two main cities, Lisbon and Oporto. Other than experiencing certain forms of rejection in Portuguese society, they very often encounter considerable difficulties in renting decent accommodation as many proprietors refuse to let apartments to Africans, or even Portuguese nationals who are 'pure Africans'. In addition, there have been incidents of police brutality and there are two cases of murder of Africans: one was allegedly beaten to death by the police and the other was shot for 'violent behaviour'. It is believed that the most racist police officers are those who fought in the colonial wars.[195]

In Portugal there is no legal statute covering immigrants, which makes the administrative process for legalization (work and residence permits) difficult and lengthy.[196] There is also a lack of information about the necessary procedures. These factors, added to the fear of deportation, often deter immigrants from applying at all. This leaves many immigrants in an irregular situation, which has serious social consequences – lack of social security, housing, trade union rights, schooling. Such people may be pushed into illegal and marginal activities like smuggling, drug-dealing and prostitution. The districts in which they live become increasingly run-down, with the inhabitants facing increasing instability, illiteracy and a lack of any social integration.

In the last couple of years, the skinheads have added to their problems. This movement, which started sometime in 1985, has been implicated in a growing number of racial attacks, mainly against black and Indian people. On 28 October 1989, they were responsible for the violent attack against the headquarters of a small left-wing party, the Partido Socialista Revolucionário (PSR), which resulted in the death of a PSR leader.[197]

Skinhead violence is such a problem for the black community that two of its representatives met with the Interior Minister on 16 January 1990 and agreed on the setting up of a committee to monitor and study the situation experienced by ethnic minorities in Portugal. It will be composed of officials from the Interior Ministry, the Judiciary and the border police, as well as representatives from associations representing Capeverdians and Guineans.[198]

The foreign population in Portugal is still rather small (about 100,000, EC nationals included). This is probably why no major opinion survey has ever been carried out on the people's attitude to foreigners. However, danger does lie ahead as there has been for some time a growing tendency for Portuguese citizens (and/or their descendants) in other countries, namely in Africa, Brazil, Venezuela and Argentina, to 'return'. There are, moreover, 100,000 or so citizens of Macau who hold Portuguese passports.

United Kingdom

England Within the period under review (1986–90), there have been annual reports of systematic and increasingly widespread racial violence which point to increasing ethnic tension.[199] Frequent arson attacks did not spare the Joint Council for the Welfare of Immigrants (JCWI) whose offices were almost burned down on 22 October 1986.[200]

In publicizing its annual report on 8 July 1987, which marked the 10th anniversary of the 1976 Race Relations Act, the Commission for Racial Equality (CRE) denounced the prevalent attacks against whole families as well as individuals and discrimination in employment and teacher-training colleges. It also criticized the press's preference for sensationalism rather than accuracy in reporting race issues.[201] Related to this are articles in some less serious newspapers which give exaggerated, and often false, accounts of immigrants and asylum-seekers who supposedly abuse the social security system.[202]

In 1989, police reported an average of six racist incidents in

London per day and an estimated 7000 known cases of racism a year, but a Policy Studies Institute survey in 1984 had suggested that racial attacks could be under-reported by a factor of 10,[203] one reason being the victims' lack of confidence in the police.[204]

Racist attacks have taken the form of hooliganism and terrorizing ethnic minority groups: their children have to put up with all sorts of racial harassment and violence, and at home they receive threatening phone calls, excreta and racist literature are pushed through their letter boxes, as well as petrol which is then ignited.[205] There was a case of an Asian mother who used to see her two children spat on and stoned as they left home. Excrement was smeared on her door repeatedly. She did not seek help until her children had knives thrown at them, mainly because she thought that this was normal behaviour and expected nothing different.[206]

The increase in racial incidents may be partially attributable to the Salman Rushdie affair.[207] Rushdie's book, *The Satanic Verses*, was condemned as blasphemous by a sizeable number of Muslims and was publicly burnt on 13 January 1989. In the same way as the Islamic headscarf affair in France and to a much lesser extent in Belgium, the Rushdie affair has created or reinforced existing prejudices among wide sections of the population who tend to regard Islam with a very negative, if not hostile, attitude and only see it as expansionist and domineering, politically-orientated religious fundamentalism. On the other hand, when in December 1989 two Muslim girls insisted on wearing their headscarves in a grammar school in Manchester, the full school governors' meeting decided on 23 January 1990 to allow them to do so on condition that they be the same colour as their school uniform.[208]

Institutionalized racism is prevalent in British society and ethnic minorities continue to be discriminated against mainly in the justice system,[209] in job opportunities and in recruitment into the police[210] and army.[211]

Action taken to combat discrimination, such as anti-racist legislation, has sometimes been manipulated to hinder rather than help black people in their efforts to get jobs.[212] In a report by the Runnymede Trust,[213] the author points out that without positive action, permitted under the Race Relations Act 1976, members of minority ethnic groups may forever fail to join mainstream economic life and the consequences would be disastrous in terms of wasted talent, social injustice and alienation. Positive action consists of active encouragement of people from ethnic minorities to apply for jobs in sectors where they are significantly under-represented. Furthermore, the Home Office has issued guidance to Chief Officers of police on dealing with racial incidents, the Department of the Environment has published good practice guidance for local housing authorities, and the Home Affairs Committee of the House of Commons produced reports in 1986 and 1989 on tackling racial incidents.

One very disturbing consequence of discrimination was pointed out at a conference in London on 24 January 1990 when participants were told that it was a major contributory factor to mental illness among black people, which had reached levels that are sometimes higher than those diagnosed among immigrant parents.[214]

Confronted with widespread discrimination, ethnic minorities are calling for 'economic empowerment' to get their fair share of power in society. Not unrelated to this is the demand within the Labour party for them to have their own 'black sections', a controversy that still continues. In terms of political representation, the party fielded 14 black candidates at the last General Election (June 1987), of whom 4 were elected; the Conservatives fielded 6, as did the Social Democrats, whilst the Liberals had 1 such candidate.

Some local councils have introduced tough measures to deal with racism. In January 1988, the council leader of Liverpool announced that council employees who persisted in racist behaviour would be dismissed.[215] In the London borough of Southwark, anyone found terrorizing or bullying ethnic minority families on housing estates would be banned from using council services and those having a market stall would lose their trading licence.[216]

Measures to prevent the spread of racist ideas have also been suggested. In education, books transmitting stereotypical ideas of the inferior role of ethnic minorities in society should be banned,[217] and young people should be more informed on politics to prevent the spread of simple extreme-right ideas.[218]

Immigration policies designed to stop as many people as possible from entering the UK,[219] through measures such as housing qualifications, the so-called 'primary purpose rule',[220] proof of family ties, etc. have had a negative effect on race relations. Family ties can now be proven with DNA blood testing, but applicants are expected to pay the high costs involved. Moreover, people wrongly refused in the past cannot enter with the help of DNA blood testing if they are now over 18 years old.[221]

There is hardly any evidence to suggest that antisemitism is a serious problem. However, this must not be taken to imply that the problem does not exist, as certain sections of the population still harbour anti-Jewish feelings. Following the desecration of the Carpentras Cemetery in France (see above), the Jewish cemetery in the London Borough of Edmonton was also desecrated, causing significant material damage.[222]

It must also be emphasized that racism and discrimination is not simply a case of whites against blacks. As pointed out by Michael Elliott,[223] Asians are sometimes victims of harassment by blacks and there have even been isolated cases of whites being victimized by blacks or Asians.

Scotland Scots used to consider racism as an 'English problem', as, true enough, Scotland had been fairly free from such difficulties. Unlike England and Wales, there are no police statistics on racial attacks, which are still treated as ordinary assaults.[224]

The extreme-right British National Party opened an office in Glasgow in 1984 and racial violence has escalated since then. A recent study at Stirling University showed that more than half of those from Strathclyde's ethnic minorities had been physically attacked and even more had experienced attacks on their homes. Ethnic minorities are now faced with the same kinds of racially motivated violence as in other parts of the UK.[225]

The media finally decided to give the problem extensive coverage after the killing of a Somali student on 16 January 1989 by three youths. Although one had proven links with the National Front, he was sentenced to 18 months in prison for 'assault'. Charges were dropped against the second and the third was never brought to trial.[226]

Wales Recently, concern has been expressed about the involvement of members of the National Front and other extreme-right groups with the extreme Welsh nationalist group, Meibion Glyndwr.

In July 1990 there was a parade through Abergele to commemorate the deaths of two terrorist 'martyrs' who blew themselves up attempting to bomb the train carrying the Prince of Wales to his investiture. The marchers were in paramilitary uniform with a banner showing two Welsh dragons wielding Kalashnikov rifles against the background of a burning cottage with the slogan '10 mlynedd o losgi. Daw ein dydd' ('10 years of burning. Our day will come').[227]

Other European Countries

Austria

There is potential danger of racism in Austria, especially in the form of antisemitism, as was demonstrated during the controversy surrounding the election of Dr Kurt Waldheim as the new president in 1987.[228]

According to a survey carried out among students in Vienna in 1988, 20 per cent of them considered the number of Austrian Jews to be several hundred thousands whereas 12.8 per cent put the figure at 'more than a million'. In reality, the number is no higher than 8000, i.e. 0.1 per cent of the population.[229]

What is also worrying, as mentioned in the previous chapter, is the progress of the Freiheitliche Partei Österreichs (FPÖ – Liberal 'Freedom Party'), with its extreme-right leanings, which captured 10 per cent of the votes in the election of the provincial government of Lower Austria in October 1988, gaining five seats, and made spectacular gains in three regional elections in March 1989: Carinthia, Salzburg and Tyrol.[230] This party takes a hard line against migrant workers, particularly Yugoslavs, from Slovenia.

Switzerland

Since 1988, there has been a serious escalation of violence against foreigners and refugees/asylum-seekers in the form of arson, armed machine-gun raids on centres for foreigners or asylum-seekers, etc. Officials carrying out an enquiry into a fire in a wooden building which resulted in the deaths of four Tamils made known on 16 August 1989 that it was probably a criminal attack. According to a journalist, Mr Frischknecht, who specializes in the Swiss extreme right, 'Never, since the last war, has there been so many Neo-Nazis in Switzerland'.[231]

The authorities have not always been quick to act. In November 1989, the police present at a transit centre for asylum-seekers in Steinhausen, in the canton of Zug, did not intervene as 30 members of a right-wing group ransacked the centre and attacked its coordinator. They did not consider the incident as a 'punishable offence', but the Swiss press denounced the scandal and recalled that a similar event happened at the end of September 1989 in the same area.[232] Such incidents have revealed that the country lacks legislation to combat racism, antisemitism and certain falsifications of history.

The last time the Federal Council was requested to introduce penal sanctions against racist acts was in 1985, with the response that such measures would be presented before the end of 1987.... Reacting to increasing pressure from MPs from both the Left and Right to institute penal sanctions against the authors of racist acts and to ratify the anti-racism UN Convention, the Federal Council promised on 13 December 1989 that a full report on all groups advocating violence would soon be issued.[233]

An institute examining opinion surveys on Swiss attitudes towards foreigners in the 1980s recently concluded that xenophobia is on the increase: only 41 per cent of Swiss people have a positive attitude towards foreigners, compared with 61 per cent in 1980. Xenophobia is strongest among older and younger people and workers, and more widespread in the German-speaking cantons than the French- or Italian-speaking ones.[234]

The worsening problem is considered to be related to the ever increasing total of asylum-seekers. The number of asylum applications reached a peak of 24,425 in 1989,[235] an increase of 46 per cent over the 1988 figure of 16,726 (10,913 in 1987),[236] which was itself considered to be the highest number since the 1956 Hungarian uprising.

Norway

Violent attacks on foreigners increased four times in 1988 and 1989, with the most dramatic increase in the latter year. There have been several murders, and shops and houses belonging to foreigners have been attacked with bombs, torches and firearms.[237]

In May 1989, a bomb went off at the Red Cross refugee centre at Eidsvoll, and narrowly missed killing 49 asylum-seekers.[238] These violent incidents followed the announcement made on 14 October 1988 by Mr A. Myrdal, ex-leader of the Folkebevegelse mot Innvandring (Popular Action Against Immigration), of plans to arm some of its members in preparation for a 'civil war'.[239]

The number of non-Europeans in Norway is comparatively small. Pakistanis form the largest group (11,000), followed by the Vietnamese (6000), although account must also be taken of those holding Norwegian citizenship. However, in the 1987 local elections, the extreme-right Fremskritspartiet (Progress Party) became the third most important political formation having gained 12.2 per cent of the votes.[240]

This party tries to project a more respectable image than the Fremskridt in Denmark with whom there are some ties and, at least in appearance, is not as violently opposed to the presence of foreigners as the more extreme Stoppinnvandring (Stop Immigration) Party.

With only two seats in the Storting from the 1985 national elections, the Fremskritspartiet gained 22 seats in the 1989 national elections with 13 per cent of the votes. Opinion polls had predicted 20 per cent. As for Stoppinnvandring, it received about 8900 votes, about 0.3 per cent.

Sweden

Among the positive steps taken to combat racism and discrimination are the approval by the Swedish Parliament of a bill to appoint an independent ombudsman as of 1 July 1986 and the tightening up of the Racial Agitation Act of 1 January 1989. A racist statement is now punishable even if it has not been made publicly or distributed to the general public. It is sufficient for the statement to be distributed, for example, within a private association.[241]

As mentioned in the previous chapter, the borough of Sjöbo in Southern Sweden became the object of a great deal of attention when its local council voted on 29 October 1987 by 25 votes against 24 to hold a local referendum in September 1988 on the reception of refugees.[242] Despite the nationwide condemnations by all traditional political parties, both Left and Right, against holding the referendum, it was held as planned and the 15,000 or so inhabitants voted by 67.5 per cent to 32.5 per cent to end receiving any more refugees.[243] The incident was played down by an expert on Swedish attitudes towards immigrants and immigration, Mr C. Westin, who claimed that Sjöbo was an exception and that the Swedish positive attitude towards foreigners has remained unchanged.[244]

However, in the summer of 1989 there was a series of violent racist incidents between refugees and Swedish youths in small towns such as Eskilstuna, Lesjöfors, Överum and Jönköping, to name just a few. Examples are as follows: a refugee was nearly killed in Jämtland after a bomb placed under his car exploded; an Eritrean family in Aneby (Smaland) was attacked in the middle of the night when a gang of young Swedish youths, dressed in Ku-Klux-Klan outfits, burned a cross on their front lawn; and hundreds of Swedish and immigrant youths fought out gang wars in Eskilstuna and Lesjöfors (Värmland) in bloody battles that made back-page news in several Swedish newspapers. Police and immigration officials have tended to describe these incidents as 'youthful pranks'.[245]

As in several other countries, the cemetery for the victims of Nazi concentration camps (mostly Soviet, Yugoslav and Hungarian deportees) in Lund was also desecrated in May 1990. Tombstones were damaged and crosses were smashed.[246]

In addition, the British National Party is known to be actively collaborating with the extreme-right Swedish racist association, Bevara Sverige Svenskt (BSS – Keep Sweden Swedish).

Finland

This is the only country where its extreme-right party, the Suomen Maaseudun Puolue (SMP – Country Party of Finland), is declining. When it captured 9.7 per cent of the votes in the 1983 legislative elections with promises such as solving the unemployment problem in 15 days, the Social Democrats gave it the portfolio of Ministry of Employment. Since then, its popularity has fallen.[247]

Besides, there is an insignificant number of foreigners in the country, and refugees total only 1500. Another 500 will be accepted during 1990.

As a new member of the Council of Europe, it is bringing forward new legislation to grant foreigners more rights.

East and Central Europe (of the Warsaw Pact)

It is difficult to measure the extent of xenophobia in the countries of East and Central Europe which are now undergoing changes towards democracy. This is not only because of the small number of foreigners in such countries, but also because racism and antisemitism have always been considered as exclusive problems of capitalism.

As the economies of all these countries undergo necessary restructuring which is already resulting in a large number of job lay-offs and high unemployment, foreigners, both migrant workers and students, are coming under increasing insecurity.

There were recently bloody riots in different towns in Czechoslovakia during which Vietnamese students were attacked, resulting in dead and wounded on both sides. There were also severe muggings of Czech gypsies by extreme-right skinheads. The situation has been described as 'increasingly tense' and 20 Vietnamese students in Pilsen wrote to President Havel to plead for their security.[248] As a result, Czechoslovakia announced the progressive repatriation of the 37,000 or so Vietnamese migrant workers and a similar announcement appeared in a Bulgarian newspaper concerning the 24,000 Vietnamese working there.[249]

Antisemitism, which has largely been played down by the authorities of these countries, including the Soviet Union,[250] is manifesting itself in a very alarming way, despite the fact that, as a result of the Holocaust and emigration, there are now scarcely 20,000 Jews in Romania, only 70,000 in Hungary, 5000 in Czechoslovakia, under 4000 in Poland, 2500 in the GDR and about 2000 in Bulgaria.[251]

During the election campaign in Hungary in March 1989, Stars of David were painted on posters, and leaflets threatening death to the Jews were distributed. Antisemitism is still very strong in Hungary, whose capital city had a population of 203,000 Jews (23 per cent of the total population) at the beginning of this century. Antisemitic Austrians used to call this capital 'Judapest'.

German Democratic Republic

As it is only a question of time as to when the GDR will be unified with the FRG, the disturbing signs of xenophobia and racial hatred in the GDR, including antisemitism and the growing skinhead movement, give cause for much concern.[252]

Of the 200,000 foreigners in the GDR, only 50,000 have a permanent right of residence. The others – mostly Vietnamese (60,000), Mozambicans (16,000), Cubans (9000) and Poles (7000) – do specific work under inter-governmental agreements which will not be renewed when they expire, mostly in the next few years.[253] Moreover, expecting to implement staff cuts in future, some firms in East Berlin have already started unilaterally to end employment contracts with these migrant workers.

Violent attacks, mainly against black workers and students, have been taken seriously by the authorities and those arrested often receive severe sentences.[254] There is also strong xenophobia against Poles.[255]

According to a study by a research institute in Leipzig shortly before the changes in October 1989, 5 per cent of the inhabitants of this town had an extreme-right tendency, double the national average. Foreign workers, such as Vietnamese and Poles, and black African students have always been separated from the native population.[256] Another study, carried out by the Central Institute for Youth Research, concluded that one in every four students and apprentices hate foreigners.[257]

Despite the rather small number of Jews in the GDR (see above), of whom about 200 live in East Berlin, antisemitism is so strong that in a letter to Rabbi Hier, Dean of the Simon Wisenthal Study Centre on the Holocaust, Hans Modrow, interim Prime Minister before the March 1990 elections in the GDR, wrote that the 'fear of resurgence of nationalism, racism and antisemitism in the GDR is absolutely justified'.[258] Antisemitic graffiti are now quite common in East Berlin and the Jewish community there receives an average of three to five threatening letters per week. Jewish cemeteries have quite often been desecrated; the most recent tombstones to be covered with antisemitic insults were those of Bertolt Brecht and his wife, H. Weigel.[259] Since the removal of the Berlin Wall, two openly antisemitic political parties have appeared: the Deutsche Alternativen and the Freiheitliche Deutsche Arbeitspartei.

4

Community Action since 1986

Introduction

Of the 40 recommendations contained in the Evrigenis Report, only a few have been fully implemented so far and none has led to significant changes in anti-racism legislation, nor to action at the Community level to confront and tackle the root causes of racism and xenophobia.

On the other hand, a number of activities carried out by the Committee of Experts on Community Relations of the European Committee on Migration (CDMG) of the Council of Europe under its five-year programme on inter-community relations fall within the scope of some of these recommendations. Such activities involve representatives of each of its (now 23) Member States, as well as a few international organizations as observers, including the Commission of the European Communities.

It can, of course, be argued that, even when fully implemented, such activities do not entail any binding obligations on the part of the Council of Europe's Member States and the reports and attached recommendations merely serve to inform and remind them of what they should do to ensure and promote harmonious co-existence among the various ethnic communities and minorities in Europe. However, a number of the recommendations of the Evrigenis Report are designed to be preventive or 'pre-emptive' measures and should have been carried out at the initiative of the Community institutions or even in collaboration with the Council of Europe to enhance the importance which these institutions attach to combating racism and xenophobia.

As we shall see, the lack of concrete measures to tackle racism and xenophobia cannot be seen as simply a lack of initiative on the part of the Commission; the matter is far more complex, and it would be unfair to deny that the Commission has, in fact, been putting forward proposals and taking initiatives to combat these phenomena.

It must be pointed out that the European Parliament as such could also have taken constructive initiatives to promote, for example by symposiums, a wider recognition and understanding of the problems identified in the previous Committee of Inquiry.

Explaining the Commission's position, Mr M. Marin, the former Commissioner for Social Affairs and Employment, said: 'It is easy for the Commission to submit documents or initiatives to the Council of Ministers, but our work does not end there'.[1] As there is strong reluctance on the part of the Council of Ministers to approve measures by a qualified majority, initiatives are either subject to long delays in the Council of Ministers or they are watered down, if not completely abandoned, by the Commission on the grounds of political necessities, believing that unanimous approval will not be obtained.[2]

It should be emphasized that Community institutions were not expected to deal with a number of recommendations of the Evrigenis Report which are clearly addressed to the Member States. As we have seen in the preceding chapter, these recommendations have virtually fallen on deaf ears in most Member States with the resulting virulent upsurge of racism and xenophobia in several of them.

Recommendations Fully Implemented at the Community Level

We shall mention here two recommendations of the Evrigenis Report which have been fully implemented so far as the Community level. These are the 1986 Joint Declaration against Racism and Xenophobia[3] and the Eurobarometer survey on racism and xenophobia in the European Community.[4] A part of the recommendation on providing information on legal recourse has also been realized within the framework of a People's Europe.[5] The Commission has also undertaken initiatives in view of implementing other recommendations, some of which are still in progress, whereas others have been abandoned or modified to avoid rejection by the Council of Ministers.

The 1986 Joint Declaration against Racism and Xenophobia

The 'declaration against racism, racial discrimination and xenophobia and in favour of harmonious relations among all the communities existing in Europe' (para. 379) was signed jointly on 11 June 1986 by the Presidents of the Parliament, the Commission and the Council, and the representatives of the Member States meeting within the Council. This Joint Declaration was significant in that it was only the second time since the signing of the Treaty of Rome in 1957 that a solemn declaration was made which would enable organizations or individuals in any Member State to urge their government to abide by the spirit of the Joint Declaration and implement measures to combat racism and xenophobia.

However, its impact was not as significant as it might have been. Described at the time by the German MEP, Mr F.L. von Stauffenberg (EPP), currently chairman of the European Parliament Committee on Legal Affairs and Citizens' Rights, as a 'simple insipid document',[6] the reply given by Mrs Adam-Schwaetzer to a question concerning the Council's follow-up action to this Declaration disappointed many. In her capacity as President-in-Office of the Council, she said on 14 June 1988 that it was 'not a question of recommendations that have been put to the various Member States: it is a declaration'.[7]

This answer given by Mrs Adam-Schwaetzer was in contrast to an earlier, more positive reply by the Council to a written question submitted by members of all political groups in the European Parliament (except the European Right), requesting the Council to state what actions it envisaged to give effect to the recommendations of the Evrigenis Report. Stressing that 'racism and xenophobia as such are a matter of public policy in each individual Member State', the Council nevertheless considered that racism and xenophobia 'may [...] be an obstacle to the actual exercise of freedom of movement of persons, and in particular of workers within the Community'.[8]

However, as the Council considers that the Joint Declaration is a 'declaration of principle' and is only a 'basis on which we work', not wanting to take stock of 'any information on what the individual Member States, acting on their own responsibility, have done to enforce this declaration',[9] and there is so far no effective structure of migrants' associations operating at the Community level that has the means to take coordinated action in influencing Member States to implement the recommendations of the Evrigenis Report, the Joint Declaration has remained mere 'sheets of paper', with no means of checking whether or not these recommendations are put into practice.[10]

Eurobarometer Study on Racism and Xenophobia in the European Community

The Eurobarometer study on racism and xenophobia in the European Community, as recommended in paragraph 386 of the Evrigenis Report, was finally conducted in October and November 1988, and the results officially presented to the European Parliament on 21 November 1989.[11]

The survey confirms the seriousness of racism and/or xenophobia in Europe, reporting that one European in three believes that there are too many people of another nationality or race in his or her country and that 'a considerable minority of those questioned' considered the presence of immigrants in their country as a rather negative factor for the future. On the other hand, 'three out of four EC citizens are in favour of improving, or at least maintaining, the rights of immigrants and they count on the European institutions to do this' and 'one European in three would like to see the adoption of Community-wide legislation in relation to non-nationals residing in a Member State'. Besides, 'only one European in five is in favour of unilateral decisions taken by individual Member States with respect to foreigners from third states'.[12]

The survey concludes: 'It is now up to the European Institutions to take the appropriate measures in the field of integration and tolerance of people with different nationality, race, religion and culture, taking the direction indicated by the opinion of the majority of EC citizens'.[13]

Recommendations on Which Some Action Was or Has Been Taken at the Community Level

Definition of the Commission's Competence on Migration Polices in Relation to Non-Member Countries

As shown in the Runnymede Trust study (see below), migrants' 'inferior status' in society is maintained and reinforced by 'institutionalized racism' permitted by national legislation which clearly discriminates against them.

Along the lines of the recommendation referring to a Community policy on migration (para. 376), an important step was taken by the Commission when it adopted, prior to the Evrigenis Report, a decision on 8 July 1985 to set up 'a prior communication and consultation procedure on migration policies in relation to non-member countries'.[14] As explained by the Commission,[15] 'this was the best way to develop its prerogatives and its jurisdiction as far as immigration problems were concerned and to try, above all, to introduce some consistency into national immigration policies'.

Using as its legal basis Article 118 of the Treaty of Rome, this Decision obliged each Member State to give prior notice to both the Commission and the other Member States of draft national or international agreements to be implemented with regard to third-country migrants and members of their families in areas of entry, residence and employment (both legal and illegal), as well as in the realization of equality of treatment in living and working conditions, wages and economic rights, the promotion of integration into the workforce, society and cultural life, and the voluntary return of such persons to their countries of origin.

Acting on this, either the Commission or a Member State would be able to set up a consultation procedure between the Commission and the Member States for the mutual exchange of information in view of identifying common problems and then proceed to seek a joint response from the Member States through Community measures and guidelines for national legislation, particularly as regards international instruments relating to migration.

Five Member States, Denmark, France, the FRG, the Netherlands and the UK,[16] failing to get the Council to annul the Commission's Decision, filed complaints with the European Court of Justice, arguing that this was not within its competence, that the legal basis used, namely Article 118, did not empower the Commission to adopt a binding decision, and that migration policies vis-à-vis third countries were outside the scope of social affairs as defined by the said Article.

The complaints by Denmark, the Netherlands and the UK were declared inadmissible as they had passed the deadline. Allowing the complaints of the FRG and France, the European Court's ruling on 9 July 1987 annulled a part of the Commission's Decision on the grounds that the latter was not competent to include the cultural integration of third-country migrants and their families among the aims of the consultation procedure. In addition, this procedure may not have the aim of ensuring that measures adopted by Member States in the above-mentioned areas (of entry, residence and employment of third-country migrants, etc.) conform with Community policies and actions.[17]

As for the claim by France and the FRG that the Commission's Decision had violated an important rule of procedure in that it had not consulted the Economic and Social Committee (ESC), as required under Article 118, the Court ruled that the Commission had to do so only when it was proposing concrete measures.

The very positive aspect of the Court's ruling is that it rejected the argument that migration policies vis-à-vis non-member countries are outside the scope of Article 118 and it emphasizes that the employment situation, and more generally the improvement of living and working conditions in the Community, is affected by member States' policies towards third-country nationals.

Taking into account the Court's ruling, the Commission's decision was amended on 8 June 1988,[18] and it was stated that cooperation between Member States in the social field was also to be applied to migration policies in relation to non-member countries 'in that the power to arrange consultation granted to the Commission [. . .] authorizes it to adopt rules of a binding nature'.

Since the publication of this decision, some Member States have adopted certain controversial migration policies vis-à-vis third countries. The Commission has, on at least two occasions, requested more information from the Member States concerned, but no consultation procedure has yet taken place.

Requested by the European Council of Hanover in June 1988, the Commission's report on the 'Social Integration of Third-Country Migrants residing on a Permanent and Lawful Basis in the Member States'[19] was presented to the European Council of Strasbourg on 4–5 December 1989. A proposal, elaborated at the beginning of the study, aimed at granting non-EC immigrants the same rights as EC nationals after a period of residence of five years for refugees, and 10 years for others, was not included in the final report.

Information Handbook

In response to criticisms of the absence of an adequate information policy on migrants' rights, and having regard to the recommendation on information of the Evrigenis Report (para. 385), the Commission issued ringbound information sheets providing systematic information on the right of migrant workers with respect to freedom of movement.[20]

Although this Handbook constitutes a most valuable collection of information on migrants' rights, equal treatment for men and women, social security for migrant workers, etc., it falls quite short of what was intended in the recommendation concerned. There is no list of names, addresses and telephone numbers of counselling and legal advice services for migrants, immigrants, refugees and persons seeking a reception centre. Moreover, it deals essentially with the rights of Community nationals and no mention is made of third-country nationals.

The Evrigenis Report recommended that copies of such a directory be made available at all points of entry into the Community. Its implementation is all the more necessary in view of more stringent controls at the external Community frontiers to compensate for the lifting of frontiers internally.

A Comparative Law Study

Soon after the adoption of the Evrigenis Report, the Commission requested a UK foundation, the Runnymede Trust, to carry out a comparative law study on the 10 member States (Portugal and Spain were not yet members).

The report, entitled 'New Approaches: A Summary of Alternative Approaches to the Problem of Protection against Racism and Xenophobia in Member States of the European Communities',[21] pointed in particular to 'institutionalized discrimination brought about by existing discriminatory national legislation and procedures, legally depriving non-national residents of equal rights with nationals. This in turn enhanced racism and discriminatory behaviour even towards naturalized ethnic minorities.'

The report notes that 'racism and xenophobia in Member States can be overcome only if a clear lead in practical action is taken by the Community institutions and by the state authorities'. It recommends not only new legislation, but also 'a detailed and determined work-out of enforcement and administrative procedures appropriate to each state's administrative system', the 'alternative approaches' it recommends 'will involve rejecting some aspects of contemporary nationalism and redefining the character of the community within a state's jurisdiction'.[22]

As almost all of these recommendations appeared to be within the exclusive competence of the Member States and the Commission was unwilling to enter into conflict with them, the report received no follow-up. Instead, the Commission's attention has been focused on more modest initiatives.

Migrant Women and Employment

The Commission organized a seminar on 'migrant women and employment' on 17–18 September 1987 during which the numerous and various forms of discrimination experienced by migrant women were revealed.[23] Included in the recommendations was the request that the Commission should encourage positive actions in all Member States to combat discrimination.

Within the Commission, the problems raised were seen by some as those which should be tackled with the programme of equal opportunities and by others as matters related to racism and xenophobia. The second line of reasoning was swept under the carpet, while in relation to the first, the Commission adopted in 1988 a Communication to the Council on the social situation and employment of migrant women aimed at promoting their social and professional integration.[24] In addition, the final report of the seminar[25] resulted in the realization of a few minor studies with some small grants from the Commission.

Youth against Racism

The Commission funded and took part in the conference on 'Youth against Racism', organized by the Youth Forum of the European Community on 18–20 April 1986.

Denouncing the empty verbal promises of measures against racism, the Youth Forum said that 'it is time for action' and issued a *Newsletter* in August 1986 'to serve as a permanent link between young people who are concerned by the problems of racism and xenophobia'. This publication never went beyond issue no. 1.

In that same year, on 9–10 January 1986, a colloquy with the same theme, 'Youth against racism', was organized by the Federation of the Green–Alternative European Link (GRAEL) of the European Parliament. In its note of address, the Youth Forum gave notice of other projects, namely a series of information brochures and dossiers aimed at promoting a new line of thinking based on the principle of respect for the particularity of each member of society. This material would be intended for schools and youth organizations.[26] However, none of it ever saw the light of day.

Funds Set Aside for Conducting Information Campaigns

As of 1987, the budget line for activities of non-governmental organizations pursuing humanitarian aims and promoting human rights (Article 303) included an amount set aside for conducting information campaigns on the dangers of racism and fascism in accordance with the 1986 Joint Declaration. This budget line has to cover a wide range of projects in the human rights field, including support for rehabilitation centres for torture victims and joint research programmes. For this reason, only a small part (ECU 50,000) is allocated for such information campaigns.

Recommendations Whose Implementation is Still in Progress

The 'Intercommunity Forum' or 'Migrants' Forum'

The one recommendation on which associations of ethnic minorities and of those working in favour of ethnic minorities have been placing great hopes is the 'Intercommunity Forum', the idea and the desired composition of which have changed since 1986. This recommendation (para. 39) proposed that 'Institutions and associations opposed to racism, and immigrants' organizations, trade unions, professional organizations and other bodies concerned' be called upon to set up an Intercommunity Forum 'under the aegis of the European Communities on the model of the Youth Forum. This body's main tasks should be to provide an exchange of information and improve the coordination and allocation of duties in action and research. The Forum would be financed by the Communities' budget'.

The proposal was not new. In the Commission's communication to the Council on 'Guidelines for a Community Policy on Migration' on 1 March 1985, among the initiatives which the Commission proposed was to 'promote the regrouping, at Community level, of migrant associations, in order to facilitate the dialogue between migrant circles and the Community institutions'.[27] This was reaffirmed by the Council in its resolution of 16 July 1985 when it recognized 'the desirability of a dialogue at the Community level with associations of migrant workers'.[28]

At a debate on immigration policy in the European Parliament's plenary session on 8 October 1986, the then Commissioner for Social Affairs and Employment, Mr M. Marin, underlined the problems of bringing together migrant workers' associations on a joint project, which he called a 'federal forum'. Nevertheless, he told Parliament that the Commission 'will succeed in setting up a federal model [. . .] for this type of association which should be able to begin its work in the coming year'.[29]

Earlier in 1986, the Commission requested a European agency[30] to carry out a study drawing up a listing of all associations of migrants/ethnic minorities in the 12 Member States. The addresses of about 1800 were obtained by this agency and a questionnaire was sent to them, asking, *inter alia,* about their interest in getting involved in a Community forum. Of the 210 replies received, 141 considered the coordination of their actions at the Community level as desirable. The Commission was not satisfied with the results.

The agency continued its research, improving its data on migrants' associations. As for the Commission, nothing more was said or done. Exactly one year later during a debate on discrimination against immigrant women,[31] Mr Marin made absolutely no mention of it. Although the matter was not forgotten, no further initiatives were taken. The dossier was considered to be too complicated and complex as it involved a very large number of immigrant associations of various nationalities, political tendencies and aims.

At a European Parliament plenary debate on racism, the

successor to Mr Marin, Ms Papandreou, referred to the forum, saying that, amongst other things, the 'sheer number of organizations of this type which exist and the varying degrees of representativeness which they could have' could bring about 'real difficulties'.[32]

The delays bred frustrations among immigrants' associations and within the European Parliament. Informed of the strong desire of some associations of migrants or those working in favour of migrants to have a forum set up as soon as possible, but lacking the means to do so, namely the 'Migreurope initiative', the European Parliament decided to give some momentum to the issue and, to mark the second anniversary of the Joint Declaration, voted for the allocation of a sum of ECU 500,000 to be set aside in the 1989 Community budget for the setting up of a 'European Forum for Migrants'.[33]

In a resolution adopted by the European Parliament in February 1989, the latter 'welcomes the establishment of the Migreurope organization which will provide a direct interface for immigrants with the Community institutions'.[34] Although it could not claim to represent all migrant associations in the 12 Member States at its constituent assembly, it was established as a structure; however, it has progressed no further because of lack of funding. At the meeting of the Committee of Inquiry on 20–21 December 1989, the Commission stated that all of the allocated sum had been spent, but there was still no 'Migrants Forum'.

One month earlier, the Spanish MEP, Ms T. Domingo Segarra, had asked when the forum of migrant workers' associations would be set up, since funds had been set aside for this purpose in the 1989 Community budget.[35] She was informed that the Commission had requested a study on existing associations of migrants in order to make a selection based on their quantitative and qualitative representativeness and the results would be made known before the end of 1989. Based on these results, the Commission would organize a large consultative meeting with these selected organizations in order to determine the beneficial and practical conditions for setting up the forum. This study was financed by the funds set aside for the forum in the 1989 budget.[36]

Although the Commission was aware of the fact that the

agency which carried out the first study had updated and improved its information on migrants' associations, it preferred to contact another agency to carry out the study, the results of which again failed to meet the Commission's approval. The 'large consultative meeting', scheduled for the beginning of 1990 did not therefore take place.

The Commission has requested yet another study and the results are believed to be more acceptable this time. The idea of the Commission now is to have a much smaller meeting, bringing together a maximum number of five delegates per Member State from representative associations of third-country migrants whose task will be to agree on the setting up of the forum which will receive an initial budget of ECU 300,000 for its operation and activities.

The kind of forum envisaged by the Commission is much more limited than that recommended in the Evrigenis Report. Not only would it exclude institutions and associations opposed to racism, trade unions, professional organizations and 'other bodies concerned', but also its composition would mainly consist of migrants from third countries, although Community migrants would not be excluded. In the light of the major institutional ruling of the European Court of Justice handed down on 22 May 1990,[37] Parliament may choose to submit this matter to the European Court for annulment of the Commission's act.

The Commission's Proposal to Combat Racism and Xenophobia

On 22 June 1988, the Commission approved a draft Council resolution on combating racism and xenophobia which was submitted to the latter on 29 June 1988.[38]

Preceding the text of the draft Council resolution is a communication from the Commission to the Council on the fight against racism and xenophobia, containing a series of proposals in three areas: legal or institutional, information, and education and professional training.

In the first area, the Commission proposes the encouragement and amelioration of existing national legislation on equal rights for all and fundamental rights as well as facilitating the possibility of groups/anti-racist associations to act as plaintiffs in cases of discrimination. In addition, it proposes a more restrictive definition of the concept of 'legitimate grounds', which often serves as a pretext to refuse to provide goods, services and employment, and proposes the setting up of mediation structures to deal with problems of employment and housing.

Measures in the field of information, education and training include initiatives on research, opinion surveys, inter-community and inter-cultural relations, sensitization of national citizens, special training for teachers and those in state bodies who work with or are in regular contact with migrants, and the development of teaching of mother tongues and cultures.

None of these proposals is new; all are contained in the Evrigenis Report. Moreover, they constitute 'merely a programme – almost just a prospectus outlining what the Council could do on this question [of combating racism and xenophobia]'.[39] The reason for this, as explained by Mrs V. Papandreou before the Parliamentary plenary on 13 February 1989,[40] was 'serious and well-founded doubts [. . .] regarding the Commission's competence to institute binding action in this field'.

This is a clear reference to the European Court's ruling of 9 July 1987 which, as earlier stated, *confirmed* the Commission's competence to adopt rules of a binding nature by virtue of the second paragraph of Article 118, with the exception of measures to promote cultural integration (see above).

The proposed Council resolution was forwarded on 12 October 1988, to the Committee on Legal Affairs and Citizens' Rights as the committee responsible, and to the Committee on Youth, Culture, Education, Information and Sport, as well as to the Committee on Social Affairs and Employment for their opinion.

On 21 September 1988, the Committee on Legal Affairs and Citizens' Rights appointed the Spanish Socialist MEP, Mr M. Medina Ortega, as the rapporteur and his report was unanimously adopted at the committee's meeting on 21–22 November 1988.

Although the Council's consultation of Parliament on this draft resolution created a precedent and was a positive step, the rapporteur described the move as 'more surprising as to the form than to the substance'.[41] Referring to the substance of the draft Council resolution, he said that it 'does not introduce any significant new element compared with the recommendations in the report of the Parliament's Committee of Inquiry and limits itself to repeating most of these. Since Parliament has not changed its opinion on this subject since it adopted the report in question, it seems rather pointless to ask it again for an opinion which it has already stated.'

When this report was presented to the plenary in February 1989, the overwhelming majority of the 265 MEPs present voted in favour of the draft resolution contained in the reply. Only some members of the European Democratic Alliance (RDE) and all but one member of the European Right (DR) voted against.

It must be noted that, in the opinion of the Committee on Legal Affairs and Citizens' Rights, a legislative text was missing from the draft Council resolution. The only legal base mentioned is the Single European Act, while Mr Medina Ortega advised specifying other legal provisions, namely Article 220 of the Treaty of Rome on cooperation between Member States on the protection of rights of persons and Article 235 of the same which provides for the extension of the Community jurisdiction and includes an obligation to consult the European Parliament.

The draft Council resolution was also forwarded to the Section for Social, Family, Education and Cultural Affairs, which appointed Lady Flather as the rapporteur to draft an opinion. The opinion, adopted by the section and by the Economic and Social Committee,[42] expresses 'deep disappointment that only a proposal for a Council resolution is presented rather than an effective policy displaying a real political commitment to combat racism' and 'insists that all EC nationals, including those who are from ethnic minorities, are assured a share of and a future in a "People's Europe"'. Moreover, it calls for effective monitoring of racial discrimination, harassment and disadvantage throughout the Community, to be followed up by effective counter-measures supervised by a 'Commissioner against Racism'.

Almost four years after the Commission submitted this proposal for a resolution, the Social Affairs Council finally adopted it at its meeting on 29 May 1990. Despite the fact that this resolution does not have a binding character, and therefore falls quite short of what Parliament would have preferred, the final text that was adopted has been so watered down that it no longer resembles the one which the Commission submitted on 29 June 1988. The Council had earlier insisted that the resolution be adopted by both the Commission and itself. The Commission refused to associate itself with it and withdrew.

In order to overcome the opposition of the UK delegation, the 11 other Member States agreed to delete from the text reference to non-EC nationals.[43] Even the phrase calling for the 'urgent introduction of a preventative education and information policy to promote intercultural understanding and a clear and objective appreciation of the situation of migrant workers' was suppressed.

Deleting the reference to third-country nationals was, in fact, the last straw as the Commission had earlier given in to several other compromises which had greatly weakened the text. The mentioning of racism and xenophobia as constituting an obstacle to the free movement of persons within the Community was deleted, as was the Commission's undertaking 'to promote the organization of migrants' associations at Community level so as to facilitate the dialogue between the migrant community and the Community institutions'.

Member States are no longer to be 'invited' to collaborate with the Commission to 'produce a report every three years assessing the position as regards the integration of migrant communities', and the 'Commission's intention to submit a report on the application of this resolution within a period of three years from the date of its adoption, having assembled the necessary information from the Member States'[44] also had to be abandoned.

Moreover, a declaration is annexed to the resolution which specifies that the implementation of the latter may not lead to an enlargement of the competencies of the European institutions as defined by the Treaties.

The Council described the final text adopted as an important step forward aimed at eliminating racism and xenophobia among citizens of the various Member States. The European Parliament's view is, that in apparently refusing to include non-EC residents within its scope, the resolution adopted signifies a step backward since it clearly goes against not only the spirit but also the contents of the June 1986 Joint Declaration against Racism and Xenophobia.

Measures Implemented by the Council/Member States

The European Dimension in Education

On 24 May 1988, the Council and the Ministers of Education of the 12 Member States meeting within the Council adopted a resolution on the European dimension in education.[45] Between 1988 and 1992, the 12 Member States would launch a series of concerted measures to, *inter alia,* 'strengthen in young people a sense of European identity and make clear to them the value of European civilization and of the foundations on which the European peoples intend to base their development today, that is, in particular the safeguarding of the principles of democracy, social justice and respect for human rights'. The resolution undertakes 'to encourage contacts and meetings across borders between pupils and teachers from different Member States at all levels in order to give them direct experience of European integration and the realities of life in other European countries'.

A 'European civic education textbook, as recommended in paragraph 392 of the Evrigenis Report, has not been prepared. Similarly, nothing has come out of the recommendation in paragraph 395 concerning the 'preparation of a European textbook of contemporary history on the basis of work already done by the Council of Europe and by UNESCO'. This is particularly desirable owing to the pressing need to insert into the school curriculum lessons on the crimes committed by the European fascist and totalitarian regimes, particularly their acts of genocide. Otherwise, the horrors of the Second World War will soon be forgotten with the disappearance of the generations who witnessed and experienced these crimes.

Moreover, in the promotion of such cultural exchanges for pupils and teachers, as well as for youths, as in the 'Youth for Europe' (YES) action programme (see below), certain Member States make no exceptions to the rules on entry visa requirements and this results in exclusion and discrimination against pupils and youths of third-country nationality.[46]

Youth Exchange Programmes

On 16 June 1988, the Council issued a decision outlining an action programme on 'Youth for Europe' (YES)[47] in order to promote international youth exchanges in the Community, as recommended in paragraph 396 of the Evrigenis Report, from 1 July 1988 to 31 December 1991.

Although the programme is designed 'in particular, to encourage the participation of young people who experience the most difficulties in being included in existing programmes of exchanges between the Member States', and aims at extending participation, 'in particular, to young people from all kinds of social, economic and cultural backgrounds', youths who are Community residents, but not Community nationals, are often excluded. Besides, as most of such youths require entry visas to travel from the Member State in which they are residing to another one, 'the various financial, legal and administrative obstacles which may inhibit participation in, or the organization of, youth exchanges', as mentioned in the Council decision, will remain for them.

1977 Directive on the Education of the Children of Migrant Workers

On 2 August 1977, the President of the Council addressed the directive on the education of the children of migrant workers to the Member States.[48] According to Article 4 of this directive, Member States were given until 2 August 1981 to comply with it. The directive itself covered only children from Community countries, but a declaration was added to the minutes of the Council meeting when it was adopted stating that the provisions made under the directive should also cover children from third countries.

According to the report presented on 3 January 1989 on the implementation of this directive by the Member States[49] the results are on the whole quite unsatisfactory as only the Federal Republic of Germany and especially the Netherlands have made adequate provisions for the teaching of the languages and cultures of origin of the children of migrant workers. In other Member States, this directive was either ignored or given very little attention, though it is certainly the case, for example, that in the United Kingdom many local authorities are implementing policies encouraging teaching in the mother tongue.

The Commission's report cites 'the situation of Ireland, which has passed no legislative or administrative measures at all, and

Greece where, despite a presidential decree providing for reception classes and tuition in the Greek language for immigrants, no implementing measure has been reported to the Commission'.[50] In addition, 'it appears that certain Member States have taken no formal measures to provide for the initial and further training of teachers who are to be responsible for reception education. These states are Ireland, Italy and Greece'.[51]

Measures Implemented by the European Parliament

A number of the measures taken by the European Parliament have already been mentioned. On various occasions, its members, representing all political groups (except the European Right), have expressed their concern over the absence of initiatives by the Community to curb the upsurge of racism and xenophobia in the Member States with questions to the Commission, the Council and the European political cooperation group of Foreign Ministers. In most cases, the replies were unsatisfactory and/or evasive.

Written Declaration on the Fight against Xenophobia and Racism

On 15 June 1988, about 270 MEPs representing the various political groups (except the European Right) submitted a written declaration to remind the Community institutions and the Member States of the 1986 Joint Declaration against Racism and Xenophobia.[52] The declaration called on its President to organize a public symposium on racism in Europe and to write to the governments of all Member States, asking them to give details of steps taken to implement the 1986 Joint Declaration, and on the Commission to earmark an appropriate amount in the 1989 budget to enable the setting up of a 'European Migrants' Forum'. Moreover, it gave notice of a future debate on the fight against racism in plenary session.

Plenary Debate on the Fight against Racism

This debate, in line with a recommendation of the Evrigenis Report (para. 404) that after two years there be a 'review of developments in the matters considered by the inquiry', and of the extent to which the recommendations had been carried out, was scheduled to be held at the end of 1988. It finally took place in February 1989 on the occasion of the joint debate on Mr M. Medina Ortega's report (see above) and on the report of Mr B. van der Lek (ARC – NL), on behalf of the Political Affairs Committee, on the Joint Declaration against Racism and Xenophobia and an action programme by the Council of Ministers.[53]

The resolution contained in the report by Mr van der Lek was approved, but not overwhelmingly (150 in favour, 90 against and 8 abstentions) because a majority felt that voting rights for both EC and non-EC migrants could not be excluded from measures to combat racism and xenophobia, and passed such an amendment accordingly.

In fact, no mention is made of granting non-nationals the right to vote among the recommendations of the Evrigenis Report. Nevertheless, on 22 June 1988, the Commission adopted a draft directive granting EC nationals residing in a Member State other than their own the right to vote and to be elected in local elections.[54] The green light was, in fact, given 14 years earlier in December 1974 at the Paris Summit of heads of Member States or Governments. However, under the permanent pretext that 'this is really not the right moment' to put it on the agenda, the draft directive has been shelved at the Council since 1988.

The resolution contained in Mr van der Lek's report reintroduced the main recommendations contained in the Evrigenis Report and called for both preventive measures – through education, information and promotion of inter-cultural understanding – and repressive ones through legislation. Once again Parliament called for a 'Forum for all ethnic communities', as defined in paragraph 399 of the Evrigenis Report.

Public Symposium on Racism in Europe

Responding to the June 1988 Written Declaration, Lord Plumb, the then President of the European Parliament, invited all Heads of State and of Governments of the 12 member countries, as well as the presidents of all political groups of the European Parliament, to a symposium on 'Europe against Racism', held in Strasbourg on 13 March 1989.[55]

Although the governments of Belgium, Greece and the

Netherlands were not represented, the statements made by representatives of the other governments and of Parliament's political groups showed consensus on the need for action to be taken in the face of the upsurge of racism and discrimination, including their new forms of expression.

Mr O. Due, in his capacity as President of the European Court of Justice, confirmed that Community legislation also protected third-country nationals and their families.

Mr Solbes, representing the Spanish presidency of the Council, affirmed the latter's total support of the Commission's proposals to intensify efforts in education, information and sensitization against the negative and intolerant attitudes of racism and xenophobia. Moreover, he guaranteed the total support of the Spanish presidency in combating racism and xenophobia using all means and with all its force.

By September 1989, Parliament was still not satisfied with the action taken by the Commission, the Council and the Member States to implement the 1986 Joint Declaration, and there were signs that racism, xenophobia and antisemitism were not only growing in some Member States, but also appearing and reaching dangerous levels in others. This led to the setting up of a new European Parliament Committee of Inquiry into Racism and Xenophobia whose composition was approved on 27 October 1989.

Recommendations Not Given Sufficient Attention by Community Institutions

Despite the European Court's ruling on 9 July 1987 (see p. 92) and the positive statement made by Mr O. Due at the public symposium just mentioned, there is still much controversy over the definition of the Community's powers and on the extent to which the institutions may implement policies against racism and xenophobia. Mr J. Delors, President of the European Commission, has, however, confirmed that initiatives and projects against racism are 'in line with the traditions and principles of human rights' and the granting of a subsidy to an anti-racism association like SOS Racisme is 'also in line with the undertakings by the Community institutions' in the 1986 Joint Declaration against Racism and Xenophobia.[56] Bearing this in mind, we mention here the recommendations of the Evrigenis Report which could have been given some or more attention by the Community institutions.

Creation of a European Legal Area to Combat International Terrorism and Extremism

As this volume has already shown, extreme right-wing groups advocating physical violence and murder of ethnic minorities are not only expanding, but are linking up with and establishing branches elsewhere. Since 1986, for example, 'skinhead groups' with their publications and their own 'music', which is repetitive with lyrics that incite violence and murder, have established themselves firmly in countries or regions which were previously free from such dangers – Portugal, Denmark, Sweden, Switzerland, Scotland, and they now constitute a major menace in France.

The TREVI Group composed of the Ministers of Justice and/or the Interior of the 12 Member States[57] is supposedly dealing with measures to combat international terrorism and extremism. As their activities and meetings are closely guarded secrets, excluding even the participation of the European Commission, it is not known whether the Group is also dealing with international terrorism and extremism against ethnic minorities.

Cooperation between the Council of Europe and the European Community

A number of activities related to the recommendations of the Evrigenis Report have been dealt with by the CMDG of the Council of Europe. The Commission of the EC has the status of observer with this committee of experts.

The Community Relations Project of the Council of Europe was launched by the Committee of Ministers in 1986 for the period 1987 to 1991 at the proposal of the Committee of Experts on Community Relations. This latter committee was set up in 1985 as a follow-up to a seminar held in 1984 on 'Making Multi-Ethnic Society Work'. It has already organized meetings on: the cultural and religious practices of migrants and ethnic groups; the role of national legislation and international instruments in combating discrimination on nationality, ethnic or racial grounds; the response of the health and social services to the needs of an ethnically and culturally diverse population; the impact of housing and town planning policies on community relations, migrants, ethnic groups and the police, etc.[58] It has also had exchange of views with experts from the USA, Canada and Australia on community relation problems.

It organized conferences on the 'Media and Cultural Diversity' in 1988 (see below), on 'Human Rights without Frontiers' in 1989 and a Standing Conference on European local and regional authorities and community relations is planned.

This committee will soon issue reports on the contribution of migrants/ethnic groups to the economic viability of urban areas through the setting up of small and medium-sized businesses, on legislation against discrimination and on racial violence and harassment.

European Year to Promote Inter-Community Harmony

The European Community has not implemented this recommendation of the Evrigenis Report (para. 379). On the other hand, certain countries already hold special events for ethnic minorities. In the Federal Republic of Germany, Luxembourg and the Netherlands, there is an annual event of several days organized specially for ethnic minorities.

In the FRG, the Woche der ausländischen Mitbürgen (Week of the Foreign Fellow-Citizen)[59] first started in 1975 as an initiative of the churches lasting only one day. In the beginning of the 1980s, it gradually expanded to a one-week event with the participation of the trade unions and government ministries. Each day is dedicated to a particular question or theme related to immigration. For example, on the first day, Monday, racism is the main topic, and since 1986, Friday has been the day for refugees.

In Luxembourg, the Festival d'Immigration is organized by migrants' associations with state funding. It is a trade union initiative in the Netherlands, and in France, concerts and other campaigns are organized at irregular intervals by the two main movements: SOS Racisme and France Plus. In Spain, for the first time, an 'Immigrants' Day' was held in November 1989, organized by church and human rights groups.

On 25–27 November 1987 the Council of Europe organized

three 'European Days' to promote inter-community harmony. The event was entitled 'Enjoying our Diversity'.

Guide for Ethnic Minorities on Community Funding

Such a guide, as mentioned in paragraph 382 of the Evrigenis Report, does not exist and, at present, the Commission has not made known any intention of issuing such a publication.

A Comparative Law Study

This was taken up by the Commission in 1986, but stopped short when the study's recommendations were considered to be beyond the Commission's competence. A more extensive study on discrimination on nationality, ethnic or racial grounds in the field of employment was carried out by the Council of Europe in 1987 and 1988.

Case Studies of Certain Community Urban Centres Experiencing High Levels of Racism

Either the European Parliament or the Commission could have taken initiatives in this direction (see para. 387 of the Evrigenis Report) by way of seminar or a study visit involving all political groups. The example has once again been set by the Council of Europe's Committee of Experts which already carried out such study visits in Birmingham (1986), Berlin (1988), Lyons (1988) and Barcelona (1989).

The Mass Media's Role in Eliminating Racial Prejudice and Promoting Harmonious Relations among Communities Resident in Europe

The role of the mass media, the question of professional ethics in the information industry and the representativeness of ethnic minorities within this industry are mentioned in paragraphs 388 and 389 of the Evrigenis Report (see also Chapter 6 below). They were dealt with in a Council of Europe colloquy on 'Migrants, Media and Cultural Diversity', held on 29 November–1 December 1988.[60]

A large number of journalists representing ethnic minorities and specializing in information on ethnic minorities were present during the two and a half day event, as well as other people working with the media and with migrants and government officials from many Member States of the Council of Europe. Despite its importance and its unprecedented character, none of the European Community institutions was represented.

Dialogue with Social Forces

Since 1986, neither the Commission nor the Parliament has paid sufficient attention to the need for European dialogue with social forces, as outlined in paragraphs 400, 401 and 402 of the recommendations. This is particularly important as evidence indicates that, as mentioned in the Evrigenis Report, there is considerable distrust, dislike and antipathy between the police and ethnic minorities.

The importance of Islam in Europe and the exaggerated reactions of intolerance and misunderstanding that we have witnessed in some Member States, particularly in the Rushdie affair and the Islamic headscarf affair, point to the urgent need for a better and fuller understanding by European governments, public authorities and the native population in general of this religion and culture. Open dialogues, via discussions and debates, with the police and the Islamic community in particular, are important measures in the fight against racism and xenophobia.

Once again, the European institutions have been shown the way by the Council of Europe, which has already looked into the relationship between migrants, ethnic groups and the police[61] and the cultural and religious practices of migrants and ethnic groups.[62]

5

General Trends in Policies and Intergovernmental Structures

The Foreign Population in the Community

There are about 13 million migrants residing in the 12 Member States of the European Community out of a total population of around 320 million. Of those migrants about eight million (2.5 per cent of the EC population) are nationals of non-Member States (so-called third-country nationals). Among them are almost two million who come from developed and industrialized countries. There are about five million migrants from Member States (1.5 per cent) living in the Community, (see Table 5.1).

Table 5.1
Total and foreign population in Member States

1987	Total (thousands)	(in thousands and % of total population) EC-migrants	Non-EC migrants
Belgium	9864.8	538.1 (5.4%)	315.2 (3.2%)
Denmark	5102.0	27.0 (0.5%)	102.0 (2.0%)
FRG	61170.5	1377.4 (2.3%)	3195.5 (5.2%)
Greece	9739.5	55.3 (0.6%)	31.3 (0.3%)
France (1982)	54273.2	1577.9 (2.9%)	2102.6 (3.9%)
Ireland	3543.0	61.7 (1.7%)	17.8 (0.5%)
Italy (1981)	56556.9	91.1 (0.2%)	112.1 (0.2%)
Luxembourg (1989)	384.2	101.6 (26.4%)	10.3 (2.7%)
Netherlands (1988)	14714.2	159.9 (1.1%)	434.9 (2.9%)
Portugal	10270.0	23.9 (0.2%)	65.6 (0.6%)
Spain	38832.3	193.3 (0.5%)	141.6 (0.4%)
United Kingdom	56075.0	810.0 (1.4%)	1651.0 (2.9%)
TOTAL	320525.7	5014.2 (1.6%)	8179.9 (2.6%)

Source: European Commission

The large majority of third-country nationals (86.9 per cent) resides in the Federal Republic of Germany (more than three million), France (more than two million) and the United Kingdom (almost two million). Of the traditional receiving countries only Belgium and Luxembourg have fewer third-country migrants than migrants from other Member States. In the traditional sending countries, Greece, Italy, Portugal and Spain, there is also a significant number of migrants from third countries.[1]

Not included in the category of migrants are those who have the nationality of host countries (for example, those coming from some former colonies of France, the Netherlands and the United Kingdom), or have acquired the nationality of a host country, the number of whom has increased substantially over the years. These people may have no problems with respect to their legal status. They do, however, suffer just as much from xenophobia and racism as other migrants. On the other hand, migrants from other industrialized countries (such as the United States, Canada and Australia) are most certainly given more friendly treatment.

Since 1985 the foreign ethnic minority population has risen despite the restrictive policies of the 12 Member States. This is largely due to natural population increase and family reunification.

The relatively higher natural growth rate for foreign ethnic minority population than for nationals contributes to the growth of the foreign population. However, foreign women's fertility is gradually coming into line with that of native women, including those foreigners whose fertility rate was much higher than that of natives on their arrival in the country.[2]

Family reunification is and will be an important channel for migratory movements. An aspect of it is that young people of foreign origin sometimes choose their spouse in the country of origin of their parents. The over-representation of males amongst the migrants in the southern Member States will probably lead to more family reunification in the coming years.

Since 1983 about 800,000 persons have applied for asylum in Europe of which 33 per cent come from the Middle East, 15 per cent from the Indian subcontinent and 10 per cent from Africa. The Federal Republic of Germany and France rank high in the countries of reception, besides Sweden and Switzerland.[3]

A set of interlinked factors will force people to move. There is the persisting imbalance between developed and underdeveloped countries. Because of crop-failures, abuse of natural resources and ecological changes, an estimated 600 million people will suffer from malnutrition and to survive many of them will have to find a better place to live. Demographic factors play a role as well. At least 60 million young people enter the labour markets of the least developed countries in the world each year.

Furthermore, the ongoing armed conflicts in the world and the many oppressive regimes also force people to leave their country to find a living elsewhere.

Notwithstanding the fact that the number of refugees and asylum-seekers who come to Western Europe is on the increase (see Table 5.2), the large majority of them stay in a neighbouring country.[4]

Table 5.2
Asylum applicants and total number of refugees

	1987	1988	Total refugee population (as per 31.12.88)
Belgium	5955	4784	24000
Denmark	2700	4668	27876
FRG	57400*	103076	800000
Greece	6950*	7992	8400
France	27352	34352	184453
Ireland	na	45	300
Italy	11050*	na	10960
Luxembourg	na	na	na
Netherlands	13460	7486	25500
Portugal	450*	287	767
Spain	2500*	4504	8691
United Kingdom	4500*	3300	100000

na: not available
***According to OECD.**

***Sources*: UNCHR activities financed by voluntary funds: Report for 1988–89 and proposed programmes and budget for 1990. Part III: Europe and North America. (A/AC.96/724 (Part III)); OECD, Continuous reporting on migration, SOPEMI report 1988. (Paris, 1989).**

Recent Developments in Central and Eastern Europe

Despite the improvements in the sphere of human rights, changes in the political system in Central and Eastern Europe, including the abolition of travel restrictions, combined with the economic crisis in these parts, led to new movements of people mainly towards West Europe. The countries most affected are the Federal Republic of Germany, Austria, and Italy; Hungary and the GDR are also receiving a significant number of people from other Eastern European countries.

In the last few years the number of people from East Germany and to a lesser extent from other Central and East European countries coming to the Federal Republic of Germany has increased enormously. There was an estimated number of 230,000 in 1988 and 370,000 in 1989 of so-called 'transferees' ('Übersiedler', Germans from the GDR) and 'resettlers' ('Aussiedler', ethnic Germans living in East European countries). They cannot be considered as refugees falling under the 1951 Geneva Convention.

Citizens of the German Democratic Republic can easily obtain the citizenship of the German Federal Republic, by virtue of which they are entitled to move freely within the Community. Mainly for that reason the signing of the Schengen Supplementary Agreement, due in December 1989, was postponed until the unification of the two German republics was further clarified. (It was renegotiated and signed on 19 June 1990.)

In the GDR there are between 180,000 and 200,000 foreign residents out of a population of 16 million. Between 40,000 and 50,000 of them have permanent rights of residence. The others have come to work for four or five years and it has been decided that their contracts will not be renewed when they expire, as most will in the next few years.[5]

In Austria there has been a strong influx of Romanian refugees of Hungarian origin. GDR nationals went to Austria as well, but moved on to the Federal Republic. There is also an increase of asylum-seekers from Bulgaria and of Soviet citizens of Jewish origin who only pass through Austria.

In Hungary the majority of the refugees comes from Romania. Since many of them are ethnic Hungarians, it is uncertain whether they will return to Romania now that the dictatorship has been overthrown.

Italy saw an increase in the number of asylum-seekers from Poland and to a lesser extent from the Soviet Union and other East European countries. Many of them intend to leave this country as soon as they can and to go the United States.[6]

It is claimed, particularly by the French Government, that countries other than those mentioned are also affected by the movements of people in Central and Eastern Europe, although in a more indirect manner. It has been pointed out that, for example, many Poles are taking over positions held by Turks in the Federal Republic and that the latter in turn also move further West (many Turks have been reported to have gone to the Alsace region).

Poles try to find work in West European countries, a practice which dates back to long before the major political changes in Poland. They work on a temporary basis with a tourist-visa in many West European countries.

It is, however, debatable whether the influx of people from Central and East Europe will lead to the increasing movement of third-country migrants who are already quite settled in Community Member States.

On the other hand, there is a fair chance that the different groups seeking admission into the Community may be played off against each other to the detriment of people from the Third World. This would be a new form of Eurocentrism which could also lead to discrimination and racist behaviour towards non-Europeans already residing in the Community.

Socio-economic developments will greatly determine whether more people will migrate to Member States of the Community. Therefore, economic aid and other economic measures by the Community and the individual Member States will also be seen as a means of discouraging people from coming to Western Europe.[7]

Tensions between traditional minority groups in Central and Eastern Europe may resurface which could lead to an increase in the number of refugees falling under the Geneva Convention.

Labour Market

For two reasons attention should be paid to the position of migrants and ethnic groups in the labour market. In the first place, social position is to a great extent determined by having a paid job. Being employed eases full participation in society considerably in a number of ways. It gives easier access to social and political power, to better health and education facilities, etc. Secondly, discrimination and racism are growing in this vital area of social life. This increases the number of unemployed migrants and members of ethnic groups, who are made more dependent on the social security system, which, among other things, will encourage negative ideas about 'foreigners' as 'profiteers' and fuel racism.

According to the OECD,[8] the number of authorized foreign workers entering the labour market is rising in almost every country under its review, including South European countries. This is due to the influx of new foreign workers (as permanent, seasonal or temporary labour) into countries like the Federal Republic, France and the United Kingdom, to the admission to the labour market for the first time of reunified family members and those born in the host country, and to the regularization of unauthorized migrants in countries like Italy and Spain.

Generally speaking, the unemployment of migrants is disproportionately high compared with Community citizens and is still rising, although not in every Member State (for example, in the Federal Republic there is a decrease in a still depressingly high number of unemployment migrants). In declining industries (basic industries, motor vehicles, building and engineering), the employment of foreigners has fallen relatively more than that of indigenous workers. This holds especially true for less skilled and older migrants. Moreover, according to the OECD, foreign workers have borne the full brunt of redundancies in manufacturing industries prompted by reduction of activities and relocation of production.

In the tertiary sector, there is a growth of foreign employment in domestic services which makes extensive use of foreign female labour. Maintenance work and caretaking (cleaning and the like) for industry, shops and government departments are increasingly subcontracted to service firms, which recruit foreign workers of both sexes.

There is an expansion in independent employment of migrants in France (Italians, Spaniards, Portuguese and North Africans in the building trade), in the Federal Republic (Turks in retail food and electronic equipment) and in the United Kingdom (Pakistanis as small shopkeepers). Moreover, flexibility, subcontracting and externalization give rise to the creation of small enterprises by foreigners.

Given the overall high rate of unemployment, competition in

the labour market is high. On various occasions migrants' associations and other organizations in various Member States have drawn attention to the fact that foreign workers are discriminated against in finding jobs by official agencies and employers and that indigenous workers try to monopolize the labour market. Moreover, it seems apparent that members of ethnic minorities often face discrimination in promotion and career advancement.

A seminar organized in 1987 to examine the findings of the Evrigenis Report stated that 'there is a need for a concerted programme of action against all forms of discrimination and exclusion against migrant workers and black minority groups in the field of employment. This programme should promote greater equality of opportunity for minority groups in the labour market.'

Measures aimed at promoting greater equality would work best if governments also took steps to promote full employment and economic regeneration, because in the context of economic recession and high unemployment it is easy for racist groups to use minority groups as scapegoats.[9]

The existence of an often complicated system of work and establishment permits makes it difficult for those falling under these rules, notably third-country nationals, to find jobs or to set up an independent enterprise. For instance, there are many restrictions as to the kind of jobs, the duration of contract, etc. Moreover, employers are discouraged from engaging foreign workers because they have to comply with many formalities.[10]

International Instruments

'Harmonization of policies' is a key phrase in the process of finalizing the Internal Market. In the next section an overview will be given of the intergovernmental bodies of the Member States dealing with, among other issues, the harmonization of migration and refugee/asylum policies. Here an overview will be given of the present state of affairs with regard to the most relevant international conventions related to the combating of racism and xenophobia.

For at least three reasons international conventions are of importance, in addition to their specific protection of the social, economic and legal rights of all citizens and those who belong to minority groups. Firstly, these international instruments, once ratified and incorporated in the respective national legislations, harmonize, at least partly, the policies of the contracting parties. Secondly, by signing and ratifying conventions, governments assume their responsibility for combating discrimination, xenophobia and racism, and, in doing so, give an example to the public.[11] Thirdly, as international norms, these conventions can be referred to by non-governmental organizations in countries having not ratified them.

To date, no UN Convention exists which deals exclusively with migrant workers and their families. A draft Convention on the Protection of the Rights of All Migrant Workers and their Families will most probably be presented to the General Assembly in autumn 1990. Unfortunately, national parliaments and non-governmental organizations seem not to be giving much attention to the drafting of this.

Only 11 of the 12 Member States of the Community have ratified the International Convention on the Elimination of All Forms of Racial Discrimination. Ireland has not. This Convention is the most widely ratified – by 128 States – of all the human rights agreements. It provides for a Committee on the Elimination of Racial Discrimination (CERD), which, among other matters, discusses the country reports regularly submitted by the contracting parties. These reports are a valuable instrument for the assessment of the situation in the various countries by both governmental bodies and non-governmental organizations.[12]

Even more important is the recognition of the competence of the Committee to receive and consider communications from individuals or groups of individuals within the jurisdiction of the contracting States, claiming to be victims of a violation of the Convention. Only four Community Member States have accepted this right of individual complaint: Denmark, France, Italy and the Netherlands. With regard to the last country, an individual complaint put forward by a Turkish woman was received which led to an opinion of the Committee in her favour (see above).

Unfortunately, the Secretariat of the CERD is working with too tight a budget, which makes it difficult to implement fully the important tasks attributed to it.

All the Member States have ratified the 1951 Convention

Relating to the Status of Refugees and the 1967 Protocol Relating to the Status of Refugees.[13] Furthermore, Italy dropped the so-called geographical restriction in December 1989, thus allowing refugees from countries other than Europe to be recognized as such under the Convention. However, governments are faced with an increasing number of people seeking asylum in West European countries who, strictly speaking, do not fall under the Convention and the Protocol.

There exists an ad hoc 'Consultations on the Arrivals of Asylum Seekers and Refugees in Europe' convened by the UNHCR in which senior government officials of participating states work together (including many European states and Australia, Canada and the USA). The consultations aim at closer dialogue and cooperation, including exchange of information on asylum-seekers and refugees. A number of working group meetings and workshops have been organized on long-term asylum/refugee policy and the migration flux from Eastern to Western Europe.[14]

Two important ILO Conventions[15] aim at ensuring non-discrimination or equality of opportunity and treatment between migrant and national workers: Convention No. 97 (ratified by 8 Community Member States: Belgium, France, the Federal Republic of Germany, Italy, the Netherlands, Portugal, Spain and the United Kingdom) and Convention No. 143 (ratified by only 2 Member States, Italy and Portugal). The latter also provides protection to so-called undocumented or clandestine migrant workers.

The ILO does not, at present, contemplate further standard-setting in this field because, among other reasons, the Organization will be involved in the supervisory arrangements foreseen for the new UN Convention on All Migrant Workers and their Families.

The legal status of migrant workers in the Member States of the Council of Europe is covered by the European Convention on the Legal Status of Migrant Workers. This Convention has been ratified by only 7 Council of Europe Member States, among them 4 Community Member States: France, the Netherlands, Portugal and Spain. At its fifth meeting in November 1989, the Consultative Committee on the European Convention took note of the fact that quite a number of countries still have to ratify the Convention. The Committee asked the Committee of Ministers to invite those States to explain their technical difficulties in ratifying and offered assistance to overcome them. Furthermore, the competent bodies of the Commission of the European Communities would be contacted in order to ascertain the current EC position with regard to the Convention.[16]

In addition, there are a number of Conventions which also have a bearing on the position of migrants and members of ethnic groups, such as the European Convention on Human Rights (ratified by all Community Member States), the European Convention on Establishment (not ratified by 3 Community Member States: France, Portugal and Spain) and the European Social Charter (not ratified by 3 Community Member States: Belgium, Luxembourg and Portugal). The European Court of Human Rights and the European Human Rights Commission aim to maintain the European Convention on Human Rights. These bodies may also receive individual complaints.

The Parliamentary Assembly of the Council of Europe proposed that an international instrument be framed to grant permanent residence rights for long-stay migrants and their families. However, it seems unlikely that the political will exists at present.

The Steering Committee on Local and Regional Authorities of the Council of Europe drafted a Convention on the Participation of Foreigners in Public Life at Local Level. This draft convention would grant foreign residents the right to form local associations, encourage the setting up of local consultative bodies for the representation of foreign residents, and grant the right to vote and to stand for election in local elections. The draft will be submitted to the Council of Ministers.

The Council of Europe has a special committee which deals with refugee and asylum policy matters. It is known by its acronym CAHAR, which stands for the Ad Hoc Committee of Experts on the Legal Aspects of Territorial Asylum and Refugees and Stateless Persons. It is the oldest of all European forums looking into asylum matters, having undertaken to study the question of the first country of asylum as from 1978. In 1988 CAHAR finalized a 'Draft Agreement on Responsibility for Examining Asylum Requests'. However, as some of the more important Member States of the Council were opposed to signing this agreement, the text was shelved and it has in a sense been superseded by the Convention on the Determination of the Member State Responsible for Examining an Asylum Request Presented in One Community State, signed by 11 of the 12 EC Member States in June 1990 (see below).[17]

In its recommendations, the Evrigenis Report calls upon the Member States of the Community to ratify the Conventions related to the subject of the Report. On various occasions it has been pointed out that States should recognize the right of individual complaint. Where this is already the case, it is necessary to educate in these matters members of the legal profession, judges and non-governmental organizations, including associations of migrants and ethnic minorities in order to make international instruments more effective.[18]

Intergovernmental Coordination

As already mentioned, there are various bodies engaged in the preparation of migration and refugee policies of the Member States. The most relevant will be described here.

The Schengen Group is composed of the five States which signed the Schengen Accord (1985), namely Belgium, the Netherlands and Luxembourg (Benelux), France and the Federal Republic of Germany. There have been attempts to enlarge this group; Italy, Spain, Denmark and Austria have been suggested as possible candidates.

The 1985 Accord is divided into two parts: the first deals mainly with the free movement of goods and services and the second with steps to be taken to allow for the free movement of persons. For that purpose it was decided to draw up a Supplementary Schengen Agreement.

Every six months meetings are held of State Secretaries and Ministers of Justice, of the Interior and/or Foreign Affairs. In between such meetings others of a lower level are held, such as those of the Editorial Committee, which is responsible for the various drafts of the Supplementary Agreement.

The Commission of the European Communities has observer status with the Schengen Group and Mr Martin Bangemann is its representative. Although all members of the Group are members of the Community, it is, however, strictly outside the competence of the Community institutions. This makes it possible for both the

Council of Ministers and the Commission to refuse to answer questions raised by members of the European Parliament on the Schengen Group.

The Supplementary Agreement rests on four main categories of policy measures: (1) measures to be taken to reinforce external borders, (2) a common visa policy, (3) a common policy on refugee and asylum and (4) the setting up of a database system, known as the Schengen Information System (SIS). Although the proposed measures under points 3 and 4 received full public attention once the draft Agreement was leaked out, this dealt with many other issues related to the free circulation of goods and persons.[19]

The scheduled signing (15 December 1989) was postponed for a number of reasons. One was the uncertainty with respect to the future relation of the GDR with the FRG and the Community. However, the Dublin Summit (April 1990) clarified this question somewhat. Other problems were ironed out during a meeting of senior officials in the Hague (April 1990). At that meeting the FRG put forward new proposals on harmonized visa policies and the protection of non-computer-stored data. The problems between the Netherlands and Luxembourg on fiscal fraud were finally solved and the SSA was signed in June 1990. This raises the question as to which Agreement will have precedence: the Supplementary Schengen Agreement or the proposed convention on asylum of the Ad Hoc Immigration Group (see below)?

The TREVI Group was set up in 1975 as an intergovernmental body under international law (outside of Community legislation) with the initial aim of coordinating efforts to combat terrorism. It is composed of the Ministers of the Interior and/or Justice of the Member States, but it is not a European Community structure. The Commission of the Communities has been excluded from the meetings of the Group.

The TREVI Group gradually extended its work to include international crime and drug trafficking and in 1988 the so-called TREVI 1992 Group was set up to examine the problems raised by the lifting of international frontiers in the field of operational matters of police and security, and propose standardized solutions to the other working groups in the TREVI framework.

The measures envisaged include: reinforced checks on persons (irregular migrants and refugees/asylum-seekers are included) at the external borders; information exchange with the database system (similar to the Schengen proposals); training of police officers for external border surveillance; harmonization of security criteria and checks at land, air and sea ports; harmonization of legislation providing for fining air, land and sea carriers for transporting passengers without adequate and/or valid travel documents; lists of deported persons and of personae non gratae; harmonization of policies on immigration, visa and asylum, etc.

Here lies the source of the unacceptable amalgam in the various TREVI groups of dealing with criminals on the one hand and with migrants and refugees on the other.[20]

The Ad Hoc Group on Immigration was set up in 1986 and is composed of the Ministers of the Interior. It has a permanent secretariat at the Council of Ministers, but is, again, not a Community structure. The Commission participates in its meetings with the status of 'member' and not as a Community institution with the right of participation under Community law. The Group drafted a convention on the determination of the State Responsible for examining an Asylum Application Presented in One of the Member States, which was signed in June 1990.

Another convention is in the making on all aspects of checks on persons at the external frontiers of the Community. This should have been ready at the same time as the convention on asylum, but there were problems with respect to proposals for a common visa policy. However, it is due to be signed before the end of 1990.

The European Council at Rhodes (1988) decided that all the ongoing activities of the various forums examining the lifting of the internal borders in January 1993 should be coordinated. The so-called Group of Coordinators, composed of high-ranking government officials, was thus established. This Group is within the framework of the Community, which means that the Council and the Commission are competent to reply to questions raised by the European Parliament.

On one occasion the European Parliament raised the question of the list of the 59 countries, decided by the Group of Coordinators, whose nationals require an entry visa for any of the 12 Member States as of the beginning of 1990. Furthermore, the Parliament wanted to know whether the Commission was aware that the exclusion of the United Nations High Commissioner for refugees from discussions within the Group of Coordinators when refugee matters are being discussed is in violation of the Treaty of Rome and the UN Convention and Protocol relating to the Status of Refugees. The question was not answered.[21]

The Group of Coordinators drew up the so-called Palma Document which contained two lists of measures to be taken to remove the obstacles for the lifting of the internal borders. The first list comprises measures that are essential and the second those which are desirable but not essential. The Document has been adopted and the Group has tried to ensure that the necessary steps are taken in the Member States so as to meet the deadlines for the remaining obstacles to a Europe without internal frontiers.

Human Rights

All matters relating to migrants, asylum-seekers and refugees must be handled in conformity with the established principles of international law as contained particularly in United Nations, ILO and European Conventions and solemn declarations. There is no reason to argue that the 1992 operation is an exception to this rule. Member States could contribute to the harmonization process of their migration and refugee policies by ratifying all relevant conventions. Moreover, these conventions could provide the basis for all kinds of additional measures.

It is obvious that the completion of the Internal Market requires many measures to make possible the free circulation of goods, capital, services and people. As far as the free movement of people is concerned, a complicating factor is the existence of many intergovernmental groups which very often operate behind closed doors, are separate from the European institutions and have their own policy-making procedures. This not only hampers democratic control, but also suggests that the various bodies are working on a very delicate and huge problem, namely how to keep as many new migrants, refugees and asylum-seekers as possible out of the Community.

The proposed measures and agreements, as far as they have become known, are not only rather restrictive – migrants and ethnic minorities often use the expression 'Fortress Europe' to characterize the proposed policy – but treat migration and refugee matters very much as related to policing. This has a very negative effect on public opinion: associating migrants and refugees with police and national security could well feed racist ideas and be used to legitimize certain forms of racist behaviour (extra identity control of those who are or look like 'foreigners').

Policies related to freedom of movement are not merely administrative arrangements between the 12 Member States, but deal with fundamental human rights. Therefore, the governments should, already at the negotiating stage, consult with the competent political bodies such as the European and national parliaments.

Commissioner Bangemann, responsible for free movement after 1992, informed the Committee of Inquiry on 7 May 1990 that although a common immigration policy was desirable, it was not essential before abolishing the internal frontiers. He felt, however, that visa and asylum policy did need to be harmonized quickly. His view was that the 13–14 million 'non-Europeans' living in the EC would be able to circulate freely throughout the Community, although they would not have universal right of residence there. He was unable, however, to state how a distinction would be made between the 'right of free circulation' and the 'right of residence'. This uncertainty lends credence to fears that non-European residents may be subjected to increased random identity checks.

6

Racism and Anti-Racism in the Cultural Field

Introduction

Culture, as defined by some authors of the Centre for Contemporary Cultural Studies in Birmingham, is the field in which people 'make sense' of their lives:

> We understand the word 'culture' to refer to that level at which social groups develop distinct patterns of life, and give *expressive* form to their social and material life-experience. Culture is the way, the forms, in which groups 'handle' the raw material of their social and material existence. . . . The 'culture' of a group or class is the peculiar and distinctive 'way of life' of the group or class, the meanings, values and ideas embodied in institutions, in social relations, in systems of beliefs, in mores and customs, in the uses of objects and material life. . . . A culture includes the 'maps of meaning' which make things intelligible to its members.[1]

This definition already hints at the importance of the 'cultural field' for the emergence and the functioning of racism and xenophobia: it is here where the images are shaped and re-shaped which can then form the basis for overt racist propaganda and activities or, on the contrary, provide some resistance against this. When racism is defined as a process of signification in which 'the Self' is defined by defining 'the Other' as a distinct, inferior 'race',[2] the importance of the different sectors of the cultural field becomes fully evident.

A thorough analysis of the unquestioned images of ethnic minorities would require an insight into the whole range of representation of minorities in the mass media, in art (literature, theatre, etc.) and in the institutions and associations of the 'civil society' of everyday life (sports, youth groups, etc.). One focus of analysis would also have to be the school as one of the most important institutions in forming images of the Self and of the Other.

This chapter, however, will concentrate on the 'information industry', the media. Its crucial role was already mentioned in the Evrigenis Report:

> Information about minorities is quite often biased, dwelling at length on the misdemeanours of some members of minority groups, giving poor coverage to the problems of such communities and ignoring almost all their achievements. . . . Lastly, by giving sensational coverage to acts of violence, . . . the media could develop a culture of violence that could foster a sort of unhealthy fascination.[3]

Whilst acknowledging that the media can play a positive role in forming knowledge about ethnic minority communities, it is undeniable that currently media presentation overall perpetuates a negative image of these communities.

Three aspects of the field of communications will be dealt with: (1) information *about* ethnic minorities, (2) information *for* ethnic minorities and (3) information *by* ethnic minorities.

Regarding the first point we shall describe some of the images of ethnic minorities in the mainstream media and ask whether and to what degree racist images are produced and reproduced. This is not to say that these representations are directly reproduced by the audience. This would be too mechanical a view and would not consider the fact that the receiver of the message 'decodes'[4] it in relation to his/her own experience and integrates it into his/her context of meaning. But nevertheless, given our definition of the cultural process, these images form the 'raw material' with which the 'maps of meaning' are designed. In this respect they do play a crucial role.

The second point deals with the other side of the coin: information *for* minorities provides the raw material for them to create an image of the society they live in as well as of the position provided for them within that society. But information for minorities can also be seen as a human right the receiving society has to provide. It should serve as an orientation in the receiving society as well as a means for keeping in touch with the society of origin, thus bridging the past and present lives of the migrants.

The third point refers to another human right formulated in the

International Convention on the Elimination of All Forms of Racial Discrimination declared by the United Nations in 1965: '5 a) viii The right to freedom of opinion and expression.' This includes the possibility to organize, plan and distribute one's own information and to produce one's own images, thus being able to re-formulate and negotiate one's own position in the new society.

The terms 'migrants' and 'ethnic minorities' are both the subject of controversial discussions: the first because it does not recognize that the majority of 'migrants' are now born in the respective countries, that is, have not themselves migrated, the second because the term 'minority' seems to have a negative meaning. But the often-proposed term 'ethnic group' assumes that the majority is not a special ethnic group. The terms 'ethnic minority' and 'migrant' will therefore be used.

Information About Ethnic Minorities

The Press

This chapter will focus mainly on material from West Germany and Great Britain, as it is interesting to compare two countries which show fundamental differences in the way in which migrants are seen and racism is dealt with. West Germany denies both being a country of immigration and the existence of widespread racism, while in Britain there is a large 'race relations industry' and an awareness of racism.

In the FRG we find a number of content analyses of the way in which migrants are portrayed.[5] In Britain research concentrates more directly on racism.[6]

The studies in the Federal Republic show that information about ethnic minorities centres around the image of the 'foreigner as a criminal': Juan Manuel Delgado[7] who analysed 3069 reports from 84 different newspapers in North Rhine Westphalia between 1966 and 1969 concerning ethnic minorities found that while 32.2 per cent of the articles dealt with information about the situation in the employment market, 31 per cent of the reports dealt with stories in which 'foreigners' were accused of committing crimes. Only 10.8 per cent of the reports were classified by the author as 'goodwill-articles', wanting to legitimize the presence of the so-called guest workers. Classifying the characteristics by which guest workers were described, Delgado found that 31 per cent were negative, 13 per cent positive and 27 per cent ambiguous. But if we look closer at those characteristics he calls positive we find the phrase used most frequently: 'We need the migrants' (32 per cent) and in second place: 'We should take care of them' (21.1 per cent). The first expression can be seen as reproducing the idea that ethnic minorities are to be viewed in a merely instrumental way, their existence being only legitimized by their contribution to the wealth of the ethnic majority. The second statement reveals a paternalistic attitude. In both cases ethnic minorities are seen as dependent on the goodwill of the majority groups.

Georgios Galanis,[8] analysing the two largest mainstream journals (*Stern* and *Quick*) between 1960 and 1982, concentrated on *the ways* in which the media report on crimes committed by members of ethnic minorities. He discovered that in times of economic depression there are many more articles dealing with crimes in general, whereas in prosperous times the articles tend to concentrate on individual criminals isolated from their economic and social context. The latter produce an individualization of crimes, whilst the former show migrants as being a general threat to Germans and to German society: not only do they threaten their economic security by taking away jobs in times of economic depression, they also threaten the personal security of the German population. Both studies found that the majority of the articles dealt with Turks. They were overrepresented in relation to their presence in the German society.

Similar images of foreigners as criminals are produced in the Spanish press[9] concerning Third World immigrants to the country. In the Netherlands 'minority members are singled out for undue attention and sometimes stigmatized as causes of social problems or as being a social problem by their very presence'.[10]

In Denmark Ole Hammer undertook a study of 'The Immigrant Issue in the Daily Press in Denmark'. The result shows that ¾ of the material concerns crime and racism. . . . The immigrants are almost never mentioned in themes like family, personalia, free time, housing and economy, children and youth – and only infrequently in entertainments.'[11]

For France, Yaya Togora from the Institut Français de Presse, writes that Le Pen's 'quadrology', 'immigration – insecurity – delinquency – unemployment of the French', is so often voiced by main political leaders that it has become a dominant ideology.

'Polls are regularly conducted on themes such as: Should migrants be expelled and will their expulsion level down unemployment of the French?' Moreover migrants/minorities appear generally in social and political disorder news stories. Although they are actually the victims of violence, they appear mostly as the actors. 'Apart from crime stories, migrants are frequently presented as a community unable to adapt to the French values.' This is made explicit, for example, in headlines such as 'Fundamentalism against Integration' ('Les Cahiers de L'Express': *Dossier Immigration*, No. 3, April 1990) or 'Immigrants: Which Threshold of Tolerance?' (*Le Point*, No. 917, April 1990).

Professor Clara Gallini, leading research on 'The image of the Arab in mass communications' in Italy, sums up her initial findings as follows:

> There is however the hard 'nucleus' of a stereotype which is *also* conceived as being real, and not a dream: it is that of the Arab who is *always* a Muslim, fundamentally a religious follower of an Islam which is presented as the source of sexual perversions (homosexuality, polygamy), of oppression and servitude (both in the family and in society at large), and of an irrationalism ('fanaticism') which realizes itself in combat (the holy war).[12]

Partly thanks to several independent agencies and pressure groups like the Runnymede Trust and the Campaign against Racism in the Media (CARM), which is part of the Campaign for Press and Broadcasting Freedom (CPBF), partly because of the sociological tradition of investigating 'Race Relations' and racism, there is a widespread literature analysing racism in the media in Great Britain.

As far as the press is concerned, migrants are treated as a 'problem', as a threat to the society because of their numbers and as posing a law and order problem. They are portrayed as cheating the British state authorities to enter the country and then 'scrounging' various forms of welfare benefit.[13]

But there are some differences between the representations in the British and in the West German press. Firstly, the form of the presentation differs. Even the worst papers in West Germany would not dare to print headlines like: 'Arab Pig Sneaks Back In' (*Sun*, 23 January 1986), or 'Get Out You Syrian Swine' (*Sun*, 25 October 1986) or to call a member of an ethnic minority a 'scum product' (*Sun*, 27 February 1989). Secondly, there are more violent images: 'Black youth' are characterized as 'rioters'/'black mob', who 'think of rioting as a form of fun and a source of profit' (*Daily Express*, 30 September 1985). Cartoons present black people in Britain as primitive cannibals in 'tribal' or 'jungle' settings. Thirdly, there is a major battle taking place in some of the British press against anti-racism. Anti-racists are labelled as 'race spies' controlling people's thoughts, imposing censorship, being 'loony leftists', etc.[14]

Obviously overt racism is much more common in the British press than it is in its West German counterpart. This must be seen in the wider context of racism being a taboo in West Germany because of that country's recent history; although it exists, it is generally denied. This might be a reason why overt forms of racism are not articulated. Instead, covert racism is the dominant feature in West German society: 'Racism is reproduced here as a set of unquestioned assumptions which are largely invisible to those who formulate the world in these terms'.[15] The unexpressed assumption is that of the superiority of the German culture and civilization and of conflicts between the different cultures being the 'natural result' of an innate preference of human beings for their 'own kind'.[16]

Television

In her study of the representation of ethnic minorities in TV programmes in 1986,[17] Hildegard Kühne-Scholand found that more than half of the programmes dealt with the issue of asylum and these mostly concerned the number of asylum-seekers and methods of preventing them entering the country. There is little on the life of ethnic minorities in the country itself, and where there is the main subject is integration but hardly ever racism or xenophobia. German nationals comprise 95 per cent of those who make the programmes and initiate discussions. To the extent that migrants appear they are only the objects of representation and are pictured mainly as groups, not as individuals: e.g. 'too many of them' trying to register as asylum-seekers or queuing for accommodation.

In Britain, covert racism is common in television. Crucial to this sometimes unconscious racism is the power to determine the terms of discussion, to pose the questions which have to be answered. In the programmes analysed in 'It Ain't Half Racist, Mum!' by Stuart Hall and others, it was shown that liberals and anti-racists, even if they were given some space, had to argue within a logic in which migrants and their numbers were the problem, for instance by saying that they were not too many yet which implicitly reinforced the view that there could be too many one day.

Angela Barry demonstrates the three 'myths' about people of Afro-Caribbean origin in British TV, which were constantly reproduced in different contexts throughout the years: the entertainer, the trouble-maker, the dependent. In the late fifties the dominant image was the one of the happy slave who knew his place, an image imported from the United States. Along with the 'race riots' in Nottingham and Notting Hill as a rebellion against racism, discrimination and violent racist attacks, emerged the picture of the 'trouble-maker': 'The blandly smiling face of the new immigrant gained definition, acquired real features which clearly spelled out menace. The reassuring penumbra of "Commonwealth" evaporated, leaving the stark "otherness" of the black intruder. The potent myth of the black as trouble-maker was born'.[18] With the Biafran war and the images of starving children, the third great myth, 'that of black dependency – was thus fixed into the consciousness of the nation'.[19] At the end of the seventies, the 'three myths had realigned themselves and flourished – the trouble-maker was now a mugger; the entertainer was the black person whose very presence triggered off hilarity; the dependency myth crossed the African continent and settled itself in Amin's Uganda'.[20]

In the eighties, people of West Indian origin started emerging in the regular programmes, reading the news, etc. Channel Four has been able to give more members of the ethnic minorities access to the media by training programmes and broadcasts programmes aimed at minority interests. But there are also debates on the extent to which these images are not just new, but now 'positive' stereotypes. There is also discussion as to whether programmes like 'Eastenders', 'Albion Market' and 'Ebony', by poking fun at racist stereotypes, are not making them more acceptable instead of criticizing them.[21]

Apart from the above, other initiatives against racism in the media include, for example, the CPBF's campaign for the 'right to reply'. Its 'Group against racism in the media' is writing a book on the historical and present images of different ethnic minorities in Britain: Irish, Afro-Caribbeans, Asians, Jews. The group has different subgroups composed of respective members of minorities examining their representations. Such organizations are non-existent in West Germany.

Information for Ethnic Minorities in Radio and Television

The function of information *for* ethnic minorities should be to enable them not only to keep ties with their countries of origin if they wish to, but also to sustain and develop their mother tongue and by doing so provide the means for a self-confidence and ability to act that could be the starting point for developing new 'maps of meaning' in the receiving society.

Very detailed information about the quantity of such broadcasting is available, but there is practically no deeper analysis of the contents of these programmes.

The Centro Studi Investimenti Sociali Censis in Rome reports that Radio Popolare in Milan and Radio Proletaria in Rome provide information for migrants in different languages, above all in Arabic.

Tables 6.1 and 6.3 show that Sweden and West Germany are the countries with the most extensive radio broadcasting service for ethnic minorities, followed by the Netherlands, whereas in Britain an exceptionally small amount of programming is available (30 minutes per week in Hindi). BBC and Channel Four offer the widest number of TV programmes, although programming offered in the mother tongue is very limited and even decreased in 1987 when the BBC's 'Asian Magazine' in Hindi was replaced by the English-language programme 'Network East' (see tables 6.2, 6.4 and 6.5). In Luxembourg there are weekly radio broadcasts in Portuguese and Italian and in 1990 daily broadcasts in Portuguese began.

In Britain as well as in France the decrease of programmes in the mother tongue is justified by claiming that the respective languages of the majority better meet the needs of the so-called second generation. This argument must be seen in the light of a deficient bilingual education, where children do not have the chance to develop their mother tongue. Perhaps it is not by chance

Table 6.1
Minutes per month of special radio programmes for migrant workers in 1975, 1979 and 1987

Station Transmitter	1975 Minutes	%	1979 Minutes	%	1987 Minutes	%	Change from 1975 to 1987 In minutes	In %
1 RTBF	1200	8.5	1200	7.8	1600	6.7	+400	+33
BRT	280	2.0	365	2.4	400	1.7	+120	+43
2 DR	0	0.0	226	1.5	1400	5.8	+1400	–
3 ARD	5600	39.4	5600	36.5	5600	23.3	0	0
HR	880	6.2	880	5.7	400	1.7	–480	–55
4 Radio France	1440	10.1	2440	15.9	2080	8.7	+640	+44
5 RTL	600	4.2	720	4.7	680	2.8	+80	+13
6 SR	2160	15.2	1855	12.1	6900	28.8	+4740	+219
7 SSR	1320	9.3	1200	7.8	1160	4.8	–160	–12
8 NOS	600	4.2	740	4.8	3640	15.2	+3040	+507
9 BBC	120	0.9	120	0.8	120	0.5	0	0
TOTAL	14200	100.0	15346	100.0	23980	100.0	+9780	+69

Countries: (1) Belgium, (2) Denmark, (3) Federal Republic of Germany, (4) France, (5) Luxembourg, (6) Sweden, (7) Switzerland, (8) The Netherlands, (9) United Kingdom.

Table 6.2
Minutes per month of special TV programmes for migrant workers in 1975, 1979 and 1987

Station Transmitter	1975 Minutes	%	1979 Minutes	%	1987 Minutes	%	Change from 1975 to 1987 In minutes	In %
1 RTBF	240	11.5	240	8.2	320	6.6	+80	+33
2 ARD	300	14.4	240	8.2	240	5.0	–60	–20
ZDF	360	17.2	540	18.4	540	11.2	+180	+50
3 RTL	0	0.0	0	0.0	240	5.0	+240	–
4 SR	720	34.5	1040	35.3	934	19.4	+214	+30
5 SSR	170	8.1	240	8.2	270	5.6	+100	+59
6 NOS	0	0.0	160	5.4	720	14.9	+720	–
7 BBC	120	5.7	120	4.1	720	14.9	+600	+500
Channel 4	–	–	–	–	480	10.0	+480	–
8 FR3	180	8.6	360	12.2	360	7.4	+180	+100
TOTAL	2090	100.0	2940	100.0	4824	100.0	+2734	+131

Countries: (1) Belgium, (2) Federal Republic of Germany, (3) Luxembourg, (4) Sweden, (5) Switzerland, (6) Netherlands, (7) United Kingdom, (8) France.

Table 6.3
Weekly radio programmes for migrant workers in 1987 (in minutes)

	Station transmitter	Language															
		Arabic	Finnish	Greek	Hindi/ Urdu*	Italian	Khmer	Laotian	Polish	Portu- guese	Serbo- Croatian	Spanish	Turkish	Viet- namese	Other[2]	Total	%
1	RTBF	60		50		60			30	50	30	60	60			400	7.7
	BRT	50											50			100	
2	DR	87			87						87		87			350[1]	5.4
3	ARD			280		280					280	280	280			1400	30.4
	NDR																
	RB			30		30					30	30	30			150	
	HR			20		20					20	20	20			100	
	SFB										150		150			300	
	SR					20										20	
4	Radio France	180**					10	10		180**	45	45	40	10	20**	540	8.3
5	RTL					95				35	20	20				170	2.6
6	SR		630	340					30		330	155	240			1725	26.6
7	SSR			25		180					30	30	25			290	4.5
8	NOS	185		30		30				30	30	95	165		345	910	14.0
9	BBC				30											30	0.5
	N	562	630	775	117	715	10	10	60	295	1052	735	1147	10	345	6485	100.0
	%	8.7	9.7	12.0	1.8	11.0	0.2	0.2	0.9	4.5	16.2	11.3	17.7	0.2	5.6	100.0	

* Hindi (BBC), Urdu (DR).
** The programmes in Arabic and Portuguese use in part French: the programme in the category 'Other' is directed to Africans and is transmitted only in French.
[1] Weekly programme time is 4 x 87.5 minutes = 350 minutes.
[2] Berber (35), Chinese (30), Malaysian (35), Papiamento (35), Dutch for Surinamese (70), Dutch Multicultural (140) = 345 minutes.
Countries:(1) Belgium, (2)) Denmark, (3) Federal Republic of Germany, (4) France, (5) Luxembourg, (6) Sweden, (7) Switzerland, (8) The Netherlands, (9) United Kingdom.

Table 6.4
Weekly TV programmes for migrant workers in 1987 (in minutes)[1]

Station transmitter	Language												
	Arabic	Estonian	Finnish	Greek	Italian	Polish	Portu-guese	Serbo-Croatian	Spanish	Turkish	Other*	TOTAL	%
1 RTBF	0				0	0	0	0	0	0		0	0.0
2 ARD				0	0		0	0	0	0		0	0.0
ZDF				0	0		0	0	0	0		0	0.0
3 FR3											90	90	10.5
4 RTL					60							60	7.0
5 SR		0	165	20		0		20		20		225	26.3
6 SSR					60				0			60	7.0
7 NOS	15							15		30	60	120	14.7
8 BBC											180	180	21.1
Channel 4											120	120	14.1
N	15	0	165	20	120	0		35		50	450	855	100.0
%	1.8	0.0	19.3	2.3	14.0	0.0	0.0	4.1	0.0	5.8	52.7	100.0	

* NOS: Berber (15), Dutch Multicultural (45) = 60 minutes.
BBC: English (120), Hindi (60) = 180 minutes.
Channel 4: English (120).
FR3: French (90).

[1] The programme services marked with 0 in this table indicate that these programmes are not transmitted every week.

Countries:(1) Belgium, (2) Federal Republic of Germany, (3) France, (4) Luxembourg, (5) Sweden, (6) Switzerland, (7) The Netherlands, (8) United Kingdom.

Table 6.5

Television programmes for migrant workers in 1987 (minutes per month)

Station transmitter	Language												
	Arabic	Estonian	Finnish	Greek	Italian	Polish	Portu-guese	Serbo-Croatian	Spanish	Turkish	Other*	TOTAL	%
1 RTBF	40				80	40	40	40	40	40		320	6.6
2 ARD				40	40		40	40	40	40		240	5.0
ZDF				90	90		90	90	90	90		540	11.2
3 FR3											360	360	7.5
4 RTL					240							240	5.0
5 SR		17	660	80		17		80		80		934	19.3
6 SSR					240				30			270	5.6
7 NOS	60				60		30	60	30	120	360	720	14.9
8 BBC											720	720	14.9
Channel 4											480	480	10.0
N	100	17	660	210	750	57	200	310	230	370	1920	4824	100.0
%	2.0	0.4	13.7	4.4	15.5	1.2	4.1	6.4	4.8	7.7	39.8	100.0	

* NOS: Berber (60), Malaysian (30), Papiamento (30), Dutch for Surinamese (60), Dutch Multicultural (180) = 360 minutes.
BBC: English (480), Hindi (240).
Channel 4: English (480).
FR3: French (360).
Countries:(1) Belgium, (2) Federal Republic of Germany, (3) France, (4) Luxembourg, (5) Sweden, (6) Switzerland, (7) The Netherlands, (8) United Kingdom.

Source for Tables 6.1–5: Taisto Hujanen (ed.), 'Final Conference of the Joint Study: The Role of Information in the Realization of the Human Rights of Migrant Workers', Lausanne, 23–7 October 1988.

that this policy is mainly supported by the two countries who were most successful in imposing their language on the peoples of their former colonies.

On the other hand the policy of mother tongue information in West Germany, Sweden and the Netherlands reflects rather different migration policies: while in West Germany the transmission of programmes in the vernacular languages was part of a policy of rotation, in Sweden and the Netherlands those programmes are an element of a minorities policy adopted by the government. Both countries recognized ethnic minorities as a new element of their society and each claimed to be a 'multicultural society'. The diversity of languages is highest in the Netherlands which broadcasts 910 minutes a week in 12 languages.

The contents of the programmes in the mother tongues and in the respective language of the receiving country include: current affairs from the countries of origin and those of residence, sports, cultural events, music and special information about legal points in the receiving countries. Only a detailed content analysis could give some insight as to how useful these programmes are for the life of ethnic minorities, their self-perception and their perceptions of the society they live in. Such investigation remains to be done.

It seems, however, that information or discussions about racism and discrimination and strategies against it are very rare. In West Germany there is a fairly regular reference to this only in the radio station of the Land Hesse: there are two magazine programmes weekly, one of two hours, the other of half an hour, in which transmissions on racism and xenophobia have occurred. This might be due to the fact that the new local authorities in Frankfurt, formed by a coalition of the Social Democrat and the Green parties, have established a committee for multiculturalism and have since then carried out some anti-racist activities (the only ones carried out by authorities of the FRG). These events have been partly reported on by the Hessischer Rundfunk (HR). Naturally, information for ethnic minorities should not deal with racism all the time, but still it is striking that it takes up so little space.

Finally, it should be noted that the decentralization and deregulation of national broadcasting in European countries has opened up possibilities for local radio stations which are either community stations, that is, are run by a particular ethnic minority, or local radio stations providing services for different minorities.

Information by Ethnic Minorities

Radio Stations

Special programmes for ethnic minorities are not necessarily made by members of the minorities but these are the examples which concern us here. The aim of the so-called ethnic media is to provide information about the country of origin as well as about the respective communities in Britain and in all other parts of the world. They also organize discussions within the community and with other communities, including the majority one.[22] The following is a short overview of existing community radio stations.

In *Belgium* there is an ethnic community radio called 'Fréquence Arabe', transmitting all day in French and Arabic. In *Britain* four community radio stations have now been licensed, several others exist illegally. In *Denmark* one out of 306 registered local radio stations serves only migrant communities using predominantly Arabic, Urdu and Turkish. In the *Federal Republic* there are cable networks in Berlin and Dortmund used for transmission of radio programmes in migrant languages, mainly Turkish. In *France* there are many community radio stations transmitting programmes for ethnic minorities either in their mother tongue, in French or bilingual. Many are illegal and operate under the threat of being closed down. Some of them were given licences recently and also receive some support from the French Government.

The Netherlands seems to have the highest number of illegal community radio stations in Europe. Here again the state has started to legalize some of them and to provide financial support for experimenting with local radio stations for migrant communities. In *Spain* there are two radio stations run by members of ethnic minorities which can broadcast all day without licence problems: the US air base station and the British Forces Broadcasting Services transmitting to their audiences in their mother tongue. In *Sweden* 23 local stations have hired 50 journalists on a permanent basis for the production of migrant programmes. Within small-circulation networks 90 clubs and organizations transmit programmes to their specific communities.[23]

The Ethnic Press

In some European countries newspapers and/or bulletins for certain communities are published in their respective mother tongues as well as in the majority languages. In Britain there are papers for the Asian, the Afro-Caribbean, Latin American, Irish and Jewish communities. The Asian weekly *New Life* (published in English) and the Gujarati weekly have, according to their publisher Mr Patel, 200,000 readers. The biggest black newspaper in Britain is *The Voice*, dealing with the life of black people in Britain and all over the world, with special pages for 'Caribbean News'. One problem for the 'ethnic press' is that they are supposed to cover *all* the interest groups of the community in one or perhaps two publications. Of course this is a virtually impossible task and so the need to represent a group characterized by diversities of age, gender, class, political beliefs, etc. as one homogeneous entity puts heavy demands on these media.

A number of newspapers published by minorities appear also in the Netherlands and in France, and there are some bulletins in Italy produced, for example, by the Philippines League, and Latin Americans. In West Germany one Turkish-German journal has just appeared. In addition there are smaller community newspapers which are available through special distribution channels (community organizations, counselling organizations like the church, etc.). Some of them are in German, like *Kontakt* for Spaniards, and some bilingual, like the Greek community's paper.

Conclusion

This brief analysis of the presence of ethnic minorities in the European media has shown that on the one hand racist images and stereotypes are common but on the other hand information for the minorities, especially in their mother tongues, is not very widespread (see tables 6.1 to 6.5). The largest foreign-language service in West Germany represents a programme of 40 minutes daily for migrants in their mother tongue. As compared to this, British, French and US soldiers in West Germany have their own programmes in their mother tongues 24 hours a day. Media run by members of the ethnic minorities are generally not distributed through the normal channels and therefore not available for a broader audience. This does not apply to papers from the countries of origin, which are easily available, at least in bigger cities, but are not especially designed for the situation of migrants.

Given this situation, the possibilities of challenging racist images on the one hand and of developing a diverse, vibrant community culture on the other are close to zero.

One way of tackling the problem has been to try to stop the production and reproduction of racist images through legislation. To the proposal for a Council resolution on the fight against racism and xenophobia,[24] for instance, the Committee on Social Affairs and Employment proposed an amendment (No. 10) to 'set up agencies in each Member State to provide information on the legal instruments that exist to protect persons against discrimination, racism and acts of incitement to hatred and racial violence'. Although such measures are very important and should be implemented, they can only be used against severe and overt forms of racism, and even then there is always a wide range of interpretations as to what is to be defined as racist and whether freedom of opinion and expression is not limited if measures are taken against cultural productions.

In the Evrigenis Report the following was recommended:

> 328 (e) The professional ethics of the information industry with respect to manifestations of violence, and especially of racial violence, should be carefully considered. The European Parliament could take the initiative in organizing a symposium on this subject. 329 (f) It should be brought home to those concerned at all levels of the information industry that the mass media have an important role to play in eliminating racial prejudice and promoting harmonious relations among communities resident in Europe. The minority communities must be fairly represented in the information media.[25]

But how can this be achieved? The fundamental problem when it comes to the cultural situation of migrants is that they lack the freedom of expression that should be guaranteed to everyone because they have hardly any access to the production and distribution of information and of cultural production. A basic precondition to counter racism, therefore, would be equal access to the media and measures to facilitate independent cultural production. This was also a concern of the Committee on Social Affairs and Employment, as expressed in an amendment (No. 11) to the proposal mentioned above to 'ensure that the minority communities are properly represented on the public information bodies'.

Members of ethnic minorities should be involved in the communication process at all levels, in the elucidation of what information is needed, through planning how information is to be collected, presented, packaged and distributed, and through active participation in those decision-making processes involved in the production and distribution of information (and cultural productions). In other words 'there needs to be a move from migrant workers being seen as passive recipients of information (and cultural productions) to being involved as active participants in the cultural processes'.[26]

As members from the British Film Institute mentioned, there is no point in reserving a section for ethnic minorities to create their culture if these productions never enter the mainstream and become a part of everyday life of the members of the majorities. At the same time ethnic minorities must have the right and the means to develop their own values, identities and self-images independently.

This need is underlined in the 'International Convention on the Elimination of All Forms of Racial Discrimination' agreed by the United Nations in its twentieth session (21 September–22 December 1965) and now signed by all countries of the EC, where in Article 2.2 it says: 'States Parties shall, when the circumstances so warrant, take in the social, economic, cultural and other fields, special and concrete measures to ensure the adequate development and protection of certain racial groups or individuals belonging to them, for the purpose of guaranteeing them the full and equal enjoyment of human rights and fundamental freedoms [including] the right to freedom of opinion and expression [and] the right to equal participation in cultural activities.'

In interviews with experts the following proposals for European Community action to ensure the right to access and equity of migrants in the process of cultural production were suggested:

- to provide funding for a European network of members of ethnic minorities working in the field of media and art production. For instance organizing smaller meetings on different fields of activities: production, distribution, technologies, etc;
- to set up a central data bank including information about organizations and individuals in the field, as well as press, films, videos and books to exchange information within Europe;
- to put pressure upon Member States to provide the means for equal access of members of ethnic minorities to media and culture by special training programmes, and by setting of quotas;
- to support independent media and artistic productions by funding distribution and translations.

This could help to ensure that the presence of ethnic minorities becomes a normal feature of the European Community, thus challenging ideologies and policies which see them and their presence as a problem.

7

Conclusions and Recommendations

The recommendations (*in italics*) were formally voted upon and adopted by the Committee of Inquiry.

The European Parliament

It is vital that there should be adequate follow-up to the research detailed in this volume. Given that the Committee of Inquiry can exist only for nine months, this follow-up will have to take place under the auspices of another committee. The Committee on Legal Affairs and Citizens' Rights, with general responsibilities for 'human rights problems in the Community', would be the logical candidate; its remit should be extended to cover 'all questions relating to combating racism, antisemitism and xenophobia'.

Recommendation 1: *That the Committee on Legal Affairs and Citizens' Rights have added to its terms of reference responsibility for questions pertaining to racism, antisemitism and xenophobia within the European Community and all matters relating to third-country nationals residing within the European Community, and that the committee should consider the possibility of proposing the setting up of a standing subcommittee under Rule 114 of the European Parliament's Rules of Procedure.*

The follow-up should be done if possible on a continuous basis, with a commitment to at least one major debate during each parliamentary session.

The present volume has been drawn up with considerable assistance from two organizations – the Churches' Committee for

Migrants in Europe (and their publication, *Migration Newssheet*), which specializes in reporting on the incidence of racism and xenophobia and action taken to combat it, and *Searchlight*, whose particular strengths lie in providing information about fascist and other extreme-right groups and organizations. It would seem that they would be extremely well-placed to undertake jointly the monitoring of developments in the field and in particular of the recommendations given here. It would be useful for a system of social and economic indicators to be developed for this field.

Recommendation 2: *That, besides its normal debates, at least once a year, one day of an EP part-session be devoted to a general debate on the situation with regard to xenophobia and racism in the Community, in the presence of the Commission and the Council.*

Recommendation 3: *That a system for monitoring developments in the field of racism, antisemitism and xenophobia (including extreme-right and fascist groups) and in particular the implementation of the recommendations contained in the present report be established.*

A large number of complaints to local and national authorities in the Member States are made by individuals. The possibility should exist for individual cases to be raised at Community level. An independent source of adjudication should be set up.

Recommendation 4: *That the attention of all Community citizens be drawn to the right to petition the European Parliament where they feel they have been victims of racist or xenophobic behaviour; that the necessary steps be taken to extend this right to all residents in the European Community; that its Committee on Petitions make a proposal to amend Rule 128 of the Rules of Procedure to this end; that the measures to be taken to endow the Committee on Petitions with the means required for its task be studied; and that the feasibility of appointing a Community Ombudsman/woman to help resolve cases of racist, antisemitic and xenophobic discrimination be examined.*

Currently, within the Parliament, the same budget line covers both actions against racism and xenophobia and actions in the field of human rights, and there seems to have been a tendency for nearly all expenditure to be devoted to the latter rather than the former. A separate budget line would remove the danger but it is vital that it should contain adequate resources to promote effective action in this field.

Recommendation 5: *That a budget line be established in the 1991 budget in order to promote and financially support pilot projects with the aim of improving the conditions for co-existence between European Community nationals and legal residents from third countries.*

Recommendation 6: *That a budget line be established in the 1991 Budget and thereafter to cover positive actions against racism, antisemitism and xenophobia, with resources commensurate with the gravity of the problem, specifically including education and the development of teaching methods that will improve people's understanding of cultural diversity.*

The European Parliament might be seen to be on weak ground in criticizing discriminatory employment practices in certain member States when its own do not explicitly permit or encourage the employment of European residents who are not Community nationals as established officials.

Recommendation 7: *That consideration be given, in negotiations with the trade union organizations concerned, to amendment of the Staff Regulations for officials of the European Communities to open the way for those from third countries with permanent resident status in one of the Community countries to permit employment as established Community officials.*

Recommendation 8: *That the Parliamentary groups employ in their secretariats non-Community citizens who have the right of residence in the Community.*

The Commission and Council should be separate signatories to all conventions in the area of the fight against racism, antisemitism and xenophobia.

Recommendation 9: *That the Commission be supported in its declared intentions of encouraging the Community's accession to the European Convention on Human Rights.*

The Social Affairs Council and the representatives of the Governments of the Member States adopted a resolution on racism and xenophobia on 29 May 1990. The draft resolution was criticized for confining itself to a recognition that certain legal measures at both institutional and administrative level could help to prevent acts inspired by racism or xenophobia. The resolution in the form adopted by the Council and the representatives of the Governments of the Member States, however, appears to fail to acknowledge the need for Community action to combat racism and xenophobia where the victims are European residents who are not Community nationals. This is a clear breach of the undertaking made in the Declaration against Racism and Xenophobia, which specifically mentions 'workers who have their origins in other Member States or in third countries' and 'the Member State in which they legally reside'.

Recommendation 10: *That, in view of the fact that the recent resolution on Racism and Xenophobia adopted by the Social Affairs Council and the representatives of the Governments of the Member States on 29 May 1990 and the European Council's declaration on antisemitism, racism and xenophobia of 26 June 1990 totally fail to respect major elements of the Joint Declaration against Racism and Xenophobia (11 June 1986), and in the light of the ruling of the Court of Justice of 22 May 1990, extending to the European Parliament the power to institute legal proceedings against the Council, we call upon its Committee on Legal Affairs and Citizens' Rights and the Legal Service of the European Parliament to examine the possibility of instituting proceedings under Article 173 of the EEC Treaty and Article 146 of the Euratom Treaty to enforce respect for its prerogatives, in accordance with its resolution of 14 June 1990.*

The Group of Coordinators (the Rhodes Group) is an official Community organization and despite undertakings by the Council to keep the European Parliament, and specifically its Committee on Legal Affairs and Citizens' Rights, informed about the work of this body, no information has as yet been given. It is vital that such information should include not only a report of the organization's activities, but also all its working documents. The same should apply to all other such organizations and ad hoc bodies.

Recommendation 11: *That its Committee on legal Affairs and Citizens' Rights assert its prerogatives to be kept informed of the activities of the Group of Coordinators (the Rhodes Group) and supplied with all its working documents; that in addition the Commission and Council be asked to keep the Committee fully and regularly informed of any discussions in which they have a presence, relating to the free movement and civil rights of residents within the Community and moves towards a common Community position on immigration rules, right of asylum and visa policy.*

The social partners have an important role to play in fostering harmonious race relations, notably through good employment practices. Coordination of Community policies should include full consultation with the employers' organizations and trade unions. The Flather Report demonstrated the Economic and Social Committee's interest and involvement in this subject. The Council of Europe has also been particularly active in the fight against racism, antisemitism and xenophobia.

Recommendation 12: *That fullest cooperation be maintained with the Economic and Social Committee and with the Council of Europe to ensure that problems relating to racism, antisemitism and xenophobia are effectively tackled in a coordinated manner.*

The widest possible publicity should be given to Parliament's activities in the field of fighting racism, antisemitism and xenophobia, particularly amongst young people.

Recommendation 13: *That any information packs produced by parliament's information offices in the Member States and particularly those for schools include a section on racism and xenophobia setting out Parliament's views.*

The Commission of the European Communities

No single Commissioner currently has specific responsibility for matters relating to racism and xenophobia – they are partly covered both by Mr Bangemann, responsible for the Single

Market, and by Mrs Papandreou, responsible for social policy. To entrust the President of the Commission with this specific responsibility, in a coordinatory role and provided with the necessary staff, would both greatly increase the efficiency of the Community's activities in this field, and be a clear measure of its resolve.

Recommendation 14: *That the President of the Commission be entrusted with ensuring coordination of the Commission activities pertaining to racism, antisemitism and xenophobia and all matters relating to nationals of third countries within the European Community, and that to this end a task force be set up spanning both the relevant directorates-general.*

Recommendation 15: *That a Community officer for immigration be appointed to monitor the preparation of the Commission report, forward regular reports to Parliament on migration policy and serve as a contact point for immigrants.*

Apart from the European Parliament's resolve to follow up the research detailed here, it would be useful for the Commission also to be involved, and this might best be done by its producing a periodic report (probably drawing on external resources). This should cover extreme-right and fascist groups as defined in the Evrigenis Report.

Recommendation 16: *That a periodic report, preferably every 18–24 months, be commissioned on the current situation with respect to racism, antisemitism and xenophobia (including extreme-right and fascist groups) with particular reference to areas with a high proportion of minority communities or those which may have exhibited a high level of tension within the Community, and that this report be presented to the European Parliament.*

All Commission legislative proposals should, in future, include a 'minority impact statement'.

Recommendation 17: *That the proposals for legislation submitted by the Commission should also indicate the effects of such proposals in combating racism and xenophobia.*

Racism, antisemitism and xenophobia should be subject areas regularly included in the Commission's sampling of public opinion around the Community, and the results widely disseminated.

Recommendation 18: *That regular surveys be conducted by Eurobarometer on the situation with regard to xenophobia and racism in the Community and on the relations between the various communities living there.*

The public at large is currently not sufficiently aware of Community action to combat racism and xenophobia, or of their rights to have their complaints heard. There is a need to foster greater awareness in the Community about the dangers which racism and xenophobia present to all its citizens, particularly in the light of the rising tide of racist attacks and crimes and of such incidents as the desecration of Jewish graves at Carpentras.

Recommendation 19: *That an information campaign be carried out to publicize measures designed to combat racism and xenophobia (both at Community and national level) and all the bodies that members of the public may contact when they consider that they have been the victims of xenophobic or racist conduct.*

Recommendation 20: *That 1995 should be designated European Year of Racial Harmony and form part of an ongoing campaign to alert residents of the Community to the dangers to them all from the growth in racism, antisemitism and xenophobia, and that adequate financial resources be made available in both 1993 and 1994 for preparation.*

Particularly important for the future will be ensuring that young people from both majority and minority communities have the fullest possible awareness both of the dangers of racism and of the benefits of a multicultural society. In fact the role of education is vital and the Commission should fully exploit what competence it has in this field. It should maintain and extend its activities to support projects in the field of the education of children from immigrant and ethnic minority backgrounds, with a view particularly to supporting and developing further the teaching to these children of their mother tongue.

Recommendation 21: *That all its educational, training and youth exchange programmes as well as teacher training programmes promote a European and non-discriminatory dimension, that it set up special training programmes to encourage the learning of minority languages and an appreciation of minority cultures as well as exchanges of young people from disadvantaged regions and minority communities, with special action programmes for gypsies and other itinerant communities.*

Recommendation 22: *That youth exchange programmes be promoted in the Community to create a critical awareness among young people of past and present forms of racism, antisemitism and fascism.*

Recommendation 23: *That the development of teaching materials for schools and instructional programmes for those working with children and young people be promoted to provide instruction on racism, xenophobia and antisemitism in the Community.*

Recommendation 24: *That the Commission use all its powers, especially those provided by Article 169 of the Treaty, to enforce full implementation of Council Directive 77/486/EEC on the education of the children of migrant workers, in all those Member States which have so far failed to fulfil the obligation imposed on them by this directive; that the Commission initiate a revision of this directive, with a view particularly to ensuring that the rights provided by it are extended so as to include the children of immigrants from third countries.*

Recommendation 25: *That the Commission significantly step up its efforts to ensure full implementation of the resolution of the Council and Ministers of Education, meeting within the Council, of May 1989, on the education of gypsy and traveller children, with a view particularly to stimulating initiatives proposed by that resolution and strengthening the development, coordination and evaluation, at Community level, of cooperative networks of initiatives at local, regional and Member State level.*

Recommendation 26: *That the Commission, by 31 March 1991, submit a recommendation to the Council on the role of education in combating and preventing racism and xenophobia.*

Recommendation 27: *That scientific research be promoted into the causes and forms of racism and xenophobia in the Community with the aim of indicating ways of overcoming racism and xenophobia.*

Attitudes to minorities are largely shaped by their portrayal in the press and other mass media; currently there is grave concern about the stereotyping of religious and ethnic minorities.

Recommendation 28: *That a campaign be conducted to raise the awareness of media professionals of the importance of their role in eliminating racial and xenophobic prejudices, particularly through appropriate treatment of the news.*

The European Community Institutions might be seen to be on weak ground in criticizing discriminatory employment practices in certain Member States when their own do not explicitly permit or encourage the employment of European residents who are not Community nationals as established officials.

Recommendation 29: *That consideration be given, in negotiations with the trade union organizations concerned, to amendment of the Staff Regulations for officials of the European Communities to open the way for those from third countries with permanent resident status in one of the Community countries to permit employment as established Community officials.*

Recommendation 30: *That the Commission carry out a detailed study of Member States' legislation governing the employment of non-Community citizens in the civil services and submit a communication thereon.*

Clearly, some Member States' legislation provides better protection for residents against racism and xenophobia than others'. It would be appropriate to coordinate legislation Community-wide to extend the same measure of protection to all Community residents. One provision of such a directive could be the establishment of a watchdog body similar to the Commission for Racial Equality in the United Kingdom.

Recommendation 31: *That, in the light of the ruling of the Court of Justice of 9 July 1987 underlining the fact that the employment situation, and more generally the improvement of living and working conditions in the Community, is affected by Member States' policies towards third-country nationals resident in the Community, a draft directive be prepared by 31 March 1991 to provide a Community framework of legislation against any discrimination connected with belonging or not belonging to an ethnic group, nation, region, race or religion, covering all Community residents.*

Extreme right-wing and fascist groups abuse the postal service by disseminating unsolicited material. They also promote racial hatred by distributing leaflets, newspapers and pamphlets outside schools and youth clubs and in other public places.

Recommendation 32: *That a draft directive be prepared by 31 March 1991 to harmonize regulations throughout the Community to prohibit the dissemination of antisemitic and racist materials.*

There persists a widespread fear that the completion of the Single Market may result in the creation of second-class citizens – Community residents without the nationality of a Member State, who may not benefit from the removal of internal frontiers and freedom of movement, and indeed Community residents with the nationality of a Member State who because of their obvious membership of an ethnic minority group may be subject to more frequent identity controls and other restrictions to their freedom of movement.

The aim of the European Residents' Charter would be to ensure that all legal residents of the Community (subject to a minimum residence qualification) enjoy the same rights and duties throughout the Community.

Recommendation 33: *That a European Residents' Charter be drafted, extending to residents of a Member State the right of residence and establishment in the other Member States of the Community, and giving them the opportunity to obtain a European Residents' Card, as part of the measures to abolish internal frontiers and establish the single area provided for in the Treaties and the Single Act; this European Residents'*

Card would allow non-Community legal residents freedom to circulate, to reside and to work within the European Community.

Important lessons can be learned from the experience of local groups and organizations around Europe, of great value to Community policies and campaigns.

Recommendation 34: *That a European network to combat racism and xenophobia be promoted with Community funding to allow the exchange of experience among the Member States and create points of contact for those affected.*

The European Parliament dealt with the question of asylum in the report by Mr Vetter (adopted January 1988), pointing out that the reasons forcing people to flee had changed since the Geneva Convention on Refugees was signed in 1951, and so the definition of the concept of refugee had to be modified accordingly. Apart from the restrictive geographical limits sometimes attached to the Geneva Convention, it is vital to ensure that no one should be returned to a country where they face persecution because of their political, religious or philosophical beliefs, or sexual orientation, or would be liable to punishment, or would face criminal prosecution for crimes not recognized as such in the Community.

Recommendation 35: *That a Convention be drafted on a common refugee and asylum policy building on the principles of the UN Convention on Refugees allowing all those threatened by persecution because of their political, religious or philosophical beliefs or convictions, or gender or sexual orientation, to benefit, including those liable to criminal prosecution for crimes that are not recognized as such in the Community, or to cruel and unusual punishment, or to an attack on or constraint of their physical, mental or social integrity.*

Recommendation 36: *That arrangements be made in cooperation with the European Parliament for the appointment of a European Community officer for questions of asylum.*

It is important that immigrants taking or facing legal proceedings should have the opportunity of being represented by an organization responsible for safeguarding the interests of their particular communities.

Recommendation 37: *That a proposal for a directive be drafted on the participation of recognized associations, including those of immigrants, as a third party in proceedings in which those they represent are the injured parties.*

Recommendation 38: *That consideration be given to the results achieved by immigrants' advisory councils and that they be encouraged on an individual basis, during a transitional phase, according to the quality of their record as regards democratization.*

Over four years after the European Parliament endorsed the call in the Evrigenis Report for a Migrants' Forum to be established, this has still not been done. The Parliament has duly voted the necessary funds in successive budgets, but the Commission has apparently spent all these credits on conducting preparatory studies, which have now led to the selection of 87 migrant organizations. The Committee of Inquiry was not provided with the information necessary to assess the representativity of these.

Recommendation 39: *That the European Migrants' Forum as recommended in the Evrigenis Report be established by 31 December 1990; the recent Commission moves in this direction are welcomed, including the convening of a conference of 87 migrant organizations in the Community; the Parliament should have representation at this conference and be kept fully informed of all developments.*

Despite the Commission's assertion of Community competence on matters relating to the achievement of the Single Market, covering particularly the harmonization of asylum rules and all other matters relating to the removal of internal frontiers and the establishment of a Peoples' Europe, Member States proceeded to remove these issues from the Community forum and therefore from accountable democratic control by creating semi-clandestine groups such as TREVI and the 'Ad Hoc Group on Immigration'. It is totally unacceptable that this lack of accountability should continue.

Recommendation 40: *That the Commission look into the question of how an action can be brought in the European Court of Justice against the decisions of the Schengen states and 'Ad Hoc Group on Immigration' of the Member States and then bring proceedings.*

Recommendation 41: *That the Commission ensure that the forthcoming Intergovernmental Conference asserts the Community's competence as indicated in the White Paper of 1985 on the Internal market and in Parliament's resolution on the right of asylum (Doc. A-227/86) in matters dealing with the harmonization of asylum rules and all other matters relating to the removal of internal frontiers and the establishment of a Peoples' Europe, such as harmonization of entry rules and common European Community visa policies, and that these efforts should be clearly reflected in the Convention on the right of asylum.*

Community funding through the European Social Fund or the European Regional Development Fund could be used, with increased financial provision, to help combat racism and xenophobia in those areas where there is a high level of social and economic deprivation and a high immigrant or minority population.

Recommendation 42: *That the criteria enabling European Social Fund and European Fund for Regional Development funding for specific positive actions be directed to a greater extent towards regions and localities with high immigrant populations, especially where minorities are concerned, and be more widely applied, but without prejudice to the claims of the disadvantaged areas of the Community.*

The Commission and Council should be separate signatories to all conventions in the area of the fight against racism, antisemitism and xenophobia.

Recommendation 43: *That the Commission be supported in its declared intentions of encouraging the Community's accession to the European Convention of Human Rights.*

The Council of the European Communities

In view of the increasing activities of the European Community as an actor on the international stage, and to underline its commitment to protecting human rights and eliminating racial discrimination, the Community itself should become a signatory to the appropriate international conventions. It should therefore revise its position of opposition to the Community's accession to the European Convention on Human Rights.

Recommendation 44: *That it reconsider its position as regards the Community's accession and take the necessary steps to ensure that the European Community become a signatory to the European Convention on Human Rights as foreseen in the Working Programme of the Commission for 1990.*

Recommendation 45: *That the necessary steps be taken to ensure that the European Community become a signatory to the UN Convention on the Elimination of all Forms of Racial Discrimination, and to the 1951 Geneva Convention on Refugees.*

The European Community Institutions might be seen to be on weak ground in criticizing discriminatory employment practices in certain Member States when their own do not explicitly permit or encourage the employment of European residents who are not Community nationals as established officials.

Recommendation 46: *That consideration be given, in negotiations with the trade union organizations concerned, to amendment of the Staff Regulations for officials of the European Communities to open the way for those from third countries with permanent resident status in one of the Community countries to permit employment as established Community officials.*

Despite the Commission's assertion of Community competence on matters relating to the achievement of the Single Market, covering particularly the harmonization of asylum rules and all other matters relating to the removal of internal frontiers and the establishment of a Peoples' Europe, Member States proceeded to remove these issues from the Community forum and therefore from accountable democratic control by creating semi-clandestine groups such as TREVI and the 'Ad Hoc Group on Immigration'. It is totally unacceptable that this lack of accountability should continue.

Recommendation 47: *That, in the light of the ruling of the Court of Justice on 9 July 1987 underlining the fact that the employment situation, and more generally the improvement of living and working conditions in the Community, are affected by Member States' policies towards third-country nationals resident in the Community, all activities related to the free movement of such third-country nationals currently dealt with in intergovernmental forums such as the 'Ad Hoc Group on Immigration' and the TREVI working groups and any other group involving all or some of the Member States of the Community should be wound up and transferred to the appropriate Community bodies.*

The Social Affairs Council and the representatives of the Governments of the Member States adopted a resolution on racism and xenophobia on 29 May 1990. The draft resolution was criticized for confining itself to a recognition that certain legal measures at both institutional and administrative level could help to prevent acts inspired by racism or xenophobia. The resolution in the form adopted by the Council and the representatives of the Governments of the Member States, however, appears to fail to acknowledge the need for Community action to combat racism and xenophobia where the victims are European residents who are not Community nationals. This is a clear breach of the undertaking made in the declaration against Racism and Xenophobia, which specifically mentions 'workers who have their origins in other Member States or in third countries' and 'the Member State in which they legally reside'.

Recommendation 48: *That if necessary a supplementary declaration be adopted as soon as possible to the Council Declaration against Racism and Xenophobia, expressly to protect immigrants to the Community from third countries in the same way as citizens of the Member States of the Community, against racism and xenophobia of which they are particular victims.*

There are alarming racist and xenophobic tendencies apparent in certain European countries which are or are soon likely to become applicants for membership of the European Community. It is inconceivable that they should accede to membership without fully subscribing to the Community fight against racism and xenophobia.

Recommendation 49: *That a declaration be made that any country seeking to join the European Community must be committed to the European democratic traditions of tolerance, the elimination of all forms of discrimination connected with belonging or not belonging to an ethnic group, nation, race or religion, and be a signatory to the appropriate international and European conventions, and take steps to combat xenophobia and antisemitism with, if necessary, denazification measures, enabling that country to meet Community standards for the prevention and repression of racism and xenophobia.*

Council Directive 77/486/EEC on the education of the children of migrant workers, despite being in force for 13 years, has still not been fully implemented in all Member States.

Recommendation 50: *That proper and full implementation of Council Directive 77/486/EEC on the education of children of migrant workers be ensured in all Member States.*

The Member States

Ireland has recently adopted legislation outlawing incitement to racial hatred and therefore should now be in a position to sign the UN Convention on the Elimination of All Forms of Racial Discrimination.

Recommendation 51: *That the only Member State which has not already signed the UN Convention on the Elimination of all Forms of Racial Discrimination, do so as soon as possible.*

It is important that immigrants taking or facing legal proceedings should have the opportunity of being represented by an organization responsible for safeguarding the interests of their particular communities.

Recommendation 52: *That an anti-discrimination law be enacted condemning all racist acts and enabling legal persons such as* *associations to bring prosecutions for racist acts or appear as joint plaintiffs.*

The 1990 decision of the Court of Justice on the interpretation of Article 48.4 of the Treaty of Rome (employment in the public service) underlines the need for unnecessary restrictions on the employment of non-nationals in the public services to be removed.

Recommendation 53: *That Member States review their legislation concerning access to posts in the public sector in order to consider the possibility of opening such access, according to specific arrangements, to nationals of third countries who have legally resided in the Member State concerned for a sufficient period, with the exception of posts which participate in the exercise of public authority in that Member State.*

In some Member States, unacceptably long administrative delays in regularization of immigrants' status occur.

Recommendation 54: *That Member States take the necessary measures to ensure that the immigrant population has access within a reasonable period to legal status as residents and workers.*

Despite the Commission's assertion of Community competence on matters relating to the achievement of the Single Market, covering particularly the harmonization of asylum rules and all other matters relating to the removal of internal frontiers and the establishment of a Peoples' Europe, Member States proceeded to remove these issues from the Community forum and therefore from accountable democratic control by creating semi-clandestine groups such as TREVI and the Ad Hoc Group on Immigration. It is totally unacceptable that this lack of accountability should continue. Access to information by the individual concerned and respect for his/her privacy are important principles, and the Schengen Information System (see pp. 121–2), for example, has been criticized for not respecting them.

Recommendation 55: *That Member States abide by the undertakings they gave in the preamble to the Single European Act and pursue their* *activities related to the removal of internal frontiers within the framework of the Community institutions.*

The forthcoming Intergovernmental Conference provides an ideal opportunity for clarification of the Community's competence in matters relating to third-country nationals resident within the Community.

Recommendation 56: *That Member States ensure that the forthcoming Intergovernmental Conference decides to introduce explicitly into the Treaties clear competence relating to third-country nationals resident in the Community, as confirmed in the ruling of the Court of Justice of 9 July 1987.*

Particularly in urban areas, one of the major elements of disadvantage for immigrants is the quality of their accommodation, often lacking access to basic amenities and suffering from severe overcrowding.

Recommendation 57: *That Member States work against the ghettoization of their ethnic minorities and adapt their housing policies to provide inexpensive and adequate housing to encourage integration.*

Recommendation 58: *That Member States encourage rehabilitation programmes to improve public housing and living conditions in the cities with large immigrant populations.*

Women are far more likely to be discriminated against on the basis of their dependent status than are men. Moreover, migrant women are often the victims of double discrimination based on both their sex and their migrant status.

Recommendation 59: *That Member States consider tackling the problems of immigrants' partners and family members who lose their resident status through divorce or separation by granting them independent resident status after a period of two years in the country, and in the case of bereavement, by granting them such status irrespective of the period of residence, and in particular that the right of residence of immigrant women should no longer be dependent on that granted to the husband.*

In some Member States, existing provisions exclude those granted asylum from gainful employment for a period of up to two years, thus ensuring that they remain in a situation of extreme poverty.

Recommendation 60: *That Member States review and then abolish the provisions forbidding refugees from taking up work and thus creating or fostering grounds for illegal employment.*

The use and exploitation of a pool of clandestine labour undermines the social protection, health and safety and the security of employment of all workers and is therefore contrary to the provisions of the Social Charter. Moreover, it is very often the case that sanctions are applied against clandestine workers rather than those who illegally employ them.

Recommendation 61: *That Member States consider adopting legislative measures providing for severe legal sanctions against those who employ and exploit immigrants without legal resident status; the aim of such sanctions should be the punishment of those found guilty of exploitation and not the victims of it.*

Many Member States perhaps unwittingly place many barriers in the way of non-Community residents wishing to acquire nationality in the form of unduly complicated or expensive administrative procedures.

It is important that dual nationality be permitted (possibly with a distinction being made between 'active' and 'passive' citizenship). Failure to do so can discourage people from seeking to acquire a Community nationality because the break with their country of origin implies a break with their traditions and family ties, perhaps removal of the possibility of an eventual return to that country, and legal and other difficulties in some cases.

Recommendation 62: *That Member States adopt measures to permit the application for nationality by immigrants who have legally resided in the Community for a continuous period of five years, keeping the costs and administrative procedures to a minimum and permitting applicants for citizenship to maintain passive citizenship in their country of origin where loss of citizenship would entail problems in relation to ownership* *of property, inheritance, etc.; and to give those born in a Member State the nationality of that state at birth.*

If immigrants are to play a full part in the life of their communities, the ability to speak and write the language of their host community as swiftly as possible is essential.

Recommendation 63: *That member States create conditions enabling any immigrant with legal status to learn a language of the Member State of residence.*

Giving resident non-nationals the right to vote is a controversial matter. However, experience in several Member States and notably the United Kingdom and the Netherlands seems to indicate that according this right does not lead to any substantial change in political structures and has distinct benefits in helping to make these residents feel part of the community. It would therefore be desirable for Member States to examine the possibilities of according this right at least at local level, alongside implementing the draft directive granting voting rights in local elections to Community nationals.

The Dutch experience has shown that public opinion swings in favour of voting rights for foreigners after seeing these rights in operation.

Recommendation 64: *That Member States consider granting the right to vote and stand, at least in local elections, first to all Community citizens and then to all legal immigrants with five years' continuous residence in the country.*

Currently there are complaints of a lack of coordination in preparing, implementing and operating many legislative proposals having a direct or indirect influence on immigrant and minority populations.

Recommendation 65: *That Member States set up appropriate mechanisms responsible for monitoring the strict application of conventions, resolutions and directives and of legislation concerning acts of racism, antisemitism or xenophobia.*

Given the extent of the problems faced by gypsies and other travelling communities, and considerable discrimination against them both in the Community and now particularly in adjoining states, it is important provision should be made for them which respects their traditional patterns of migration.

Recommendation 66: *That Member States respect the traditional way of life of gypsy and other travelling communities, encouraging the provision of the necessary facilities to make this possible, at external frontiers as well as within the Community.*

It is often in the workplace that the problems of racial discrimination are at their most acute, and collective rather than individual action has often been proved to be the most effective. Full participation in collective bargaining would also help improve the general situation of all workers on low pay and with poor working conditions.

Recommendation 67: *That Member States encourage full and active participation by immigrant workers in trade unions.*

Considering the political aspect of racist crimes and the fact that they are in a sense the negation of the civic rights of their victims, it seems incongruous that the perpetrators of racist crimes sufficiently serious for a custodial sentence to have been imposed should be permitted to exercise full civic rights while they are serving such a sentence.

Recommendation 68: *That Member States tighten up their law to repress racism and antisemitism, and in particular take measures to ensure that those who are sentenced and imprisoned for such offenses are deprived of their civic rights for the period of detention.*

There is a common, often misguided, belief that persons of authoritarian and racist inclinations are attracted to employment in the police and customs authorities. Numerous complaints are received throughout the European Community about racist behaviour in these services.

Recommendation 69: *That Member States renew the instructions given to the various services responsible for carrying out checks to avoid any discriminatory harassment likely to suggest to the persons being checked that external characteristics pertaining to a particular race or category may have predisposed them to the checks concerned.*

A central aspect of tackling problems of racism, antisemitism and xenophobia lies largely within the competence of the Member States – education. It is vital that children should not absorb racist attitudes at school but that, on the contrary, they should learn about the benefits to be derived from living in a multicultural society.

Recommendation 70: *That all Member States undertake to fully and effectively implement the terms of Directive 77/486/EEC on the education of the children of migrant workers and to apply the Directive equally to the children of both Community and non-Community citizens resident in the Community.*

Recommendation 71: *That Member States introduce teaching against racism into the curriculum of their primary schools as a compulsory subject.*

Recommendation 72: *That Member States adopt policies enabling children from the majority population and from ethnic minorities to be educated together.*

Recommendation 73: *That Member States step up the support that education systems can provide for the campaign against racism, antisemitism and xenophobia through the teaching of human rights and history at school, through teacher training and through university research.*

Lack of information about immigrants' rights and about the bodies responsible for administering, monitoring and implementing legislation can often prove to be a barrier to alleviating discrimination.

Recommendation 74: *That Member States ensure that the persons concerned are better informed of the means available to them to oppose any discrimination to which they may be subject.*

The Foreign Ministers Meeting in European Political Cooperation

There has been considerable growth both in racist, antisemitic and xenophobic incidents and in the strength and number of extreme right-wing organizations in the countries of Eastern Europe. In considering its foreign policy links with these countries and ever-closer cooperation with them, the Community must seek to help them to resolve these problems.

Recommendation 75: *That the growth of racism, antisemitism and xenophobia in many countries of Eastern Europe be discussed in the light of the Community's relations with them.*

The ACP–EEC Joint Assembly adopted a resolution on 29 March 1990 assessing the need for the ACP states to be associated with the fight against racism and xenophobia in the Community, in particular as this involved citizens of ACP states. The foreign policy aspects of this must be carefully considered both in respect to the ACP states and the Community's attitude towards other states.

Recommendation 76: *That problems faced by non-Community nationals of ACP states and other states resident in the Community be examined in the light of the Community's relations with the ACP states (paying particular attention to the procedure for dialogue provided for in Lomé IV) and other states.*

There are alarming racist and xenophobic tendencies apparent in certain European countries which are or are likely shortly to become applicants for membership of the European Community. It is inconceivable that they should accede to membership without fully subscribing to the Community fight against racism and xenophobia. The foreign policy aspects of this must be carefully considered.

Recommendation 77: *That the Foreign Ministers meeting in Political Cooperation fully discuss the implications of the above recommendation that the Council make a declaration that any country seeking to join the European Community must be committed to the European democratic traditions of tolerance, the elimination of all forms of discrimination connected with belonging or not belonging to an ethnic group, nation, race or religion, and be a signatory to the appropriate international and European conventions, and take steps to combat xenophobia and antisemitism with, if necessary, denazification measures, enabling that country to meet Community standards for the prevention and repression of racism and xenophobia.*

Appendix 1
Written Evidence to the Committee of Inquiry

By Individual

Bovenkerk, Prof. Frank. Willem Pompe Instituut voor Strafrechtswetenschappen, Rijksuniversiteit te Utrecht
Chombart de Lauwe, Marie-José
Elss, Werner
Essed, Dr Philomena
Fisch, Jean-Albert
Jäger, Prof. Dr Siegfried
Jensen, Erik, & Sejersen, Jens
Pearsall, Phyllis

By Organization

Avrupa Milli Görüs Teskilatlari, Cologne, Germany
Agence Nationale pour L'Insertion et La Promotion des Travailleurs D'outre-mer, France
Associação Guineense de Solidariedade Social, Lisbon, Portugal
British Rommani Union, Great Britain
Commission for Racial Equality, London, Great Britain
The Danish Center of Human Rights, Copenhagen, Denmark
Folkebevægelsen mod Nazisme, Denmark
Irish in Britain Representation Group, Great Britain
Instituto de Estudios Islamicos, Lima, Peru
Joint Council for the Welfare of Immigrants, London, Great Britain
Mouvement contre Le Racisme, L'antisemitisme et La Xenophobie, Centre D'accueil Pour Immigrés, France

Nottingham & District Community Relations Council, Great Britain
The Organisation of International Human Relations, Brussels, Luxembourg
The Board of Deputies of British Jews, Great Britain

Documentation Received

Belgium

Belgian parliamentary documents (House of Representatives) (submitted by Mr Ernest Glinne)
Chambre des Représentants
Réunion publique de la Commission de l'Interieur des Affaires générales, de l'Education et de la Fonction publique – *compte rendu* analytique 17 janvier 1990
L'intégration: une politique de longue haleine
Vol. I: *repères et premières propositions*
Vol. II: *philosophies, politiques et opinions*
Vol. III: *données argumentaires*
Commissariat Royal à la politique des immigrés, novembre 1989

Denmark

A Guide to the Danish Refugee Council
December 1989
En asylsøgers vej igennem systemet – An Asylum Seeker's Way through the System
Edited by Dansk Flygtningehjælp
The Role of Airline Companies in the Asylum Procedure – Group of Experts under the Auspices of European Consultation on Refugees and Exiles (ECRE)
Edited by Dansk Flygtningehjælp
'Victims of Neutrality: Race Discrimination in Denmark'
Meredith Wilkie, *Nordic Journal of International Law, Acta scandinavica gentium*, pp. 4–87
'Kan det ske igen?', Povl. E. Nøragen, Udgivet af Folkebeægelsen mod Nazisme i samarbejde met Forlaget Tommeliden

Federal Republic of Germany

'Schulische Bildung der Kinder von Wanderarbeitnehmern' Modellversuchsprogramm der Europäischen Gemeinschaften, Landau 1989

Information from Aigali Dshunussow, National Executive member responsible for foreigners, SPD in der DDR, East Berlin, 6 February 1990

'Zwischen Toleranz und Besorgtheit – Einstellungen der deutschen Bevölkerung zu aktuellen Problemen der Ausländerpolitik – Vertraulich – Institut für Demoskopie Allensbach

'Public Beliefs about Anti-Jewish Attitudes in West Germany: A Case of "Pluralistic Ignorance"' by Werner Bergmann, *Patterns of Prejudice*, Vol. 22, No. 3, 1988

'Présentation de la politique et de la législation concernant les étrangers en République Fédérale d'Allemagne', Le Ministre Fédéral de l'Intérieur, situation: juillet 1989

'Arbeitsplatz Deutschland' Informationszeitschrift für ausländische Arbeitnehmer in der Bundesrepublik Deutschland

'Ausländer – Daten' Herausgegeben vom Bundesminister für Arbeit und Sozialordnung, Dezember 1989

'Situation der ausländischen Arbeitnehmer und ihrer Familienangehörigen in der Bundesrepublik Deutschland – Repräsentativuntersuchung '85' Der Bundesminister für Arbeit und Sozialordnung

'Faschismus, Rechtsextremismus, Sprache', von Siegfried Jäger, Duisburger Institut für Sprach- und Sozialforschung

'Rassismus. Zur Klärung eines Begriffs', Siegfried Jäger; Thesen zum Rechtsextremismus – Colloquium des DISS an 16–18 March 1990 in Radevormwald

France

French report to Rocard on Racism and Xenophobia: Recommendations – Conclusions

Texte d'une proposition pour lutter contre le racisme et l'antisémitisme, et moderniser la démocratie France Plus

Dossier de la section Marseille-Nord Sud
Ligue des droits de l'homme

Dossiers relatifs à des attentats racistes et au front national
MRAP

Dossiers relatifs à l'intégration des émigrés et aux agressions racistes à l'égard de la communauté algérienne et *Bulletin de l'association Amicale des Algériens en Europe*

Bilans, bulletin de l'association Fédération APAC

Dossier élaboré à l'occasion de la visite de la commission d'enquête par le Collectif Marseille Fraternité et les Verts

Brochure du CLAF

'Le Méridional', dossier remis par Radio Galère

Dossier relatif au scénario d'un film sur le racisme et l'intégration à Marseille
Mme Caroline Chomienne

Dossier remis à l'hôtel de région lors de la visite de la commission d'enquête à Marseille
Conseil régional

Dossiers remis par la municipalité lors de la visite des quartiers de Marseille:

- dossier de presse de la ville de Marseille
- dossier sur l'activité de l'office public d'HLM
- étude sur 'le sentiment et les réalités de l'insécurité à Frais-Vallon'
- publication de M. Parisis: 'Paroles de locataires 1919–1989'
- Mairie des 11ème et 12ème arrondissements: 'projets, escalades, métiers, espaces verts, parapentes. Données sur population, logement et emploi'
- Mission jeunes: dossier d'activités
- Maison de l'étranger: dossier d'activités

Dossier remis par Radio Gazelle

Immigration, Islam, Le problème des représentations, Université Paris 7, Ligue de l'Enseignement, et Centre de Documentation, Institut du Monde Arabe

Greece

Human Rights and Balkan Minority Treaties
George B. Zotiades, Thessalonika, 1968

Ireland

Racial Discrimination in Ireland: Realities & Remedies
A Harmony Report, Dublin, March 1990

Italy

Italian parliamentary documents

Luxembourg

Aspects demographiques de l'immigration
Bulletin du Statec, 1989
Devenez propriétaire! L'Etat vous aide!
Brochure éditée par le Service de l'immigration en collaboration avec le Service des Aides au Logement (Construction-Acquisition), 1988
Les prestations familiales au Grande-Duché de Luxembourg
Brochure éditée par la Caisse Nationale des Prestations Familiales du Grand Duché de Luxembourg, 1988
Projekt OECD/CERI und SIRP: 'Bildung und Migration in Luxemburg – Statische Bilanz: 2. Teil'
Courrier de l'Education Nationale
Ministère de l'Education Nationale et de la Jeunesse, octobre 1986
'A propos de "l'Année des Droits de l'Homme": textes et commentaires'
Courrier de l'Education Nationale,
Ministère de l'Education Nationale, octobre 1978

Netherlands

Minderhedennota
Tweede Kamer der Staten-Generaal, Nederland, Zitting 1982–1983 – Nr. 16102
Overzicht onderzoek minderheden
Adviescommissie Onderzoek Minderheden (ACOM), Ministerie van Binnenlandse Zaken Nederland, juli 1985
Onderzoek minderheden in opdracht van de Rijksoverheid,

Ministerie van Binnenlandse Zaken Nederland, mei 1984 en november 1986

Onderzoek etnische minderheden
Bibliografie samengesteld door de Adviescommissie Onderzoek Minderheden
(ACOM), Ministerie van Binnenlandse Zaken Nederland, juli 1989

Allochtonenbeleid
Wetenschappelijke Raad voor het Regeringsbefeid, Rapport aan de Regering Nr 36, 1989, Nederland

Een beter beleid?
Commentaar op het rapport 'Allochtonenbeleid' van de WRR, september 1989

Minderheid – Minder recht?
Ministerie van Justitie, Nederland, 1983

Een eerlijke kans
F. Bovenkerk, Ministerie van Binnenlandse Zaken, Ministerie van Sociale Zaken en Werkgelegenheid, februari 1986

Overheid, Godsdienst en Levensovertuiging
Eindrapport van de Commissie van adviez inz. de criteria voor steunverlening aan kerkgenootschappen en andere genootschappen op geestelijke grondslag, Nederland, maart 1988

Petitie en Memorandum: Een sociaal Europa voor iedereen
Adviesraad Buitenlanders, Gemeente Den Haag, Nederland, oktober 1989

Minderheden in Nederland, Statistisch vademecum 1989
Centraal Bureau voor de Statistiek en Instituut voor sociologisch-economisch onderzoek, Nederland

Actieprogramma minderhedenbeleid 1990
Tweede Kamer der Staten-Generaal, vergaderjaar 1989–1990

'Naar omstandigheden redelijk'
Rapport van de Evaluatiecommissie van de Landelijke Advies- en Overlegstructuur Minderhedenbeleid (LAO), Ministerie van Binnenlandse Zaken, Nederland, April 1988

Portugal

O projecto 'Nô djunta môn', projecto integrado de educação de base nas áreas de alfabetização, saúde, planeamento familiar
Associação Caboverdeana, Lisboa

Associação Guieense de Solidariedade Social, Lisboa
Assembleia Da República, Lisboa

Spain

'Normativa española vigente sobre protección del principio de igualdad frente a discriminaciones de carácter racista o xenófobo'
Ministerio del Interior, Secretaría General Técnica

United Kingdom

Unequal Migrants: The European Communities on Equal Treatment of Migrants and Refugees,
Report from the Joint Council for the Welfare of Immigrants, ed. Don Flynn
New Right, New Racism,
Paul Gordon and Francesca Klug, Searchlight Publication, London, 1986
The Other Face of Terror: Inside Europe's Neo-Nazi Network, by Ray Hill, with Andrew Bell, Grafton Books, London, 1988
'Linked By a Common Thread'
Video presented to the Committee of Inquiry on the Growth of Racism and Fascism
Migrants Film and Video Collective
Institute of Race Relations:
- Catalogue
- Bulletin No. 58 (Media Research Project)
- Bulletin No. 59
- Code of Practice (for the elimination of racial discrimination and the promotion of equality of opportunity in employment)
- Code of Practice (for the elimination of racial discrimination in education)

Indian Workers' Association, London
- 'The Regeneration of Racism'

Irish in Britain Representation Group about a policy on anti-Irish racism, ed. Patrick Reynolds PEO OBRG

Searchlight
- *From Ballots to Bombs: The Inside Story of the National Front's Political Soldiers*, January 1989

The Southall Day Centre, Hounslow
- Annual report 1988/1989

Ealing Family Housing Association Racial Harassment Casework Report (Casework to December 1989)
Ealing Family Housing Association – annual report 1988–1989

Sunrise Radio – Hounslow

Letter of Waltham Forest NALGO 'Black Workers Group to all black workers' referred to by Ms Goldsmith (assistant to Mr Tebbitt, ex-minister – Cons.)

Copies of *Asian Times* and *Caribbean Times* collected at Selby Centre

Patterns of Prejudice – Vol. 23, No. 3
- Anthony M. Messina: 'Anti-Immigrant Illiberalism and the "New" Ethnic Minorities in Western Europe'

Institute of Jewish Affairs
- Research Report Nos 2 and 3, 1990, No. 1, 1990, No. 7, 1989
- Report of Activities – July 1988–December 1989

Home Office (Minister John Patten)
- Immigration and Nationality Department – Policy Statement of race relations
- Circular Instruction 32/1986 – To all Prison Department Establishments (Race Relations)
- Home Office Circular No. 75/88 – Probation Service policies on race
- Home Office Notice 23/1989 – Working procedures – Equal Opportunity Proofing
- Home Office News Release – 'Muslims in Britain Today' by John Patten
- Home Office News Release – 'On Being British' by John Patten
- Home Office Circular No. 84/1989 – Magistrates' Courts service policies on race
- Home Office Circular No. 87/1989 – Equal opportunities policies in the police service
- Home Office Circular No. 33/1990 – Ethnic minority recruitment into the police service

- Home Office Circular No. 42/1990 – Government reply to the Home Affairs Committee report on racial attacks and harassment
- Section 11 of the Local Government Act 1966 – Grant Administration: proposals (+ annex C)
- Report of the Inter-Departmental Racial Attacks Group: 'The response to racial attacks and harassment: guidance for the statutory agencies'

Office of Population Censuses and Surveys (OPCS)
- Press notice: Government decides on ethnic group questions for 1991 census

House of Commons Home Affairs Committee
- 'Racial Attacks and Harassment'

House of Lords Select Committee on the European Communities
- '1992: Border Control of People'

KAAMYABI
- '1992 & the Black Community'

Eastern Europe

'Accordez des droits à la plus grande minorité d'Europe'
SOS Transylvanie – Comité de Genève et Hungarian Human Rights Foundation
Committee for Human Rights in Romania
Genève, New York, December 1989

European Commission

'Libre circulation des persones dans la communauté'
par Jean-Claude Seche (Commission Européenne)

Council of Europe

'Need to combat resurgent fascist propaganda and its racist aspects', Report by Robet Krieps

United Nations

Reports on the International Convention for the Elimination of all forms of Racial Discrimination (CERD)

General Documentation

Internationaal Instituut voor Sociale Geschiedenis/Stichting Historische Racisme Studies
- 'Racism and the Labour Market', D. Van Arkel and R.C. Kloosterman

Beate Ritter
- 'Racism and Xenophobia against Migrants in Europe'

Lillian Mumbua Kitusa
- 'Race Relations in the European Community' (transmitted by Ian White, MEP)

Appendix 2
Resolution on the Report by the Committee of Inquiry into Racism and Xenophobia (1)

The European Parliament, having regard to the report of its Committee of Inquiry into Racism and Xenophobia (A3-195/90):

1. Resolves to give effect to the recommendations to the European Parliament contained therein;
2. Calls on the Commission, the Council, the Foreign Ministers meeting in European Political Cooperation and the governments of the Member States to study in detail the recommendations contained in the report of its Committee of Inquiry;
3. Undertakes to publish and distribute widely the report in the Member States, including at local and regional level, and calls on the Commission and Council to do the same;
4. Instructs its President to forward this resolution and the report of its Committee of Inquiry with the recommendations contained therein to the Council, the Commission, the Foreign Ministers meeting in European Political Cooperation and the governments of the Member States.

Appendix 3
Resolution on the Report by the Committee of Inquiry into Racism and Xenophobia (2)

The European Parliament, having regard to Oral Questions with debate B3-1327 and 1329/90 on the recommendations of the Committee of Inquiry and the Commission's response,

- having regard to the findings of the Committee of Inquiry into Racism and Xenophobia,
- having regard to the Joint Declaration against Racism and Xenophobia of 11 June 1986,

A. having noted the recommendations set out in the Committee of Inquiry's report,

B. whereas particular vigilance is required to prevent any threat of racism and xenophobia becoming more widespread in Europe:

1. Approves the appropriate measures which will enable the Community's specific role in this field to be strengthened alongside national bodies and welfare and religious authorities;
2. Takes the view that a solution must also be sought in a wide-ranging programme encompassing employment, housing, education and the development of harmonious coexistence at grass-roots level;
3. Calls, accordingly, on the Commission, Council and other Community institutions, as well as on the governments and parliaments of the Member States, to work towards that goal and calls more specifically on its Committee on Budgets to enter in the budget at an early date the budget headings proposed in the Committee of Inquiry's recommendations;
4. Instructs its President to forward this resolution to the Commission, the Council and the other Community institutions and to the governments and parliaments of the Member States.

Afterword: 1992 and Beyond

The political watershed embodied in the 1992 process in Western Europe, combined with the tumultuous events throughout Eastern Europe, have served to magnify the problem now posed to the entire European continent by racism and xenophobia.

Since the conclusion in July 1990 of the Committee of Inquiry's investigation, the trends outlined in the foregoing chapters have, all too unfortunately, continued. In parliamentary terms there have been further electoral victories for the extreme right. In extra-parliamentary terms there have been marked increases in the violent expressions of racial hostility.

If the 'New Europe' is to avoid nurturing the anti-democratic and exclusionary culture of racism, then this phenomenon must be resolutely tackled at an institutional level. To this end, following the recommendations of the Ford Report, the European Parliament set up a new Committee on Internal Affairs and Civil Liberties which first met in January 1992.

The remit of the committee broadly encompasses the 'third pillar' of the Maastricht Treaty signed in December 1991, of which one of the most pressing concerns is the agreement for a common immigration and asylum policy by the beginning of January 1993. The committee will additionally consider the problems of racism and xenophobia on a day-to-day basis with the intention of producing annual reports on racism.

However, one of the foremost aims of this report has been to identify, not simply the action being taken in this field, but perhaps more importantly, the action *not* being taken at a local, national and European level. In this sense the preceding chapters represent a handbook for action along cross-political lines.

The members of the Committee of Inquiry were drawn from across the political spectrum (with the exception of the extreme right/neo-fascists).

It is telling to note that the broad trends documented within the report (specifically an increase in the power and *influence* of the extreme right, and a corresponding shift in the politics of the traditional right) were actually reflected in the final vote itself within committee in so far as the traditional right found itself split five ways, displaying considerable disarray: Mr Nordmann (LDR – Liberal) voted against; Ms Fontaine (EPP – Christian Democrat) abstained; Mr Nianias (RDE – The European Democratic Alliance) voted in favour; Mr Cooney (EPP) refused to participate; and members of the EDG (British Conservatives) refused to be present at all, requesting in fact that a Liberal member be allowed to vote for them.

The European Parliament adopted the report in the October plenary session of 1990. The follow-up debate a year later in October 1991 confirmed, on the one hand, the trends outlined in the report, and on the other, the lack of action taken by the Community institutions. Only two groups voted against: the European British Conservatives (the European Democratic Group), and the extreme right/neo-fascists (the Technical Group of the European Right).

Just one month later in November the Belgian elections provided a grim example of political advantage sought through blatantly racist propaganda. The leaflets distributed throughout Brussels by the PRL, the Belgian (Francophone) Liberals, amounted to nothing less than a thinly-veiled incitement to racial hatred. In Antwerp the Vlaams Blok (an extreme right Flemish nationalist party) won 25 per cent of the vote, becoming the largest party.

The elections illustrated the extent to which the parties of the traditional right throughout Europe have succoured xenophobic sentiment and succumbed, willingly or otherwise, to the racist backwash of the extreme right.

In France, former President Giscard d'Estaing, smarting from the electoral success of the Front National and its leader Jean-Marie Le Pen, has found it expedient to declaim the 'immigrant' population, and continues to rail against the 'invasion'. He has called for the 200-year-old 'law of the soil' (*jus solis*), by which anyone born in France has a right to French citizenship, to be replaced by the 'law of blood' (*jus sanguinis*), requiring French parentage. This would preclude, for example, French citizenship from all those born in France to Moroccan parents.

Giscard d'Estaing has justified his stance by hinting privately that his own xenophobic position will encourage racist voters to pledge their support to him rather than Le Pen, avoiding any need to negotiate with a stronger Front National after the next elections.

General fear and uncertainty towards the future across Europe have resulted in political polarization, ethnic division, outpourings of nationalist fervour and, of course, the marginalization of the easily-targeted immigrant communities. Politicians of all persuasions remain wary of tackling legislative deficiencies for fear of exciting the toxic nationalism so expertly guided by the ideologues of the extreme right.

Tory ministers in Britain now privately claim that Britain's racist immigration policies throughout the 1980s have served to forestall the rise of a British Le Pen.

Mr Le Pen himself declares there are 'one million immigrants too many', and then gladly listens to his political opponents, lured into a debate on his own terms, argue that 'no, no, Mr Le Pen is wrong, there are only *half* a million immigrants too many.' In this respect he and others like him have been successful in redrawing the parameters of debate.

Le Pen's politics have not changed dramatically since 1979 when he stood in the European elections and received 0.3 per cent of the vote, and the two subsequent European elections in 1984 and 1989 when he received 10 and 11 per cent of the vote respectively and ten members of parliament. It is instead the political climate that has changed. Since 1984 he has been able to utilize the political platform afforded him by electoral success, and as a result is no longer merely a *symptom* of racism and xenophobia, but now also a *cause*.

In Germany the governing Christian Democrats have called for a change in the Constitution granting automatic asylum to political refugees, on the grounds of immigration control. Proposals have included, amongst other things, the construction of special camps to contain asylum-seekers.

The EC's '13th State', comprising between 12 and 14 million ethnic minority residents and immigrants, continues to languish with virtually no protection from race discrimination legislation. Where legislation exists, notably Britain, a lack of effective enforcement machinery has led to a long history of judicial inaction in areas where racism remains a daily phenomenon.

After the 1992 process is complete there will be *de facto* rather than *de jure* free movement around the Community. Unemployed EC residents, like EC citizens, will inevitably gravitate towards centres of economic activity, but once there, their status will be transformed from legal EC resident to illegal immigrant. These illegal immigrants, like the ones currently unprotected by legislation, will face social, political and economic exploitation.

The maintenance of a pool of exploited illegal workers undermines the social provisions covering minimum health and safety regulations, hours of work, and rates of pay that the Social Charter seeks to guarantee. Thus, in order to protect *all* Europeans, *all* European residents must have the same rights and duties. In simple terms, harmonization must occur in both the economic *and* the social sphere. Moreover, the latter is able to influence positively the former. After all, in Britain it is not the low-wage, low-skill economies of Greece or Portugal that strike fear into the heart of British industry. It is the high-wage, high-skill economies of Germany and Japan.

Moving forwards into the post-1992 Europe, we must be clear that this date, set aside as it has been for history, may either mark the beginning of hope or the commencement of fear. We must not allow the code-word '1992' to be used as a tool in the construction of Fortress Europe. Racism is not merely scientifically fallacious and morally bankrupt. It is politically dangerous. Moreover it only serves to benefit a small coterie of intellectual and ideological racists and neo-fascists who bargain with the politics of hate.

The American neo-nazi leader George Lincoln Rockwell was well aware of this when he astutely observed that 'the easiest thing in the world to sell is hatred.' This is an ominous augury for all those involved in building a frontier-free Europe, and surely one which cannot afford to be ignored.

Glyn Ford
February 1992

Notes

Chapter 1

1. Details of Committee membership are as follows: Mr Elliott, Mr Ford, Mr Kneps, Mr Rothley, Mrs Van Hemeldonck and Mrs Mebrak-Zaïdi on behalf of the Socialist Group, Mr Cooney, Mrs Fontaine and Mr Garcia Amigo on behalf of the EPP Group, Mr Nordmann on behalf of the LDR Group, Lord Bethell on behalf of the ED Group, Mrs Tazdaït on behalf of the Green Group, Mrs Valent on behalf of the EUL Group, Mr Nianias on behalf of the RDE Group and Mrs Elmalan on behalf of the CG. The groups also appointed the following substitute members: Mr Avgerinos, Mr Baget Bozo, Mrs Belo, Mr Christiansen, Mr Glinne, Mr Ramirez Heredia, Mrs d'Ancona (all Socialists), Mrs Cassanmagnago Cerretti, Mrs Oomen-Ruijten, Mr Saridakis, Mr von Stauffenberg (all EPP), Mr Wijsenbeek (LDR), Mr Prag (ED), Mrs Roth (Green) and Mrs Domingo Segarra (EUL). Mrs d'Ancona, who became a minister in the Dutch government in November 1989, was replaced by Mrs van Putten (Soc.). Towards the end of the Committee's appointed term Mrs Elmalan was replaced by Mr de Rossa (Left Unity Group). Taken as a whole the members of the Committee and their substitutes represent all the nationalities of the European Community.
2. At its constituent meeting the Committee also elected Mr Jean-Thomas Nordmann Chairman, Mrs Djida Tazdaït first Vice-Chairman and Mrs Nicole Fontaine second Vice-Chairman.
3. The participants were as follows: *Belgium*: Mr Bruno Vinikas, Acting Royal Commissioner for Immigration Policy, Brussels; *Denmark*: Mr Hans Jensen, Head of Division, Ministry of Justice, Copenhagen; *Federal Republic of Germany*: Mr Titus Kokai and Mr Jürgen Haberland, Chiefs of Section at the Ministry of the Interior, Bonn; *France*: Mr Louis Joinet, Adviser in the Prime Minister's Private Office, Paris; *Greece*: Mr Konstantinos Economidis, head of the legal service of the Ministry of Foreign Affairs, Athens; *Spain*: Mr Victor Moreno Catena, Secretary-General (technical) of the Ministry of the Interior, Madrid; *Ireland*: Mr Cathal Crowley, Assistant Secretary of the Ministry of Justice and Mr P. Murray, Principal Assistant at the same ministry, Dublin; *Italy*: Mr Antonio Cavaterra, head of the Aliens Section of the Emigrations Directorate of the Ministry of Foreign Affairs, Rome; *Luxembourg*: Mr Michel Neyens, adviser at the Ministry of Family Affairs, Luxembourg; *Netherlands*: Mr Henk Molleman, Director, minorities policy, Ministry of the Interior, The

Hague; *Portugal*: Mr Antonio Gomes Lourenço Martins, deputy Attorney-General, and Mr Vernelho Curral, Director of the Aliens and Frontier Department of the Ministry of Foreign Affairs, Lisbon; *United Kingdom*: Mr Richard Fries, Assistant Under-Secretary of State at the Home Office, London.

4. The participants were as follows: Mrs Nora Rathzel and Mrs Annita Kalpaka, Institut für Migrations- und Rassismusforchung (Institute for Research into Migration and Racism), Hamburg; Mr Alf Dubs (The British Refugee Council), London; Mr Walter Jansen, Assistant Director of the Nederlands Centrum (Dutch Centre for Foreigners), Utrecht; Mr Abdelatif Imad, Mr Ahmed Benyachi and Mr Moussa, Mémoire Fertile (Fertile Memory), Paris; Mr Kiticki, Mr Gnomis F. Gnaty and Mr T. Safu, representatives of the Organisation Unitaire des Syndicats Africains (Organization of African Trade Unity), Paris; Professor Hakki Keskin, representative of the Bündnis Türkischer Einwanderer (Association of Turkish immigrants), Hamburg; Mr Bob Cools, Mayor of Antwerp; Mrs Laura Balbo, President of Italia Razzismo (an Italian race relations organization), Rome; Mr Perez, Deputy Secretary-General of Union Romani (Romany Union), Barcelona; Mr Arne Piel Christensen, Secretary-General of Dansk Flygtningehjaelp (Danish Refugee Council), Copenhagen; Mrs Youtopoulou-Marangopoulou, President of the Marangopoulos Human Rights Foundation, Athens; Mrs Sabine Missistrano, president of the francophone section of the Belgian League of Human Rights, Brussels; Mr J. Lapeyre, Secretary-General of the Confédération Européenne des Syndicats (European Trade Union Confederation), Brussels; Mr Francisco Tomar, president of the Associação Caboverdeana (Cape Verdean Association), Lisbon.
5. The same is true of the reply (dated 7 September 1990) by the Italian Government to a letter (dated 11 April 1990) from the Committee Chairman, Mr Nordmann, to the Italian Foreign Minister, Mr de Michelis, in connection with comments by the Italian Vice-Premier, Mr Claudio Martelli, concerning the deployment of the Italian army against clandestine immigration in the country.
6. The following voted in favour: Mrs Tazdaït, first Vice-Chairman; Mr Ford, rapporteur, Mrs Belo (deputizing for Mr Krieps), Mr De Rossa, Mr Elliott, Mr Glinne (deputizing for Mrs Mebrak-Zaïdi), Mr Nianias, Mr Rothley, Mrs Valent and Mrs Van Hemeldonck. Mr Nordmann, Chairman, voted against. Mrs Fontaine, second Vice-Chairman, abstained. Mr Cooney declined to take part in the vote.

Chapter 3

1. Some of the most blatant cases of discrimination include the ruling in the Gravier Case on 13.2.85 when Belgium was condemned for requiring foreign students, including EC nationals, to pay a supplementary registration fee for tertiary education, the 'minerval'. Following its reluctance to comply with the Court's ruling, Belgium was condemned again on 3.2.88 in three new rulings of the Court of Justice against the payment of the 'minerval' (see *Migration Newssheet*, May 1987 and March 1988). In matters of family allowances, France was ordered by the Court on 15.1.86 (the Pinna Case, No.

44/84) to put an end to the discrimination system of paying Community migrant workers a lower family allowance if the children reside in the country of origin. In the face of France's persistent refusal to comply, the matter dragged on until 13.6.89 at a meeting of the 'Social Affairs' Council when a compromise was reached between France and the 11 other Member States (see *Migration Newssheet*, July 1989). On 16.6.87, it was Italy's turn to be condemned for discriminating against EC nationals in so-called public service jobs by granting EC citizens limited two-year contracts at the National Research Council whereas their Italian colleagues received permanent ones (see *Migration Newssheet*, July 1989). The situation is worse in Belgium where simple, ordinary posts in the public sector are also reserved for Belgian nationals (see *Le Soir*, 6.4.90). Until the Court's ruling on 18.5.89, the Federal Republic of Germany was abusing the application of a 1968 EEC directive stipulating that EEC nationals must have decent lodgings to obtain a residence permit. The authorities there sometimes inspected the lodgings again when the permit was up for renewal.

2. Continuing his reply to the question raised by Mr Thomas Maher (LDR, Ireland), Mr Sutherland said that 'it would be preferable that complaints be made through the petition procedure' (see *Migration Newssheet*, July 1987). At the hearing of the Committee of Inquiry on 3 May 1990, the Commissioner for Social Affairs and Employment, Ms V. Papandreou, acknowledged that very few EC nationals were aware of the petition procedure.
3. In the Single European Act, the 12 Member States voice their determination 'to work together to promote democracy on the basis of fundamental rights recognized in the constitutions and laws of the Member States, in the Convention for the Protection of Human Rights and Fundamental Freedoms and the European Social Charter, notably freedom, equality and social justice'.
4. Quoted from a lawyer participating in a colloquy 'Law and Discrimination', held on 19–20.6.87 in Paris, organized by human rights associations such as MRAP and LICRA to evaluate the 15 years of the application of the 1.7.1972 law against racism (*Le Monde*, 26.6.87).
5. Report on the conference on 'New Expressions of Racism – Growing Areas of Conflict in Europe', held in the Amsterdam City Hall on 19–21.10.87. Issued by the Netherlands Institute of Human Rights (SIM), Utrecht, Special Issue No. 7. Equally informative are the following publications: A. Spire (ed.), *Vous avez dit Fascismes?*, Ed. Montalba, Paris, 1984; P. Gordon and F. Klug, *New Right, New Racism*, Searchlight Publication, London, 1986; various authors, *The New Right, Image and Reality*, Runnymede Trust Publication, London, 1986.
6. Chapour Haghighat, *Racisme 'Scientifique' – Offensive contre l'égalité sociales*, Ed. L'Harmattan, Paris, 1988; Michael Billig, *Psychology, Racism & Fascism*, Searchlight Booklet, A.F. & R. Publications, Birmingham.
7. Eurobarometer, Public Opinion in the European Community, Special issue on 'Racism and Xenophobia', Commission of the EC, November 1989.
8. Working Document by Mr E. Glinne (PE 139.226).
9. Working Document by Mrs M. van Hemeldonck (PE 139.154).
10. S. Lucki, 'Le racisme et sa répression dans la loi belge', in *MRAX Information*, No. 58, March 1990.
11. See note 9.

12. *Solidaire* (18.4.90), Brussels.
13. Mr Pepermans, an MP (Agalev) expressed surprise at the speed at which the 'victim', Mr H. Simonet, an MP of the Parti Réformateur Libéral (PRL) obtained satisfaction (*Le Soir*, 4.12.87).
14. *Le Soir*, 10.3.88.
15. The recorded statement of Mr Michel (Parti Social-Chrétien – PSC) was: 'We risk being like the Romans – invaded by barbarians. The barbarians are the Moroccans, Turks, Yugoslavs, the Islamic people. . . You cannot call them anything else. They are people who come from very far away and who have nothing in common with our civilization' (*Migration Newssheet*, December 1987).

    One of the many unsuccessful cases concerns a complaint filed by an anti-racist association against the extreme-right association, DELTA, whose posters and text speak of non-Europeans who 'invade and attack Belgians who will soon cease to exist'. The Brussels Court of Appeal simply judged DELTA to be 'discourteous' (*Migration Newssheet*, October 1987).
16. See note 9.
17. *La Libre Belgique*, 30.1.90; *Le Soir*, 1.2.90.
18. *Le Soir*, 2.2.90.
19. *Migration Newssheet*, February and March 1987.
20. For details, see: *La Libre Belgique*, 2., 17., 25.11.89; *Le Soir*, 3., 8., 18/19., 23.11.89; *De Standaard*, 14., 18., 17.11.89 and 2., 3.12.89.
21. After leaving the PRL, he formed his own list with the acronym, NOLS – Nouvelle Organisation de Libération de Schaarbeek.
22. This Socialist mayor, Mr C. Picque, is also against banning the notice 'The owner reserves the right of entry' on the front door or window of restaurants, bars, etc. which is quite often used as a pretext to refuse entry to foreigners. He considers it indispensable for owners to keep out drunkards (*Le Soir*, 7.4.88). He was also one of the two authors of a policy document submitted to the Brussels Federation of the Socialist Party (adopted on 16.6.87 with 159 in favour, 2 against and 30 abstentions) calling for, *inter alia*, a halt to all forms of immigration, tougher measures to expel irregulars and delinquents (of foreign origin), spreading out of the immigrant populations and strict control of Islamic religious lessons to combat fundamentalism, as well as the refusal of voting rights for foreign residents. In addition, the authors accuse the right-wing parties of having been too soft in dealing with expulsions (see *Migration Newssheet*, July 1987).
23. *Migration Newssheet*, December 1989 and February 1990. The Ministry of Education had not only refrained from taking action, but also provided other boroughs with a pretext to take a similar measure. According to this Ministry, a royal decree of 3.5.78 provided for the setting up of committees to supervise temporal matters of recognized Islamic communities. As this decree has never been implemented, local authorities can claim 'not to be concerned by the agreement between the National Ministry of Education and the Islamic and Cultural Centre in Brussels on Islamic religious courses in local schools (See also: *Le Soir*, 4.4.89, and *Migration Newssheet*, May 1989).
24. *Migration Newssheet*, July 1986.
25. *Migration Newssheet*, October 1986.
26. *Le Soir*, 28.4.88.
27. *La Libre Belgique*, 2.5.88.

28. *Le Soir*, 16.12.88.
29. *Le Soir*, 10. and 18./19.6.88. Mr Nols's departure brought no real changes: this borough's council voted a new rule in June 1989 making it illegal as from 23.6.89 for public places, cafés, restaurants, shops, etc. to put up signs in a non-EC language under the pretext of favouring integration. The Council claimed that non-EC language signs 'cannot be understood by the Belgian population and will not fail to create an atmosphere of aggression and insecurity and that is excessively harmful to public tranquillity and to the upkeep of good order in public places'. This rule had to be withdrawn as it violated Article 23 of the Belgian Constitution, Articles 10 and 14 of the European Convention on Human Rights and Article 23 of the UN Convention on Political and Civil Rights (see *Migration Newssheet*, July 1989).
30. In reality, the overwhelming majority of foreigners is not affected by this law. It gave rise quite often to undue fears and has had the perverse effect of discouraging immigrants from moving, as they were afraid of being refused registration elsewhere, thereby aggravating the concentration of immigrants, which the law aimed to avoid! Derogations were made in many cases and the victims have mainly been poor foreigners and asylum-seekers (*La Libre Belgique*, 26.4.90: *Le Soir*, 18., 26., 27.4.90).
31. *Le Soir*, 21./22.4.90.
32. *La Libre Belgique*, 18.4.90.
33. *Le Soir*, 10.5.90; *La Libre Belgique*, 10., 11.5.90.
34. *Le Soir*, 29./30.9.87.
35. *Le Soir*, 5.8.88.
36. Vlaams Blok received a total of 23 council seats in Flanders. It received 17.7 per cent of the votes in Antwerp, giving it ten seats on the city's council. The Nieuwe Partij (the 'New Party' which existed officially only for the election), even more extreme, gained 1 per cent of the votes (about 2,600) in Antwerp. Unlike other national front movements, Vlaams Blok is not antisemitic, at least according to the official party line (see *Migration Newssheet*, November 1988).
37. The Royal Commissioner for Immigration and her Deputy were appointed by Royal Decree on 7 March 1990.
38. The report is entitled, 'L'intégration, une politique de longue haleine'.
39. Statement by Mr Bruno Vinikas, the Belgian representative to the Committee of Inquiry at the meeting held in Brussels on 30 January 1990 (PE 139.432).
40. Meredith Wilkie, *Racial Discrimination in Denmark*, Danish Centre for Human Rights, Copenhagen, 1990.
41. Working document by Mr E.H. Christiansen (PE 139.296). Paragraph 266b states: 'Anyone who publicly or with the intention of dissemination to a wider audience expresses an opinion or makes any other statement threatening, insulting or degrading a group of persons on the grounds of their race, colour, national or ethnic origin, religion or sexual orientation shall be punishable with a fine, detention or imprisonment for up to two years'.
42. *Migration Newssheet*, August 1986.
43. *Migration Newssheet*, June 1989. 'The Danish Supreme Court did not find that the interests of freedom of expression on topics and events of general concern were such as to warrant acquittal when confronted with the interests of protection from racial discrimination' (see also contribution by Mr Hans Jensen – PE 140.241).

44. Christiansen, see note 41. Immigrants have also been victims of systematic harassment, including threatening letters and phone calls. In 1987 in the Østerbro quarter of Copenhagen, the police were unable to keep such racist gangs under control and the immigrants had to resettle in other parts of the city (see *Migration Newssheet*, June 1987).
45. Christiansen, see note 41.
46. There are at present 15 as the position of the 16th member depends on the outcome of criminal charges that are pending.
47. *Migration Newssheet*, June 1988.
48. *Migration Newssheet*, June 1990.
49. *Politiken*, 17.4.88.
50. *Migration Newssheet*, August 1989.
51. Christiansen, see note 41. See also Chapter 2, p. 12 above.
52. *Vinduet*, 5.4.90, Copenhagen.
53. *Migration Newssheet*, October 1987, April 1988 and February and August 1989.
54. *Migration Newssheet*, April 1988.
55. Art 1(1) states: 'The dignity of man shall be inviolable. To respect and protect it shall be the duty of all State authority' and, according to Art 3(3): 'No one may be prejudiced or favoured because of his sex, his parentage, his race, his language, his homeland and origin, his faith, or his religious or political opinions.'
56. Statement by Mr Haberland (PE 139.276).
57. Working document by Mrs C. Roth (PE 139.279).
58. For example, on 1 July 1986, a Hamburg court sentenced a band of skinheads to prison terms ranging from three and a half to ten years for the murder of a Turkish worker in December 1985. Although the band had proven links with extreme right-wing groups in Hamburg, the judge refused to accept the view that the killing was racially motivated and ruled that, in his view, revenge was the main motive. (*Frankfurter Allgemeine Zeitung* and *Süddeutsche Zeitung*, 1., 2.7.86.)
59. *Tageszeitung*, 26.8.88; *Stuttgarter Zeitung*, 30.6.88 and 1.7.88; *Stuttgarter Nachrichten*, 28.6.88.
60. *Frankfurter Rundschau* and *Süddeutsche Zeitung*, 16.1.89.
61. See note 57.
62. *Ganz Unten* ('The Lowest of the Low') was the result of two years of 'undercover work' during which he disguised himself as a Turkish worker (called 'Ali'), accepting all kinds of 'dirty jobs', as well as dangerous assignments. He not only had a number of lawsuits filed against him by firms who had employed 'Ali', but also received numerous death threats, not to mention the bugging and the wiretapping of his telephone. He was eventually obliged to leave the FRG to take up residence in the Netherlands, near the Dutch–German border.
63. One example among many is that of a Turkish resident in the FRG for 16 years who was sentenced to two and a half years' imprisonment. After 20 months, he was released for good behaviour, only to be deported, leaving behind his wife and children (see *Migration Newssheet*, February 1987). Many non-EC families, mainly Turkish, have also been affected by the Federal Government's decision of 2.12.81, recommending certain criteria to the Federal States with the aim of restricting the immigration of spouses of foreigners in the FRG. The partner in the FRG would have to have lived there

for eight years and the marriage to have been of at least one year's duration. The States of Bavaria and Baden-Württemberg, however, increased the marriage period requirement to three years. In November 1987, the Federal Constitutional Court decided that a three-year period was too long a time for a spouse to wait to unite with his/her married partner and that such a requirement was against the Constitution. The Government of Bavaria, however, refused to inform foreigners of the Court's decision, claiming that the persons concerned could learn from social workers and their own news service (see *Süddeutsche Zeitung*, 11.12.87, and *Migration Newssheet*, January 1988).

64. Article on the 4th World Romany Congress, held in Warsaw in *The Economist*, 21.4.90.
65. *Migration Newssheet*, December 1986.
66. Black people were victims of Nazi persecution in the same way as gypsies and Jews. Now they are suffering from 'social death' by being ignored by society. See *Frankfurter Rundschau*, 9.12.86. They have their own publication called *Afrekete* (Friesenstr. 12, D-2800 Bremen, FRG).
67. These video games have commentaries like 'Play in Treblinka', 'Clean society of all parasites', 'When the gas has accomplished its work, you will have won'. The player gains points by 'killing' Jews, Turks, homosexuals and ecologists with the sound of 'Deutschland über alles' (*La Libre Belgique*, 26./27.3.89).
68. These games portray Turks as 'dangerous non-Aryans' who destroy society. One of the ways to destroy them is the concentration camp (*Frankfurter Rundschau*, 19.3.90).
69. These figures were put forward in 1987 by a Sociology Professor in Cologne after a study of several years. He claimed that the figures were higher in rural areas (*Die Welt*, 22.5.87). This has been confirmed by studies carried out by the Allensbach-based opinion poll organization 'Institut für Demoskopie', mentioned in Mrs Roth's working document (see note 57). The institute claims that the potentially antisemitic proportion of West Germans has remained relatively constant, at 15 to 20 per cent, since the 1950s.
70. Gill Seidel, *The Holocaust Denial – Antisemitism, Racism and the New Right*, Beyond the Pale Collective, Leeds, 1986.
71. *International Herald Tribune*, 6./7.1.90.
72. *Frankfurter Allgemeine Zeitung* and *Süddeutsche Zeitung*, 5.1.90; *Neue Zürcher Zeitung*, 6.1.90.
73. Working Document by Mr Willi Rothley (PE 139.153).
74. *Stuttgarter Zeitung*, 25.1.90; *Frankfurter Rundschau*, 1., 12.2.90; *Süddeutsche Zeitung*, 6.2.90.
75. *Die Welt*, 25.1.90.
76. *Der Spiegel*, September 1989, quoted in doc. PE 139.279, see note 57.
77. Working document by Mr P. Avgerinos (PE 139.278).
78. Statement by Mr Ekonomidis (PE 139.277).
79. Law 927/1979 prescribes penalties for acts or measures aimed at racial discrimination. Article 25 of Law No. 1419/1984 adds religious discrimination to discrimination on the ground of race and ethnic origin which is covered by Law No. 927/1979. Article 4 of the Greek Civil Code provides that foreign nationals shall enjoy absolutely equal rights with Greek nationals and, according to Article 5(2) of the 1975 Constitution, 'all persons living

within the Greek territory shall enjoy full protection of their life, honour and freedom irrespective of their nationality, race or language and of religious or political beliefs . . . .'

80. Commission Report: 'The Social Integration of Third-Country Migrants Residing on a Permanent and Lawful basis in the Member States' (SEC (89) 924 final), 22.6.89.
81. *Greek News*, 5–12.2.90.
82. *Greek Weekly*, 5.2.90. Greece recognizes only the religious identity of the minority and references to ethnicity have been banned since 1987. *Athens News*, 9.2.90.
83. *Guardian*, 2.4.90.
84. See note 77.
85. Contribution of Mr Morena Catena (PE 139.214) at the hearing of the Committee of Inquiry in January 1990.
86. 'Los Inmigrantes en España', issued by Documentación Social of Cáritas Española, 1987. The dossier claims that after the amnesty period for irregular migrants (July 1985 to March 1986), there were still about 320,000 'irregulars', prior to the introduction of the new law on foreigners on 1.7.85. The amnesty was a failure. Only 12.5 per cent had their situation regularized, representing a mere 16 per cent of all cases presented, since the prerequisites were too stringent.
87. *Cambio 16*, 7.12.87.
88. *Cambio 16*, 21.3.88.
89. Summary of report in *El País*, 18.4.90.
90. See note 85.
91. In May 1988, the parents' association of the La Salle College of Santa Coloma de Ferners (Gerona) voiced, in a letter, its opposition to the entry of 11 black children of African agricultural workers, mostly Gambians. The College Director affirmed his total disapproval of the contents of this letter (see *El País*, 22.5.88).
92. *El País*, 6.11.89. The organizers also praised the petition presented to the Constitutional Court by the Ombudsman (Defensor del Pueblo) against the Organic Law of 1.7.85 on the rights and freedoms of foreigners. The petition, which criticized this law for denying certain fundamental human rights, such as the right of association, resulted in a positive ruling by the Constitutional Court about two years earlier. However, public authorities, especially the police, misapply certain principles of the July 1985 law and human rights abuses continue. See summary of the Annual Report by the Defensor del Pueblo in *El País*, 18.4.90.
93. *El País*, 8.11.87; *Migration Newssheet*, December 1987.
94. *El País*, 22.12.87.
95. See note 85.
96. *Guardian*, 19.7.86; *Migration Newssheet*, August 1986.
97. *El País*, 9.10.86.
98. Forty-five gypsy children aged between 4 and 12 of the community of Ripollet in Barcelona were denied entry into the local schools in 1988 for the second consecutive year on the grounds that they had not been 'sponsored' (*El País*, 5.4.88; see also: *El País*, 19.4.88). Later in September, before the start of the academic year, the responsible alderman announced a new measure obliging the 45 children to provide medical proof of good health, considering

this measure logical as these children may transmit any kind of disease (see *El País,* 14.9.88).

99. Working Document by Mr Juan de Dios Ramírez Heredia (PE 140.275).
100. Quoted from Mr Juan Ramírez Heredia, ibid.
101. Working Document by Mrs Elmalan (PE 139.260).
102. He was killed in the bombing of the immigrant hostel in Nice in December 1988. Eleven others were injured. *Le Monde* and *Libération,* 20./21.12.88.
103. *Migration Newssheet,* September 1987.
104. A 'Harki' is a French national of Algerian origin who fought on the French side during the Algerian War of Independence. They are in the unenviable situation of being disliked by North Africans in France, in particular, Algerians, who treat them as traitors, and discriminated against by the French, who look down on them as Arabs. Their children, also French citizens, are confronted with very high unemployment and many take to alcohol and drugs, with some requiring psychiatric hospitalization (see *Libération,* 8.3.88).
105. That same day, a Tunisian was stabbed to death after a quarrel with an Italian, and a Moroccan died of knife wounds after a dispute in a bar in which he refused to pay his bill (see *Migration Newssheet,* August 1989).
106. *Le Monde,* 1.9.87. The article points out that negative feelings against foreigners are now acceptable and openly voiced and that it is more difficult to convict someone for making a racist remark. Nowadays, people who do 'not like Arabs' say so openly, speaking of 'foreign invasion', is a 'polemical' expression of an 'admissible' degree; racists, instead of denying being such, admit openly their feelings in the name of 'honesty'. Complaints against people for racist remarks are dismissed for reasons such as 'not exceeding the limits of simple polemics' or 'expressing a political opinion'.

     While it is difficult, if not virtually impossible, to convict a policeman for making a racist remark, foreigners calling policemen racists face quick conviction for racism if they dare call a policeman a 'sale Français!' (Dirty Frenchman) – see *Le Monde,* 24.12.87, and *Libération,* 8.9.89.
107. *Le Monde,* 29.3.90.
108. On 5.12.86, an Algerian national was killed by a drunken policeman as he tried peacefully to break up a fight. The next day, a French student of Algerian origin was beaten to death by policemen. Between these two deaths, racists emptied a jerry-can of petrol on an Algerian who became a human torch (see *Migration Newssheet,* January 1987). In 1990, a French youth of Algerian origin was shot three times in the back at close range by a policeman who felt threatened. He was accompanied by another policeman and the youth was handcuffed.
109. Another victim was the managing director of a computer firm who was also a friend of the MP who chairs the Committee on Social, Family and Cultural Affairs of the National Assembly. *Le Monde,* 13.4.89.
110. *Le Monde,* 27./28.9.87.
111. *Migration Newssheet,* April 1990. The appeal of the Public Prosecutor's Office in Marseilles against the decision to release the police officer responsible was turned down. On 15 May 1990, a court in Aix-en-Provence confirmed the officer's release (*Libération,* 16.5.90).
112. Contribution by Mr Joinet (PE 140.240).

113. On 29.4.87, Mr P. Seguin (RPR), the then Minister of Social Affairs, spoke before the Commission for Human Rights and claimed that the legal measures aimed at combating racism and the special policies of favouring the integration of foreigners into French society were far from reaching their target. At his initiative, the National Assembly unanimously adopted on 11.6.87 amendments to the 1972 anti-racist law aimed at extending to associations the possibility of instituting court action in cases involving individuals who claim to be victims of discrimination (*Migration Newssheet*, July 1987). He also proposed the setting up of a structure of mediation and communication with immigrants which would be under the responsibility of a well-known person whose tasks would include intervening in situations of conflict regarding accommodation or injustice involving youths of foreign origin (*Libération*, 30.4.87). Almost three years later, Mr M. Rocard put forward the same proposal. Earlier that same month, the State Secretary in charge of Human Rights, Mr C. Malhuret (UDF), implicitly referring to the Front National, declared on television on 13.4.87 that the problems of co-existence among ethnic communities could not be solved by 'shouting down in public the heads of associations who work in favour of immigrants' or 'by organizing demonstrations tarnished by confrontation' (*Le Monde*, 11, 17./18.4.87; see also *Le Monde*, 2.7.87). However, when the Gaullist MP, Mr M. Hannoun (RPR), issued his major report in November 1987 entitled 'L'homme et l'espérance de l'homme – rapport sur le racisme et la discrimination en France', his proposals came under attack from his own colleagues (see *Migration Newssheet*, December 1987 and January 1988).

114. This incident was preceded by four other similar ones in the region: 12.2.1988: the premises and a minibus of an Islamic Cultural Association near Nice were intentionally damaged by fire; 9.5.88: a gas bomb exploded in another immigrant hostel, injuring two persons; 8.6.88: an explosive device which was found under the car of the director of SONACOTRA (which manages immigrant hostels) in Nice was defused in time; 4.10.88: a jerry-can of ignited petrol was thrown into the Algerian Consulate in Nice, causing a fire (*Le Monde* and *Libération*, 20./21.12.88).

115. The proposed measures were: (1) to put an end to the practice of people making statements inciting racial hatred under the pretext of freedom of expression; (2) to extend the application of the 1972 anti-racist law to some 'private places', instead of exclusively 'public places'; (3) the possible loss of civil rights for people convicted for racism, and; (4) the establishment of an arbitration procedure in case of discrimination to ensure that tensions in places of conflict be eased. However, the bill that was passed on its first reading on 3 May 1990 was more limited in its scope and application (see below).

116. The opinion survey, requested by the Information and Documentation Service of the Prime Minister's office, indicates that 90 per cent of those questioned considered racism to be very or fairly widespread and 83 per cent recognized that North Africans were the first victims of racism. Seventy-six per cent considered that there were too many Arabs (too many black people – 46 per cent; too many Asians – 40 per cent; too many Jews – 24 per cent). Aversion is probably strongest against Arabs (39 per cent), followed by gypsies (36 per cent), black people (21 per cent), Asians (20 per cent) and Europeans from the South (12 per cent). Even North African youths of French

nationality (beurs) are unpopular: only 22 per cent of those questioned considered the 'beurs' to be French, whereas 45 per cent classified them as 'Arabs'.

Moreover, the survey confirms strong xenophobia: 15 per cent of those questioned felt that immigrant workers were very well treated and 49 per cent considered that they were 'rather well treated'. In addition, 59 per cent considered that they were a burden for the French economy and only 25 per cent felt that they were 'an asset'. Besides, 47 per cent (compared to 43 per cent who shared the opposite view) favoured sending them back to their countries of origin if they lost their jobs (*Le Monde* and *Libération*, 28.3.90).

117. Under the new bill, those convicted for 'the most serious violations' of racism/antisemitism would be deprived of the right to be an election candidate for a maximum period of five years during which the person would be also barred from public posts. He/she would, however, retain the right to vote. Contrary to the initial draft text, these sanctions would not be applied to journalists and directors of publications who report on racist remarks. This was considered necessary to avoid situations similar to that in Denmark (see above). In fact, when carrying out opinion surveys on racism, statements that are clearly racist have to be formulated to find out the opinions of respondents (see *Libération*, 18.5.90). As for the newly introduced 'offence of revisionism', aimed at taking action against those who deny the Holocaust and the existence of gas chambers, it would only concern crimes against humanity committed under the Nazi regime and recognized as such by the Nuremburg Tribunal. Moreover, the proposal to hold an anti-racism day of information, requested by the Parti Communiste Français (PCF), has been replaced by an annual report by the government.

118. *Libération*, 7.8.89, and the article on the colloquy in June 1987 entitled 'Law and Discrimination' in *Le Monde*, 26.6.87. See also the book issued by two anti-racist associations: MRAP and LICRA (*Le Racisme*, 1989) covering 390 court rulings in cases of racism and discrimination in the last 40 years. Between 1.1.1986 and 11.10.89, there were 120 court rulings.

119. The difficulty in proving racism is shown in the case of three North Africans who tried to prove the existence of a racial door policy in two night clubs in Moulins (Central France). A journalist who offered to help them entered the two clubs, dressed with a tie and in blue jeans. The three Arab youths who followed him, neatly dressed and with a tie, were refused entry. The representative of the Public Prosecutor denounced their action, saying: 'It is not an enquiry that you have carried out – it is a provocation and, in France, provocations are thrown out of the court room' (*Libération*, 8.1.88).

120. *Libération*, 7.8.89.

121. *Le Monde*, 1.2.88; *Libération*, 16.9.88: *Migration Newssheet*, March and October 1988, November 1989, January and February 1990.

122. *Libération* and *Le Monde*, 4.11.89. After his re-election, confronted with the Front National, which gained 30 per cent of the votes, this (ex-) Mayor of Seine-Saint-Denis, Mr André Dechamps, described black people and Arabs as a 'pack of hyenas'. 'Rather than aggress our poor, innocent women, they ought to move [to work]', he said. 'If they have nothing to do, let them go back to their own country' (*Libération*, 28.3.90).

123. *Migration Newssheet,* November and December 1989.
124. An opinion survey by SOFRES, published in *Le Monde* (6.1.89), the third of its kind in three years, confirmed that as the French people became better informed about Mr Le Pen, they tended to consider him and the Front National as representing a danger for democracy. In three years, the percentage of people who declare that they would not, under any circumstances, vote for the Front National rose from 60 to 77 per cent.
125. *Le Monde,* 11.6.88, and *Libération,* 10.6.88.
126. *Le Monde,* 24.11.89.
127. According to the UDF candidate, Mr Mattei, in a constituency in Marseilles who only managed a narrow victory over his Front National rival, he met 'for the first time people who proclaimed their pride in voting for the Front National'. An opinion survey carried out at the polling stations in Dreux reveals that 41 per cent of Front National voters were very much influenced in their choice of vote by the debate over the Islamic headscarf affair and another 22 per cent said that the debate played a somewhat important role. Equally disturbing is the indication that 35 per cent of those who voted for the Front National (FN) candidate in Dreux in the first round had never before voted for the FN. This percentage climbed to 41 per cent in the second round. (*Libération,* 4.12.89; *Le Monde,* 5.12.89).
128. On 16.11.87, Mr Le Pen was convicted for 'provocation of racial hatred, discrimination and violence' in two separate judgements, one for a leaflet he published in March 1983 and the other for his statements in a TV programme in February 1984. With regard to the leaflet, the judge ruled that 'In wanting to persuade the electors . . . that there are too many immigrants in France, that they are expensive to society, that it is necessary to reduce the number of them or else risk losing the identity of the French people, Jean-Marie Le Pen is inviting the readers to [take] discriminatory measures against them [immigrants]'. On his televised statements, the judge ruled that 'In attributing to foreigners a negative and evil behaviour, soon to menace the French people in their liberty and future, he [Mr Le Pen] is only inciting the latter to consider them [the immigrants] as undesirables. He is provoking the listeners to discrimination, hatred and even violence against them' (see *Le Monde,* 19.11.87).

    Furthermore, on 28.1.88, the 14th Chamber of the Court of Appeal of Versailles confirmed the ruling rendered on 23.9.87 by the Departmental Court of Nanterre which condemned Mr Le Pen to pay a symbolic one franc indemnity to each of nine associations and three survivors of the deportations who filed complaints against him (see *Migration Newssheet,* October 1987). In describing the gas chambers as a 'detail' of the Second World War, the Versailles Court ruled, *inter alia,* that it was 'consenting to the horrible [event]' (see *Le Monde,* 30.1.88).
129. *Libération,* 6.4.90. An increasing number of Mr Le Pen's opponents fear that he may be benefiting from all the publicity surrounding the requests to lift his parliamentary immunity. Such actions can serve to reinforce the image he tries to project of being a 'poor victim' and a 'martyr' for expressing openly views on immigrants which millions of French people supposedly share, but do not dare to say so.
130. *Guardian,* 22.10.87.
131. *Libération,* 8.12.87; *Migration Newssheet,* January 1988.

132. *Le Monde*, 29.3.90; *Libération*, 19.3.90.
133. *Le Monde*, 3.4.90; *Libération*, 2./3.4.90.
134. *Libération*, 1.3.88. It has been alleged that the Socialists, in control of this city, are apprehensive of the negative feelings of the local French population towards the mosque.
135. The Front National obtained 25 per cent of the votes in this borough in the first round of the 1988 presidential election. The mayor, Mr A. Dezempte (RPR), who promised not to allow the Muslim community to build a mosque and warned the local population that 'the value of real estate would fall by 30 to 60 per cent if a mosque were built,' assumed office with 66.7 per cent of the vote in March 1989 (the several thousand-strong Muslim community only had a room in an old building for worship and this was destroyed by a bulldozer). The Socialist–Communist alliance who favoured the building of a mosque saw their popularity drop to 26 per cent of the vote (see *Migration Newssheet*, September 1989). The Mayor's deputy was later convicted (in February 1990) for inciting racial discrimination during the electoral campaign (*Le Monde*, 9.2.90; *Le Figaro*, 8.2.90). A few months later, on 14 May, Mr Dezempte was himself charged by a court in Lyons for 'hindering the freedom of worship and demolishing goods belonging to others [with reference to the Islamic prayer room]' (*Le Monde*, 16.5.90).
136. *Le Monde*, 24.6.89; *Libération*, 31.8.89.
137. *Le Monde*, 14.6.86.
138. *Migration Newssheet*, September 1986. The dead included the chairman of SOS France and a former Front National candidate at a municipal by-election in 1984. SOS France was supposedly the political wing of the 'Commandos de France'.
139. *Le Monde*, 31.5.88, 1.6.88, 15.11.88; *Libération*, 2.11.88, and the *International Herald Tribune*, 14.6.88. In one of the most serious incidents, 13 skinheads were convicted in June 1988 for unprovoked physical violence against a French youth and three other French persons of non-European origin. The sentences passed were light and the judge ruled out racism (see *Le Monde*, 6.7.88).
140. *Le Monde*, 26.1.90.
141. *Le Figaro* and *Le Monde*, 18.1.90; *Libération*, 10.10.89.
142. *Le Monde*, 1./2.4.90.
143. *Libération* and *Le Figaro*, 11.5.90; *Le Monde*, 12.5.90. Two other smaller Jewish cemeteries were desecrated a few days earlier. On 4 May 1990, 22 tombstones in the Jewish cemetery in Wissembourg (Northern Alsace) were found to have been overturned and damaged. In another Jewish cemetery, in Yvelines, 44 tombstones were discovered in a similar state on 10 May 1990 (*Libération*, 12./13.5.90).
144. The former president, Mr V. Giscard d'Estaing, could not be present because of the opening session of the May plenary of the European Parliament in Strasbourg (*Le Monde*, 16.5.90). At the European Parliament on 17 May 1990, a resolution referring to the desecration of the Carpentras cemetery was adopted with 167 votes in favour, 12 against (members of the European Right) and one abstention (*Libération*, 18.5.90).
145. *Le Monde*, 17.5.90. That same day, a female teacher who had mentioned the desecration of the Jewish cemetery to her pupils in relation to the 1949

Universal Declaration of Human Rights was severely beaten up by two attackers who broke into her home.

146. In 1989, the Director of *National Hebdo* and member of the political bureau of the Front National, Mr R. Gaucher, wrote in the November issue of his publication (with a circulation of about 100,000): 'We are at the start of a tremendous power struggle, a great planetary struggle between the international Jewish movement and the international Christian, primarily Catholic, one. Depending on the outcome of this combat, which will be the great religious and political confrontation of the year 2000, or of this battle, either Christianity will succeed in preserving its position in the face of the fantastic force of the Jewish world, or else we, believers and non-believers, will come under a new religious law, that of the shoah' (*Le Monde*, 15.5.90). According to an opinion survey by CSA published in *Le Parisien* (17.5.90), 55 per cent of respondents considered the Front National to be an antisemitic party compared to 22 per cent who held an opposite view. Another survey carried out at the same time, namely on 14 and 15 May 1990, by SOFRES and published in *Le Nouvel Observateur*, shows that 66 per cent of respondents believe the Front National to be responsible for what happened at Carpentras. The CSA survey also shows that 96 per cent of respondents were shocked by the desecrations, but 35 per cent (compared to 56 per cent holding an opposite view) considered it 'normal' to make 'remarks hostile to Jews' (*Le Monde* and *Libération*, 18.5.90).
147. *Migration Newssheet*, September 1989.
148. During the Nazi occupation of France, the same Field-Marshal Pétain, without being asked to do so by the Nazis, decreed a new law on the status of Jews which, *inter alia*, prohibited them from taking up posts of director, manager, editor of newspapers, reviews, bulletins, with the exception of publications of a strictly scientific character.
149. *Migration Newssheet*, October 1989.
150. *Le Monde*, 5., 7., 10.4.90.
151. *Libération*, 28.3.90.
152. *Migration Newssheet*, May 1990, and *Le Monde*, 17.5.90.
153. *Libération*, 16.5.90.
154. The administrative council also decided to request the Minister of National Education, Mr L. Jospin, to adopt the necessary measures so as to prevent Mr Notin from exercising his profession as of the next academic year (*Le Monde*, 17.5.90).
155. Working Document by Mr P. Cooney (PE 139.156).
156. *Racial Discrimination in Ireland: Realities & Remedies*. A Harmony Report, Dublin, March 1990.
157. This Act was passed to comply with Article 20 of the United Nations 1966 Covenant on Civil and Political Rights, signed and ratified by Ireland.
158. Evrigenis Report, December 1985, para. 119.
159. Written Statement made by Dr A. Cavaterra (PE 139.431).
160. Working Document by Ms D. Valent (PE 140.464).
161. *Corriere della Sera*, 1.3.90; *Migration Newssheet*, March 1990.
162. *Migration Newssheet*, April 1990.
163. *Migration Newssheet*, April 1990; *Guardian*, 13.4.90.
164. *Migration Newssheet*, April 1990.

165. The law, No. 416, is entitled: 'Emergency regulations governing asylum, the right of entry and residence of non-Community citizens and the regularization of the status of non-Community citizens and stateless persons already residing within the territory of the Italian State'. Article 1 deals with the status of refugees and revokes the geographical reservation made by Italy when it signed the 1967 Protocol of New York.
166. *Migration Newssheet*, April 1990.
167. See note 159.
168. *Libération*, 5.4.90; *La Repubblica*, 4.4.90.
169. *Migration Newssheet*, March and April 1987.
170. *Migration Newssheet*, June 1988.
171. *Migration Newssheet*, September 1989.
172. *La Repubblica*, 7./9.10.89.
173. The survey was carried out by a daily in the North, *Bergamo Oggi*: 62 per cent of the respondents said that they would never marry an Italian from the South; 66 per cent were convinced that the rise of delinquency in the North coincided with the arrival of Southern Italians; and 70 per cent believed that incompetence within the public administration was caused by the predominance of staff members originating from the South. Only 32 per cent of those questioned considered these Italian 'immigrants' as an important contribution to the regional economy. *Libération*, 17.7.89.
174. Written Statement by Mr Michel Neyens (PE 139.212).
175. See note 80. See also Working Document by Mr R. Krieps (PE 139.155).
176. See note 174.
177. *Le Monde*, 14.4.90.
178. See note 174.
179. Working Document by Ms M. van Putten (PE 139.239).
180. Ibid.
181. Document submitted by Mr H.A.A. Molleman to the hearing of the Committee of Inquiry on 31 January 1990 (PE 139.213).
182. In a statement issued in July 1989, the Mayor of Amsterdam expressed his shock at the fact that half of all young foreigners were without a job. He denounced this as discrimination and blamed the private sector. *NRC Handelsblad*, 4.7.89.
183. In her report, Maartje van Putten notes that 'It is interesting that the majority of local authorities and housing associations refuse to report voluntarily and only act under pressure from publicity and the ethnic organizations.' See note 174.
     See also article on the problems of housing discrimination in the municipality of Haarlem, *NRC Handelsblad*, 23.9.89, 29.12.89.
184. The LBR is subsidized by the Ministry of Justice and is responsible for combating discrimination by means of investigation and legal action.
185. This government initiative was the result of criticism voiced by the UN Committee on the Elimination of Racial Discrimination (CERD) which supervises the UN Convention on the Elimination of All Forms of Racial Discrimination. Before the bill, no effective means to prohibit racist organizations existed in The Netherlands. See *AFdruk*, No. 28, October 1986, Amsterdam.
186. See note 178.

187. This right of individual complaint became effective only in 1988. The Commission ruled in favour of a Turkish woman who was dismissed by her Dutch employer on racist grounds when she became pregnant. As the local judge had approved the dismissal and an appeal had been rendered impossible, the UN Commission considered that the Dutch Government had to pay compensation to the woman (see Communication No. 1/1984, *Yilmaz-Dogan v. The Netherlands,* in the Report of the Committee on the Elimination of Racial Discrimination, General Assembly, Official Records: 43rd Session, Supplement No. 18 (A/43/18), New York, 1988).
188. According to the report complaints of Moroccan and Turkish immigrants are mostly related to discrimination in the employment field, while persons of Caribbean descent complain about racism in the personal sphere. Most complaints come from employees. Long-term unemployed migrants or independent migrants can avoid contacts with the Dutch population and therefore have fewer negative experiences (see *NRC Handelsblad,* 10.2.88).
189. In an interview with the *NRC Handelsblad* (11.5.88), the Chief Constable of the Amsterdam Police admitted that discrimination occurs in the force. Only 4 per cent (instead of the targeted 10 per cent) of the force belongs to a minority group. Ethnic minorities often leave the force because of racial harassment. Besides, ethnic minorities often hesitate to join the police force.
190. *Migration Newssheet,* September 1986.
191. *Migration Newssheet,* April 1990.
192. Written Contribution by Mr Lourenço Martins to the hearing on 29/31 January 1990 (PE 139.210).
193. Working Document by Ms M. Belo (PE 139.257).
194. *O Emigrante,* 9.3.90.
195. See note 193.
196. Ibid.
197. *Diário Popular* and *Diário de Notícias,* 29.10.89.
198. *Diário de Notícias,* 17.1.90.
199. Report by the Runnymede Trust (1986), entitled 'Different Worlds', which states that racial discrimination is 'tenacious, rampant and still on the increase'. It reports on widespread discrimination in employment and low-cost housing and intimidation by the police (see *Migration Newssheet,* October 1986).
200. *The Times,* 23.10.86.
201. The report also denounces the failure to employ or to offer services to ethnic minority citizens on equal terms with others and underlines that the number of young black teachers is declining as well as black students in teacher-training institutions, resulting in an ageing minority teacher workforce. The CRE warned that unless the trend was reversed, there might eventually be no more black teachers. *The Times,* 9.7.87.

The Commission for Racial Equality was established by the Race Relations Act 1976 with the following duties:

(a) to work towards the elimination of discrimination;
(b) to promote equality of opportunity and good relations between persons of different racial groups generally; and
(c) to keep under review the working of the Act, and, when required by the Secretary of State or when it otherwise thinks it necessary, to draw up and submit to the Secretary of State proposals for amending it.

202. For example the article in the *Daily Star* (17.5.89) calling Kurdish asylum-seekers from Turkey '"refugee" scroungers'.
203. Two reports issued by the CRE: one in 1987 entitled *Living in Terror* and the other in 1988, *Learning in Terror*. The latter, published after a two-year investigation into racial abuse in educational institutions in the UK, points out that racial harassment and violence in schools and colleges is widespread and persistent and that the teachers, lecturers and parents are as much to blame as pupils and students. The Government responded by recommending that all schools keep records of all racial incidents involving pupils. See *Migration Newssheet*, April 1988 and June 1989.
204. Several campaigns have been launched to recruit more ethnic minorities into the police force, without much success. About 1 per cent of police officers in England and Wales are from ethnic minority communities, although they make up 3.9 per cent of the UK population (*Independent*, 21.12.89). Recently, Asian youths in East London decided to defend themselves. Breaking from their traditionally passive attitude towards racial attacks, they have formed a group of about 350 members trained in martial arts for defensive reasons (*Independent*, 12.3.90).
205. *Independent*, 20./26.4.89, and Colin Brown, *Black and White Britain: The Third PSI Survey*, 1984.
206. *The Independent*, 24.4.88. In another article, *The Independent* (9.12.88) reported on a pregnant Bengali woman who lost her baby after youths set a dog on her.
207. For more information on this affair, see *Migration Newssheet*, February 1989, and subsequent issues.
208. *Independent*, 15. and 17.1.90; *Guardian*, 19.1.90; *Daily Telegraph*, 25.1.90.
209. According to the Chairman of the Commission for Racial Equality, most black people under 30 will have been sent to prison or youth custody by the year 2000. Figures show that the proportion of black people in custody was twice that of their proportion in the population. Black people had fewer previous convictions than white prisoners sentenced for similar offenses and were more likely to be remanded in custody (*The Times* and *Guardian*, 15.9.88). His views were confirmed by the research carried out by the Institute of Criminological Research at Oxford which reveals that black prisoners are discriminated against in jails and are given worse jobs than whites. According to the *Daily Telegraph* (22.9.88), these findings were presented to the Home Office in December 1986, but were never published.
210. An Asian police officer won the first ever case against the Nottinghamshire police force, alleging racial discrimination and harassment. The plaintiff's lawyer submitted to the industrial tribunal written examples from reports by Nottinghamshire officers, in which coloured people were referred to as 'coons, spooks, darkie, and nigger'. *Guardian*, 12.9.89; *Daily Telegraph*, 12.9.89; and 20.3.90; *Independent*, 5.10.89, and 20.3.90.
211. In March 1990, a black ex-Grenadier Guardsman, the second black person ever to serve with the Guards, withdrew his racial discrimination case against the army, although he was supported by the Commission for Racial Equality and had won the right to have his case heard before an industrial tribunal. His withdrawal followed advice by lawyers that he was unlikely to succeed (*Guardian*, 21.3.90).

212. Results of the research carried out by N. Jewson and D. Mason of the University of Leicester in *Sociology*, vol. 20, No. 1, 1989, p. 43. The authors suggest that management can manipulate the formal rules to their own advantage and keep management white and male.
213. Elisabeth Burney, *Steps to Racial Equality: Positive Action in a Negative Climate*, Runnymede Trust, London, 1988. Ms Burney points out that in spite of legislation and campaigns to improve the situation, non-whites have not made a breakthrough into the mainstream of economic life. Job prospects for them remain as bad as when the Race Relations Act was passed in 1968. In its reaction, the Commissioner for Racial Equality said that the report underlined its own findings: that it was twice as hard for black people to get jobs as it was for whites (*The Times* and *Guardian*, 15.3.88).
214. One psychiatrist at the conference pointed out that the rate of diagnosed schizophrenia was sixteen times higher for British-born blacks aged 16–19 years than for British-born whites (*Independent*, 25.1.90). A study published in October 1988 in the review *Psychological Medicine* already warned that children of immigrants from the Caribbean living in the UK were up to ten times more likely than white children to develop schizophrenia in adulthood. The study concludes that the discrepancy may be due in part to reactions induced by racial discrimination, but strongly warns against oversimplification. It notes that higher rates of mental illness have been found in some other first-generation immigrants, compared with those in their adopted country. But in these cases, rates of mental illness have dropped to around those of the adopted country in the second generation. Among Caribbeans, the trend is just the opposite (*Guardian*, 31.10.88).

    See also Roland Littlewood and Morris Lipsedge, *Aliens and Alienists*, Unwin Hyman, London, 1989.
215. *The Times*, 4.1.88.
216. *Daily Telegraph*, 2.1.90.
217. An examination of reading material used in 196 primary schools in a Northern industrial city in 1986 showed that ethnic minorities are massively underportrayed by comparison with white people and are often characterized in terms of racial stereotypes. One of the more 'enlightened' series of books showed that blacks and other minorities were presented in roles including that of cannibal chief, house painter, construction worker and magician (*Independent*, 22.7.87).
218. According to the findings of a research programme published on 2.12.87, the overwhelming majority of young people were politically illiterate with no conception of how Parliament, political parties or the economy operated. The only party whose policies were well-known was the National Front and its commitment to the enforced expulsion of non-whites. 'Feeling that something must be done in the face of economic decline, they were drawn to the conclusion that the repatriation of non-white immigrants was the only possible policy', says the report. The researchers found that many young people conceded that with greater knowledge they would have reached different conclusions and expressed regret that they had not been taught more about politics in school (*Guardian*, 3.12.87).
219. Written statement by Mr M. Elliott (PE 139.280).
220. Under this rule, a foreign spouse of a UK resident is required to prove that the 'primary purpose' of their marriage was not to gain entry into the UK.

221. As of March 1988, it became known that the Government was refusing to incorporate DNA blood testing into immigration procedures. To have such tests done privately, applicants have to pay several hundred pounds (see *Migration Newssheet*, April 1988, June and July 1989; *Independent*, 27.7.88).
222. *Mail on Sunday*, 20.5.90.
223. See note 218.
224. *Migration Newssheet*, September 1986.
225. According to a survey carried out in 1988 by the Scottish Council for Racial Equality, more than 80 per cent of Pakistanis and Indians experienced racist abuse, with 58 per cent of Indians registering a physical attack. Asian women out shopping have been bombed with polythene bags full of urine. Dogs have been set on them. They have had excrement, burning mats and firecrackers thrust through mail boxes. (*Guardian*, 13.4.88.)
226. *The Scotsman*, 5. and 8.6.89; 16. and 17.1.90; *Evening News* (Edinburgh), 5–18.5.89; 6., 8. and 10.6.89.
227. *Western Mail*, 9.7.90.
228. The Deputy Mayor of Linz provoked a scandal in July 1987 when he wrote to the President of the World Jewish Congress, criticizing the latter's actions against Dr Waldheim, saying that he was behaving like his fellow Jews who 'condemned Christ to death 2,000 years ago' (*Le Monde*, 11.7.87).
229. *Libération*, 9.11.88.
230. Its most important gain was in Carinthia where it increased its score by 13 percentage points to 29 per cent, receiving 11 seats out of a total of 36. It gained 6 seats in Salzburg (+2) and 5 (+3) in Tyrol (*Le Monde*, 11. and 14.3.89).
231. *Le Monde*, 18.8.89.
232. *Neue Zürcher Zeitung*, 9., 11., 14., 27.11.89.
233. *Tribune de Genève*, 13.12.89.
234. *La Libre Belgique*, 17.4.90.
235. *Neue Zürcher Zeitung*, 14. and 20.1.90.
236. *Neue Zürcher Zeitung*, 15. and 16.1.89.
237. *Independent*, 21.8.89.
238. *Migration Newssheet*, June 1989.
239. *Libération*, 15. and 16.10.88.
240. *The Independent*, 21.8.89.
241. *News & Views* (Stockholm), 19.1.89.
242. The initiator, Mr S.O. Olsson of the local Centre Party, is believed to have a pro-Nazi past and is very much against the presence of foreigners. His action was condemned by his own party's national leader, Mr Johansson (see *Le Monde*, 29. and 31.10.1987).
243. Like the decision one year earlier to hold the referendum, the outcome caused great indignation throughout the nation. The only 'visible' foreigners in this farming borough are a Chilean couple. The others, mostly Poles, have been residing there for a long time and have married Swedes. One member of its local council who voted against holding the referendum, Baroness Ramel of the Conservative party and president of the local Committee on Social Affairs, offered parts of her family's property to accommodate refugees in response to the Council's claim that there was a housing shortage (see *Le Monde*, 20.9.88; *News & Views*, 22.9.88; *El País*, 17.9.88).
244. *News & Views*, 17.12.87.
245. *Sydsvenskan*, 13.8.89.

246. *Le Monde*, 16.5.90.
247. *Le Monde*, 22.8.87; *Die Welt*, 14.9.87.
248. *Frankfurter Rundschau*, 30.4.90.
249. *Frankfurter Rundschau*, 4. and 19.4.90; *Frankfurter Allgemeine Zeitung*, 17.4.90; *Süddeutsche Zeitung*, 19.4.90; *La Libre Belgique*, 14.4.90.
250. Article by Vitaly Vitalyyev, 'Seeds of a Racist Disaster', *Guardian*, 20.2.90.
251. *American Jewish Year Book*, 1989. See also collection of articles on antisemitism in East and Central Europe entitled 'L'anti-sémitisme dans les pays de l'Est', *Le Nouvel Observateur*, 20.3.–4.4.90.
252. Already in 1987, the *Guardian* (16.11.87) reported that there was a growing problem with neo-nazi youths who 'patrol' the streets clad with black paramilitary dress, with parachute boots and closely shaven heads. Armed with chains and knuckledusters, they raid youth clubs and beat up punks, pacifists and environmentalists and even State youth groups. They tell jokes about Jews which older people thought they would never hear again – and similarly racist ones about Turks. Slogans such as 'gas them all' and 'blacks out' have appeared on walls.
253. See note 57. See also Information from Aigali Dshunussow, National Executive member responsible for foreigners, SPD in the GDR, East Berlin, 6.2.90.
254. *Frankfurter Allgemeine Zeitung*, 1.8.88; *Libération*, 20.10.88.
255. *Stuttgarter Zeitung*, 4.1.90; *Frankfurter Rundschau*, 19.1.90.
256. Ibid.
257. *Süddeutsche Zeitung*, 4.4.90.
258. Catherine David, 'RDA: le retour du refoulé' in *Nouvel Observateur*, 29.3.–4.4.90.
259. *Libération*, 7.5.90.

Chapter 4

1. Debates of the European Parliament, No. 2-343/109, 8.10.86.
2. 'Qualified majority' here is in the sense of Article 118A of the 1986 European Single Act for the implementation of social policy. The cautious and hesitant attitude of the Commission in such matters was confirmed by Mr Marin when he pointed out that initiating legislation in the field of migration was 'a very delicate issues' and 'that it would be preferable to arrive at an agreement with the various Member States so that we put forward a document which will enable progress rather than one which is rejected from the outset'. 'I therefore prefer', he added, 'the pragmatic approach'. Debates of the European Parliament, No. 2-434/109, 9.10.86.
3. OJ No. C 176, 14.7.86.
4. *Eurobarometer*, Special Issue, 'Racism and Xenophobia', November 1989, Directorate-General Information, Communication, Culture, Surveys, Research, Analyses.
5. *A People's Europe*, Information Handbook, issued in 1987 by the Directorate-General Information, Communication and Culture of the Commission of the EC.
6. Speaking on behalf of the European People's party, Mr F.L. von Stauffenberg (EPP – D) criticized the wording of the Joint Declaration: 'We would like to

have seen such a Joint Declaration from the institutions of the Community couched in more inspiring, colourful and forceful language than the simple insipid document in front of us'. Debates of the European Parliament, No. 2-340/108, 11.6.86.

7. Mrs Adam-Schwaetzer was replying to a question raised by the Socialist MEP, Ms R. Dury (S – B) requesting the Council that as one way to commemorate the second anniversary of the Joint Declaration, it could 'send a note to the Member States to find out exactly what they have done towards this (anti-racism/xenophobia) campaign'. According to Mrs Adam-Schwaetzer, the aim of the Joint Declaration 'cannot [. . .] be [. . .] to set individual actions by the Council in this respect in train but to bring about a change of attitude so that people in our Member States really accept this declaration of principle.' Debates of the European Parliament, No. 2-366/66, 14.6.88.
8. Written Question No. 2381/86, of 10.3.87 (87/C 117/89). Reply given on 23.3.87.
9. Debates of the European Parliament, No. 2-366/66, 14.6.88.
10. Intervention of Mr J. Ramírez Heredia (S – E) in Debates of the European Parliament, ibid.
11. In reply to a written question (No. 599/87 of 22.6.87–88/C 23/78) by Mr D. Baudis (EPP – F), Mr Ripa di Meana, on behalf of the Commission, said on 19.8.87 that the necessary funds to carry out the Eurobarometer survey on racism and xenophobia were not available in the 1987 budget and the operation had to be postponed. The amount of ECU 200,000 was allocated to the 1988 'information' budget to enable the survey to be carried out.
12. *Eurobarometer*, Special issue, see note 4.
13. Ibid.
14. Commission Decision of 8.7.85 setting up a prior communication and consultation procedure on migration policies in relation to non-member countries (OJ No. L 127, 19.8.85), *Bulletin of the European Communities*, Supplement 9/85, pp. 19–20.
15. Speech by Commissioner M. Marin, Debates of the European Parliament, No. 2-356/72, 13.10.87.
16. FRG (Case 281/85); France (Case 283/85); the Netherlands (Case 284/85); Denmark (Case 285/85); the United Kingdom (Case 287/85).
17. The following phrase was thus deleted from the Commission Decision: 'To ensure that the agreements and measures referred to in Article 1, including those relating to development aid, are in conformity with, and do not compromise the results of, Community policies and actions in these fields, in particular as regards Community labour market policy'.
18. Commission Decision of 8.6.88 setting up a prior communication and consultation procedure on migration policies in relation to non-member countries (88/384/EEC) (OJ No. L 183/35, 14.7.88).
19. Commission Report: 'The Social Integration of Third-Country Migrants residing on a Permanent and Lawful Basis in the Member States', SEC (89) 924 final, 22.6.89.
20. *A People's Europe*, see note 5.
21. 'New Approaches: A Summary of Alternative Approaches to the Problem of protection against Racism and Xenophobia in Member States of the European Communities', prepared by the Runnymede Trust, 1986, V/387/87 – EN.
22. Ibid., p. 20.

23. 'Migrant Women and Employment', V/928/87 - FR.
24. COM(88) 743 final.
25. 'Migrant Women and Employment', Community Seminar, Brussels, 17–18 September 1987, Final Report, V/902/88 - FR.
26. 'Youth against Racism', ARC/GRAEL-87-, p. 30.
27. 'Guidelines for a Community Policy on Migration', *Bulletin of the Commission of the European Communities*, Supplement 9/85, p. 15.
28. Ibid., p. 19.
29. Debates of the European Parliament, No. 2-343/110, 8.10.86.
30. The European Centre for Work and Society whose main office is in Maastricht, the Netherlands.
31. Debate on 'Discrimination against immigrant women'. Subject of debate: Report (Doc 1-133/87) by Mrs Heinrich, drawn up on behalf of the Committee on Women's Rights, on discrimination against immigrant women in Community legislation and regulations.
32. Debates of the European Parliament, No. 2-374/20, 13.2.89.
33. Chapter 30 of the Community budget on 'Subsidies for Balancing Budgets', Article 303 for 'Subsidies for certain activities of non-governmental organizations pursuing humanitarian aims and promoting human rights'. Under 'Remarks', it is stated: 'Part of the additional appropriations requested would be used to set up the European Forum for Migrants (numbering some 13 million), as recommended at point 3 in the Joint Declaration of 11 June 1986'.
34. Resolution on the Joint Declaration against Racism and Xenophobia and an action programme by the Council of Ministers (PE 126.109/fin.) (150 in favour, 90 against and 8 abstentions.)
35. Oral question no. 82 by Mrs Domingo Segarra (S – E) (H-378/89) with reply by the Commission published in the 'Verbatim report of proceedings', 'Question Time', 22.11.89.
36. Working Document of the Commission of the EC, submitted to the Committee of Inquiry (PE 139.485).
37. The ruling of the European Court of Justice on 22.5.90 constitutes a major recognition of the powers of the European Parliament which, according to Article 173 of the Treaty of Rome and Article 146 of the Euratom Treaty, is not included among the institutions that can take proceedings to annul acts of other institutions. The two aforementioned articles explicitly grant this power only to a Member State, the Council or the Commission. However, in the case submitted by the European Parliament requesting the annulment of a Council regulation of 22.12.87, which determines, after Chernobyl, the admissible levels of radioactive contamination in foodstuffs after a nuclear accident, the European Court ruled that it had to guarantee respect for the 'institutional equilibrium' prescribed by the EC Treaties. The Parliament, ruled the Court, 'like the other institutions, [. . .] cannot have its prerogatives ignored without being able to take legal recourse [. . .] that can be exercised surely and effectively.' From now on, the European Parliament will have the power to submit a request to the European Court for annulment of a Council or Commission act 'on the condition that these proceedings only involve safeguarding its prerogatives'.
38. Proposal for a Council resolution on the fight against racism and xenophobia (COM(88) 318 final) in OJ 88/C 214/12 of 16.8.88.

39. Reaction by Mr M. Medina Ortega in the debates of the European Parliament, No. 2-374/18 of 13.2.89.
40. Debates of the European Parliament, No. 2-374/20, 13.2.89.
41. Explanatory statement of the report (Doc. A2-265/88) drawn up by Mr M. Medina Ortega on behalf of the Committee on Legal Affairs and Citizens' Rights on the proposal by the Commission to the Council for a Council resolution on the fight against racism and xenophobia (COM(88) 318 – C2-102/88).
42. Opinion of the Economic and Social Committee on the proposal for a Council resolution on the fight against racism and xenophobia (COM(88) 318 final), SOC/164 Racism and Xenophobia, CES 1232/88 AH/co/hm, 23 November 1988. The ESC adopted the opinion by 105 votes in favour and three abstentions.
43. The suppressed phrase was: 'Whereas any measure taken in this connection must protect all persons on Community territory, whether they are nationals or Member States or of non-member countries, foreigners in a Member State or nationals who are perceived or who perceive themselves as belonging to a foreign minority.'
44. OJ No. C 214/36, 16.8.88.
45. OJ No. C 177, 6.7.88, p. 5.
46. One related incident which managed to get a lot of media attention, probably because of the reaction of the Mayor of Orléans in France, concerned a group of seven children who were refused permission to transit through Belgium to the Netherlands in May 1988. Five were Moroccans with a 'group passport' issued by the Moroccan consulate and the two others, a Zaïrian and a Laotian, whose parents had refugee status in France, were in possession of a safe-conduct pass. They were part of a group of 55 children from a school in Orléans, travelling by coach to the Netherlands on a two-week cultural trip after one and a half months of preparations. Another child, of Caribbean origin, was allowed to enter Belgium only after efforts were made by the accompanying teachers to explain that citizens from French overseas territories had the same rights as French nationals. The seven children, shocked by the discriminatory treatment and separation from their classmates, had to return to Orléans by train. When he learnt of the incident, the Mayor of Orléans addressed a strongly worded telegram of protest to the Belgian Ambassador in Paris (see *Libération* and *Le Monde*, 23.5.88).
47. OJ Np. L 158, 25.6.88, p. 42.
48. Directive 77/466/EEC of 25.7. 77. OJ No. L 199/32, 6.8.77.
49. Report on the implementation in the Member States of Directive 77/486/EEC on the education of the children of migrant workers, Brussels, 3.1.89, COM(88) 787 final. As the reference year for this second Commission report is 1984–5, it does not cover Spain and Portugal.
50. Ibid., p. 25.
51. Ibid., p. 26.
52. OJ No. C 187/117, 18.7.88.
53. COM(88) 318 final (OJ 88/C214/12).
54. OJ No. C 246, 20.9.88. (COM(88) 371 final.)
55. 'Europe against Racism', European Parliament, Strasbourg, 14.3.89. Verbatim report of Symposium.

56. Written question No. 323/87 by Mr O. d'Ormesson (DR – F) to the Commission of the European Communities on 'Subsidies for SOS Racism' dated 6.5.87. Reply given by Mr Delors on behalf of the Commission on 8.10.87. (ON No. C 42/17 of 15.2.88.)
57. António Cruz, 'An Insight into Schengen, Trevi and other European Intergovernmental Bodies', Churches' Committee for Migrants in Europe (CCME). Briefing Paper No. 1, Brussels, May 1990. Available also in French and German.
58. Community relations and solidarity in European society, Interim report on the community relations project prepared by the Committee of Experts on Community Relations (MG-CR), Strasbourg 1989, Doc MG-CR (89) 3 rev.
59. Details from: Ökumenischer Vorbereitungsausschuss zur Woche der ausländischen Mitbürger, Neue Schlesingergasse 22-24, D-6000 Frankfurt am Main 1. Tel: 49 (69) 29 31 60.
60. Documents of the Colloquy on Migrants, Media and Cultural Diversity (MG-CR/coll 1 (88) 3,4,5,9,10,11, 12 and MG-CR/coll 1 (89) 1), Council of Europe.
61. Conclusions of the meeting of experts on migrants, ethnic groups and the police, Strasbourg, 15.12.88, Addendum to MG-CR (88) 25, Council of Europe.
62. Conclusions of the meeting of experts on cultural and religious practices of migrants and ethnic groups, Strasbourg, 26–28.6.89, Addendum to MG-CR (89) 4, Council of Europe.

Chapter 5

1. Figures based on a report of the Commission entitled: The Social Integration of Third-Country Migrants Residing on a Permanent and Lawful Basis in the Member States. (Sec (89) 924 final.)
2. OECD, Continuous reporting on migration, SOPEMI report 1988 (Paris, 1989).
3. Jonas Widgren, 'Asylum Seekers in Europe in the Context of South–North Movements', *International Migration Review*, Vol. 23, 1989.
4. Ibid. See also his paper, 'International Migration. New Challenges to Europe' (Council of Europe, 1986). Furthermore, Gilbert Jaeger, 'Study in Irregular Movements of Asylum-Seekers' UNHCR, 1985, and for recent statistics and analysis, *The World Refugee Survey 1989*, published by the US Committee for Refugees, Washington, 1990.
5. Mrs Roth's submission to the Committee of Inquiry into Racism and Xenophobia. See also *Migration Newssheet*, May 1990.
6. Based on: Parliamentary Assembly of the Council of Europe, Report on refugees from countries of Central and Eastern Europe. Rapporteur: Mr Fuhrmann. 22.1.90. Doc. 6167.
7. A clear example is the decision of the government of the Federal Republic to offer a 1-for-1 exchange rate when the Deutschemark replaces the East German mark. Bonn admitted that this was based on political rather than economic factors to keep the East Germans from emigrating. *International Herald Tribune*, 25.4.90.
8. SOPEMI report 1987 and 1988.

9. 'New expressions of racism. Growing areas of conflict in Europe', *SIM Special No. 7*. Report of the Seminar held in Amsterdam (19–21 October 1987), organized by International Alert and the Netherlands Institute of Human Rights. Compare: British Council of Churches, 'Account of Hope. Report of a Conference on the Economic Empowerment of the Black Community' (London, 1990). See also the Evrigenis Report and the Council of Europe's Interim Report on the Community Relations Project (1989). MG-CR (89) 3 rev.
10. Jan Niessen, 'Migrants' Rights. Migration and (Self) Employment. Residence and Work Permit Arrangements in Seventeen European Countries' (Maastricht, May 1990). For self-employed persons see also Ali Najib, 'The Contribution of Migrant/Ethnic Groups to the Economic Viability of Urban Areas Through Setting Up Small and Medium-Sized Businesses in Western Europe' (Council of Europe, November 1989). MG-CR (90) 4.
11. For the major role of the government as an opinion leader see the Interim Report of the Community Relations Project of the Council of Europe (MG-CR (89) 3 rev). For the importance of international instruments see Ann Dummett's discussion paper for the 'Meeting of Experts on the Role of National Legislation and International Instruments in Combating Discrimination on Nationality, Ethnic or Racial Grounds'. Council of Europe, 4–6 October 1989. (MG-CR (89) 14). See also the report prepared by the Runnymede Trust at the request of the Commission entitled 'New Approaches. A Summary of Alternative Approaches to the Problem of Protection against Racism and Xenophobia in Member States of the European Communities' (1986). V/387/87=EN.
12. The reports can be obtained from the Secretariat of the CERD. See further its reports to the General Assembly. See also A. Eide, 'Study on the Achievements Made and Obstacles Encountered during the Decades to Combat Racism and Racial Discrimination'. Report to the CERD (New York, 1989).
13. Centre for Human Rights, 'Status of International Instruments' (New York, 1987) and its yearly updated survey on ratifications.
14. The Development of the Informal Consultations on Asylum-Seekers between UNHCR and Governments in Europe and North America. Internal UNHCR-paper (Geneva, 1989). See for further information *Migration Newssheet*, May 1990, and Antonio Cruz, 'An Insight into Schengen, Trevi and other European Intergovernmental Bodies', Churches' Committee for Migrants in Europe (CCME), Briefing-Paper, Brussels, May 1990. Also available in French and German.
15. ILO, 'Equality in Employment and Occupation: General Survey by the Committee of Experts on the Application of Conventions and Recommendations', Report III (Part 4B), 1988.
16. Consultative Committee on the European Convention on the Legal Status of Migrant Workers. Meeting Report – 5th meeting, Strasbourg, November 1989. Council of Europe (T-MG (89) 11).
17. CAHAR, 'Final Activity Report. Draft Agreement on Responsibility for Examining Asylum Requests'. Council of Europe, 1989. CM(89) CAHAR (88) 9 def.
18. Summary of Conclusions. Meeting of experts on the role of national legislation and international instruments in combating discrimination on nationality, ethnic or racial grounds. Council of Europe (MG-CR (89) 20).

19. Convention. L'Application de l'Accord de Schengen du 14 Juin 1985 entre les Gouvernements des Etat de l'Union Economique Benelux, de la République Fédérale d'Allemagne et de la République Française, relatif à la Suppression Graduelle des Contrôles aux Frontières Communes, Version finale.
20. It is noteworthy that the Declaration of TREVI Group Ministers (Paris, 15 December 1989) almost exclusively deals with fighting international crime, terrorism, narcotics and illegal trafficking of every sort. This last seems to include 'the attraction represented by the freedom and prosperity of our societies is in itself becoming a source of profit and exploitation of misery for networks of illegal immigrants, taking advantage of our wish not to impose over-rigorous controls at frontiers on the vast majority of travellers'. That is about all that deals explicitly with migration.
21. European Parliament, document B3-286/90, 15 January 1990.

Chapter 6

1. John Clarke, Stuart Hall, Tony Jefferson and Brian Roberts, 'Subcultures, Cultures and Class: A Theoretical Overview', in Stuart Hall and Tony Jefferson (eds), *Resistance Through Rituals*, Hutchinson, London, p. 10.
2. For these concepts see Robert Miles, *Racism*, Routledge, London, 1989.
3. Committee of Inquiry into the Rise of Fascism and Racism in Europe, Report on findings of the inquiry. Rapporteur: Mr Dimitrios Evrigenis. December 1985, pp. 87–9.
4. For the concepts of encoding and decoding see Stuart Hall, 'The "Structured Communication" of Events', in *Getting the Message Across. An Inquiry into Success and Failures of Cross-Cultural Communication in the Contemporary World*. UNESCO Press, Paris, 1975.
5. For instance Juan Manuel Delgado, *'Die Garstarbeiter' in der Presse*, Leske Verlag, Opladen, 1972. Georgios N. Galanis, *Migrantenkriminalität in der Presse*, Express Edition, Berlin, 1987. Hildegard Kühne-Scholand, 'Die Darstellung der Ausländer im deutschen Fernsehen', in *Ausländer und Massenmedien. Bestandsaufnahme und Perspektiven*, Bundeszentrale für politsche Bildung, Bonn, 1987. Klaus Merten, 'Das Bild der Ausländer in der deutschen Presse', in ibid.
6. For instance: Paul Gordon and David Rosenberg, *Daily Racism. The Press and Black People in Britain*, The Runnymede Trust, London, 1989. Nancy Murray and Chris Searle, *Your Daily Dose: Racism and the Press in Thatcher's Britain*, The Institute of Race Relations, London, 1989. Chris Searle, *Your Daily Dose: Racism and the Sun*, Campaign for Press and Broadcasting Freedom, London, 1989. John Twitchin (ed.), *The Black and White Media Book. Handbook for the Study of Racism and Television*, Trentham Books, Stoke-on-Trent, 1988. Stuart Hall, 'The Whites of their Eyes', in G. Bridges and R. Hunt (eds), *Silver Linings: Some Strategies for the 80s*, Lawrence and Wishart, London, 1981. Stuart Hall, 'Media Power and Class Power', in J. Curran et al. (eds), *Bending Reality: The State of the Media*, Pluto Press, London, 1986. Paul Hartmann and Charles Husband, *Racism and the Mass Media*, Davis Poynter, London, 1974.
7. Delgado, *'Die Gastarbeiter' in der Presse*.
8. Galanis, *Migrantenkriminalität in der Presse*.

9. Alice-Gail Bier, 'Mass Media and the Foreign Immigrant in Spain', in Taisto Hujanen (ed.), 'Final Conference of the Joint Study: The Role of Information in the Realization of the Human Rights of Migrant Workers', Lausanne, 23–27 October 1988.
10. Denis McQuail, 'National Report of the Netherlands', in Taisto Hujanen (ed.), 'The Role of Information in the Realization of the Human Rights of Migrant Workers: Report of International Conference', Tampere, 19–22 June 1983. University of Tampere, Tampere.
11. Taisto Hujanen (ed.), 'The Role of Information in the Realization of the Human Rights of Migrant Workers: Progress Report of the Joint Study', University of Tampere, Tampere, p. 47.
12. Clara Gallini, 'Arabesque: Images of a Myth', *Cultural Studies*, 2.2, May 1988, p. 179. See also by the same author: 'Le Radici dell'immaginario esotico', *Democrazia e diritto*, no. 6, 1989.
13. Gordon and Rosenberg, *Daily Racism*; Murray and Searle, *Your Daily Dose: Racism and the Press in Thatcher's Britain*; Searle, *Your Daily Dose: Racism and the Sun*.
14. Gordon and Rosenberg, *Daily Racism*, and Searle, *Your Daily Dose: Racism and the Sun*.
15. Gordon and Rosenberg, *Daily Racism*, p. 64.
16. Annita Kalpaka and Nora Räthzel, 'Rassismus als Form ideologischer Vergesellschaftung', in Kalpaka and Räthzel (eds), *Die Schwierigkeit, nicht rassistisch zu sein*, (2nd edn), Mundo Verlag, Leer, 1990.
17. See note 5.
18. Angela Barry, 'Black Mythologies: Representation of Black People on British Television', in John Twitchin (ed.), *The Black and White Media Book*.
19. Ibid, p. 90.
20. Ibid, p. 96.
21. Therese Daniels and Jane Gerson, *The Colour Black. Black Images in British Television*, The British Film Institute, London, 1989.
22. These aims were described by the London-based publisher of three Asian journals, Mr Patel.
23. Hujanen (ed.), 'Final Conference of the Joint Study', p. 91–100 and 114.
24. COM(88) 318 final – OJ No. C 214, 16.8.88.
25. Evrigenis – Report, p. 97.
26. Hujanen (ed.), 'Final Conference of the Joint Study', pp. 206–7.

Index